D1880977

THE MOHAMMADAN DYNASTIES

THE MOHAMMADAN DYNASTIES

Chronological and Genealogical Tables with Historical Introductions

By

STANLEY LANE POOLE

GYAN

Published by

GYAN

Gyan Publishing House
5, Ansari Road
Daryaganj, New Delhi-110002
Phone: 011-47034999, 9811692060
E-mail: books@gyanbooks.com

Distribution Network
gyanbooks.com
India, USA, Canada, UK, Australia, France

© Publisher

All rights reserved. No part of this work may be reproduced, stored, adapted, or transmitted in any form or by any means, electronic, mechanical, photocopying, micro-filming, recording or otherwise, or translated in any language, without the prior written permission of the copyright owner and the publisher.

ISBN : 978-81-212-9836-0 (PB)
First Published, 1894

2nd Impression 2023

Printed at: Gyan Press, Delhi.

The book is sold subject to the condition that it shall not, by way of trade or otherwise, be lent, resold, hired out, or otherwise circulated without the prior publisher's written consent.

THE MOHAMMADAN DYNASTIES
Author: STANLEY LANE POOLE

THE

MOHAMMADAN DYNASTIES

CHRONOLOGICAL AND GENEALOGICAL TABLES WITH HISTORICAL INTRODUCTIONS

BY

STANLEY LANE-POOLE

MDCCCXCIV

PREFACE

THE following Tables of Moḥammadan Dynastics have grown naturally out of my twenty years' work upon the Arabic coins in the British Museum. In preparing the thirteen volumes of the *Catalogue of Oriental* and *Indian Coins* I was frequently at a loss for chronological lists. Prinsep's *Useful Tables*, edited by Edward Thomas, was the only trustworthy English authority I could refer to, and it was often at fault. I generally found it necessary to search for correct names and dates in the Arabic historians, and the lists of dynasties prefixed to the descriptions of their coins in my Catalogue were usually the result of my own researches in many Oriental authorities. It has often been suggested to me that a reprint of these lists would be useful to students, and now that the entire Catalogue is published I have collected the tables and genealogical trees in the present volume.

The work is, however, much more than a reprint of these tables. I have not only verified the dates and pedigrees by reference to the Arabic sources and added a number of dynasties which were not represented in the Catalogue of Coins, but I have endeavoured to make the lists more intelligible by prefixing to each a brief historical introduction. These introductions do not attempt to relate the internal history of each dynasty: they merely show its place in relation to other dynasties, and trace its origin, its principal extensions, and its downfall; they seek to define the boundaries of its dominions, and to describe the chief steps in its aggrandisement and in its decline. In the space at my command these facts could only be stated with the utmost brevity, but in the absence of any similar attempt to arrange, define, and explain the relative positions and successions of all the Moḥammadan Dynasties in every part of the Muslim world, I hope the manual may be useful to students of history. To the collector of Arabic coins and

Saracenic antiquities I know, from personal experience, that it will be practically indispensable.

The plan I have followed is to arrange the dynasties in geographical order, beginning with Spain, which first threw off the control of the Caliphs of Baghdād. From the extreme west of the kingdoms of Islām I gradually work eastwards, till the end is reached in India and Afghānistān. Certain deviations from the strict geographical order are explained as they arise (see p. 107). Each dynasty has its historical introduction, a chronological list of its princes, and (when necessary) a genealogical tree. The years of the Christian era are given as well as those of the Hijra,* and when the latter occur in the introductory notices they are distinguished by italic

* The Hijra date is of course the more exact, as it is derived from Arabic historians; whilst the date A.D. is merely *the year in which that Hijra year began*, and does not necessarily correspond with it for more than a few months. The correspondence is near enough, however, for practical purposes; and a reference to the conversion tables in my *Catalogue of Indian Coins* will render it more precise. When the Hijra year began at the close of the Christian year the following year A.D. is given.

type. Beneath each chronological list is given [in square brackets] the name of the succeeding dynasty.

The two synoptic Tables of the Moḥammadan Dynasties, (1) during and (2) after the Caliphate, will give a general idea of their relative positions, and roughly indicate the comparative extent of their dominions. The numismatist will find almost all the coin-striking dynasties within the limits of time assigned; and the Oriental student in general may find this map of the Moḥammadan Empire instructive in its rough delineation of the relative territorial extent of the various dynasties, its assignment of each dynasty to its proper geographical position in the Muslim world, and its attempt to indicate the interweaving of the several houses and the supplanting of one by another in the various kingdoms and provinces of the East. It is interesting to trace the gradual absorption of the vast empire of the Caliphs from the opposite quarters of Africa and the Oxus provinces. We see how the

Omayyads of Cordova were the first to divide the authority of the head of the religion, and then how the Idrīsids, Aghlabids, Ṭūlūnids, Ikhshīdids, Fāṭimids, and many others, destroyed the supremacy of the 'Abbāsid Caliphs of Baghdād in their Western provinces; and how, meanwhile, the Persian dynasties of Ṭāhirids, Ṣaffārids, Sāmānids, Ziyārids, and Buwayhids gradually advanced from the Oxus nearer and nearer to the City of Peace, until, when the Buwayhids entered Baghdād on Dec. 19, 945, the Caliph ruled little more than his own palace, and often could not even rule there. Then a fresh change comes over the scene. The Turkish tribes begin to overrun the Moḥammadan Empire. The Ghaznawids establish themselves in Afghānistān, and the Seljūḳs begin their course of conquest, which carries them from Herāt to the Mediterranean, and from Bukhārā to the borders of Egypt. When the Seljūḳ rule comes to be divided among many branches of the family, and division brings its invariable consequence of weakness, we find several dynasties of Atābegs, or generals of Seljūḳian armies, springing up in the more western provinces of Syria and Diyār-Bakr and Al-'Irāḳ, whilst the Shāh of Khwārizm founds further East a wide empire, which increases with extraordinary rapidity, and eventually includes the greater part of the countries conquered by the Seljūḳs as well as that portion of Afghānistān which the Ghaznawids, and after them the Ghōrids, had subdued to their rule. And then comes the greatest change of all. The Mongols come down from their deserts and carry fire and sword over the whole eastern Moḥammadan Empire; the Turkish slaves, or Mamlūks, of Saladin found their famous dynasty in Egypt; the Berber houses of Marīn and Ziyān and Ḥafṣ are established along the north coast of Africa; and the Christians are rapidly recovering Andalusia from the Moors, who had given it so much of its beauty and renown. And here the epoch is chosen for beginning the second table, which begins at the Mongol invasion and brings the history down to the present day.

Vertically the tables are divided under the headings of the chief divisions of the Moḥammadan Empire. The various dynasties have been placed as nearly as possible, not only under their proper geographical head, but in the proper portion of the space allotted to that head: but the difficulties of arrangement and the necessity of economizing space have brought about a certain number of exceptions. The Turkish and Mongol tribes who wandered in Siberia, Turkistān, Kipchak, etc., are altogether omitted, because no exercise of ingenuity availed to provide a convenient place for them.

Horizontally the tables are divided, though the lines are not ruled through, into centuries, an inch representing one hundred years. The date of the beginning is taken at A.H. 41, the year of the foundation of the Omayyad Caliphate, because the Moḥammadan Empire was scarcely organized until this house came into power, and it would have been very difficult to indicate in any satisfactory manner the tide of Muslim conquest with its flow and ebb. Where space permits the names of a few leading kings and caliphs are inserted in the space allotted to their dynasty, especially when such names are familiar to European students.

In the orthography of Oriental names I have thought it best to be precise and consistent, except in some instances of names which have been adopted into the English language and cannot now be amended. Every letter of the Arabic and Persian alphabet is represented as a rule by one character, as shown in the table on p xix. The final *h*, which has an inflexional use, is omitted, since it serves no purpose in Roman writing: but it must be remembered that every name ending in short *a* (as -Baṣra, but not *ā* as Ṣan'ā) has a final *h* in Arabic. To indicate the elision of the *l* in the article *al* before certain letters, (as *d*, *s*, *r*), the *l* is printed in italic type: thus 'Abd-a*l*-Raḥmān is to be pronounced 'Abd-ar-Raḥmān.* The *l* is retained (though not pronounced) because it is so written in Arabic. On the other hand I omit the article altogether *before* a name. All the Caliphs and a multitude of other dynasts have names with the prefixed *al*, and a considerable saving of space and some added clearness is gained by omitting it. To show, however, that the article is to be used in the original I retain the hyphen: thus -Ḥākim stands for Al-Ḥākim. The only sign not generally employed by Orientalists is the Greek colon (·) which I use to denote the quiescent *hamza* in the middle of a word: as -Ma·mūn, where there is a catch in the breath between the *a* and *m*.

To students who are not Orientalists, and who wish to be accurate without elaboration in the orthography of

* If the inflexion of the Arabic is to be reproduced the name would be 'Abdu-r-Rahmān, and would require to be modified in accordance with its government in the sentence; but this would be carrying accuracy to an extreme of pedantry.

Eastern names, I would recommend the omission of all the diacritical points and the prefixed hyphen, and the assimilation of the italic *l* to the letter which follows it: thus for popular purposes one might write Abd-ar-Rahman instead of ‘Abd-a*l*-Raḥmān, Hakim instead of Al-Ḥākim. No system of transliteration can possibly represent the pronunciation of all parts of the Moḥammadan world: what would suit the accent of Fez would not fit the mouth of an Egyptian, still less of a Panjābī. One simple suggestion may, however, be made. Whereas for consistency I have adopted the *a* throughout to represent the Arabic vowel *fatḥ*, an *e* may advantageously be substituted for the *a* in spelling Egyptian or Algerian names, where *el* is nearer the native pronunciation than *al*, and Shems-ed-dīn than Shams-al-dīn.

The European reader when confronted with the long string of names and titles commonly affected by Oriental potentates is naturally puzzled to select the name by which a Moḥammadan ruler may be called ‘for short.’

In the early days of Isālm a great man was content to be known by a single or at most a double name. There would be his proper name, or what we should call his 'Christian name,' such as Moḥammad, Aḥmad, 'Omar; and to this would sometimes be added a patronymic (or rather hyionymic), as Abū-l-Ḥasan, 'the father of -Ḥasan,' or the name of his father as b. Ṭūlūn or ibn Ṭūlūn, 'the son of Ṭūlūn.' The patronymics beginning with *Abū* may always be omitted (except Abū-Bakr) in shortening the name, and so may the sonship prefixed by the abbreviation *b.* They are necessary in the dynastic lists for purposes of identification, but Aḥmad the Ṭūlūnid is a sufficient designation for Aḥmad b. Ṭūlūn, and the Ziyānid Mūsā I is adequately defined without his patronymic Abū-Ḥammū.

But very soon other titles of an honorific or theocratic character began to be added. Such epithets (laḳab) as Nūr-a*l*-dīn, 'Light of the Faith,' Nāṣir-a*l*-dīn, 'Succourer of the Faith,' Sayf-a*l*-dīn, 'Sword of the Faith,' were prefixed to the proper name; and adjectives or participles such as Al-Manṣūr 'the victorious,' A*l*-Sa'īd 'the Fortunate,' A*l*-Rashīd 'the Orthodox,'' were appended to the title *Khalīfa* (caliph) or *Malik* (king). Thus we find the caliph Hārūn a*l*-Rashīd, 'the Orthodox,' or 'rightly-directed,' caliph Aaron; and Saladin's full title was Al-Malik A*l*-Nāṣir Ṣalāḥ-a*l*-dīn Yūsuf b. Ayyūb, 'The Victorious* King, Redresser of the Faith, Joseph son of Job.' In the case of compound names such as these, the owner is generally called either by the participial title A*l*-Nāṣir, Al-Manṣūr, A*l*-Rashīd, etc, or by the laḳab with the termination a*l*-dīn ('of the Faith') or a*l*-dawla ('of the State'), etc. Thus the brother of Saladin is known both as Al-'Ādil, 'the Just [King]' and as Sayf-a*l*-dīn, 'Sword of the Faith.' On the other hand the Atābegs of Al-Mōṣil are generally cited by both

* Lit. 'Helping': one who helps the religion of Islām by his victories.

MOHAMMADAN DYNASTIES I DURING THE CALIPHATE. AD 661 - 1258 (face page XVII)

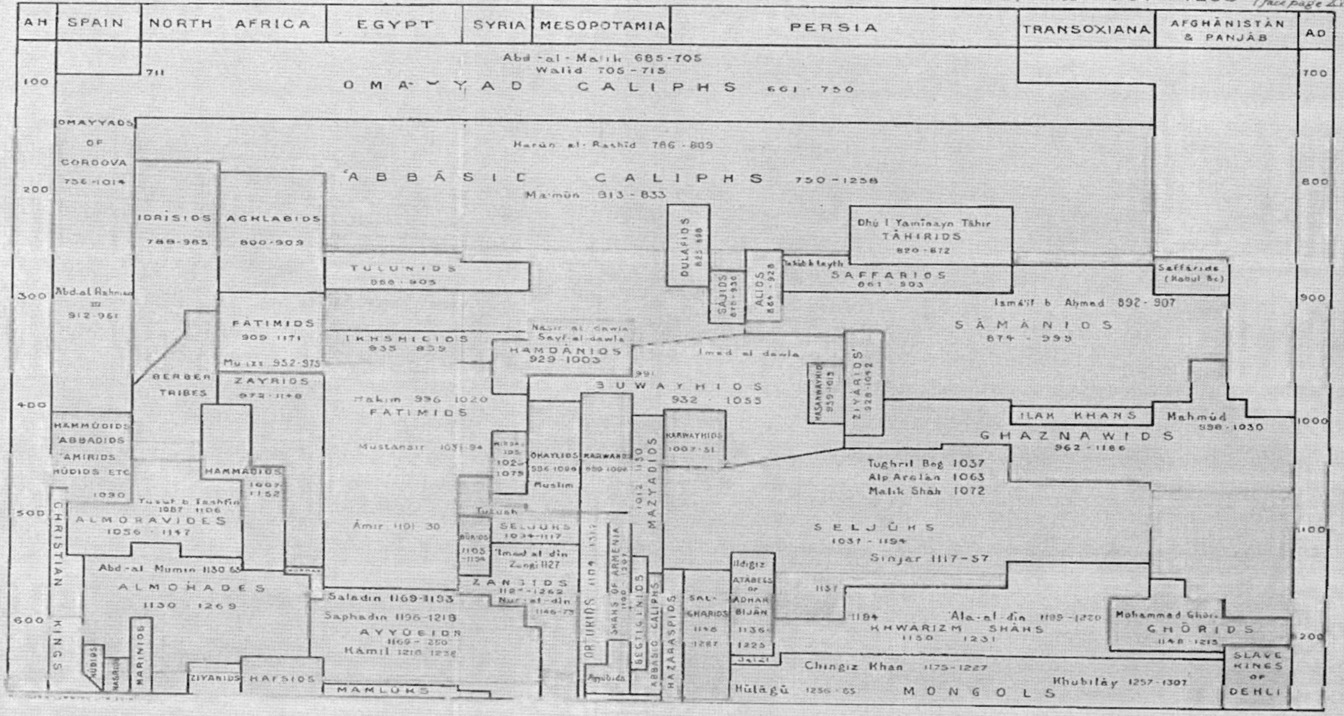

the proper name and the epithet, as 'Imād-al-dīn Zangī, 'Izz-al-dīn Mas'ūd; though the epithet by itself is sufficient. As a general rule the first name given in the chronological lists (omitting the patronymic Abū-such an one) may be used to designate the ruler, to the exclusion of the rest. When there are several similar titles it is better to add the proper name: for instance there are eight Al-Manṣūrs among the Mamlūk Sulṭāns, and it is necessary to distinguish them as Al-Manṣūr Kalā'ūn, Al-Manṣūr Lājīn, etc.

To give a list of the authorities I have used in compiling the lists of dynasties and historical notices would involve publishing a catalogue of an Orientalist's library. I have referred to all the leading Arabic historians, consulted special histories, and derived considerable help from articles in the Asiatic and numismatic journals. Where I am specially indebted to a particular author I refer to his work in a footnote. The coins, however, are the backbone of the book and the historian's surest documents, and upon them I have relied throughout.

In a work abounding in names and figures it would be strange if misprints and mistakes did not occur. I shall be grateful to any scholar who will convict me of error; for those who 'serve tables' know the danger and annoyance of even slight inaccuracy.

S. L.-P.

THE ATHENÆUM,
1st October, 1893.

TABLE OF TRANSLITERATION

أ	ʼ	ض	ḍ
ب	b	ط	ṭ
پ	p	ظ	ẓ
ت	t	ع	ʻ
ث	th	غ	gh
ج	j	ف	f
چ	ch	ق	ḳ
ح	ḥ	ک	k
خ	kh	گ	g
د	d	ل	l
ذ	dh	م	m
ر	r	ن	n
ز	z	ه	h
س	s	و	w
ش	sh	ی	y
ص	ṣ		

VOWELS

ـَ a (rarely e)	ـَا ā	ـَو aw (rarely ō)
ـُ u (rarely o)	ـُو ū	ـَی ay
ـِ i	ـِی ī	

CORRIGENDA

Page 46 *line* 3 *for* Ḥammūdid *read* Ḥammādid

,, 71 *lines* 2, 5 *for* Ḳayruwān *read* Ḳayrawān

,, 78 *for* [*Tatars*] *read* [*Mongols*]

,, 79 *line* 7 *from bottom*, *for* Tughtakīn *read* Ṭughtigīn

,, 157, 172 *for* FĀRIS *read* FĀRS

,, 168 *heading* B. *for* 712, 1312, *read* 811, 1408

MOHAMMADAN DYNASTIES I DURING THE CALIPHATE. AD 661 - 1258 (face page XVII)

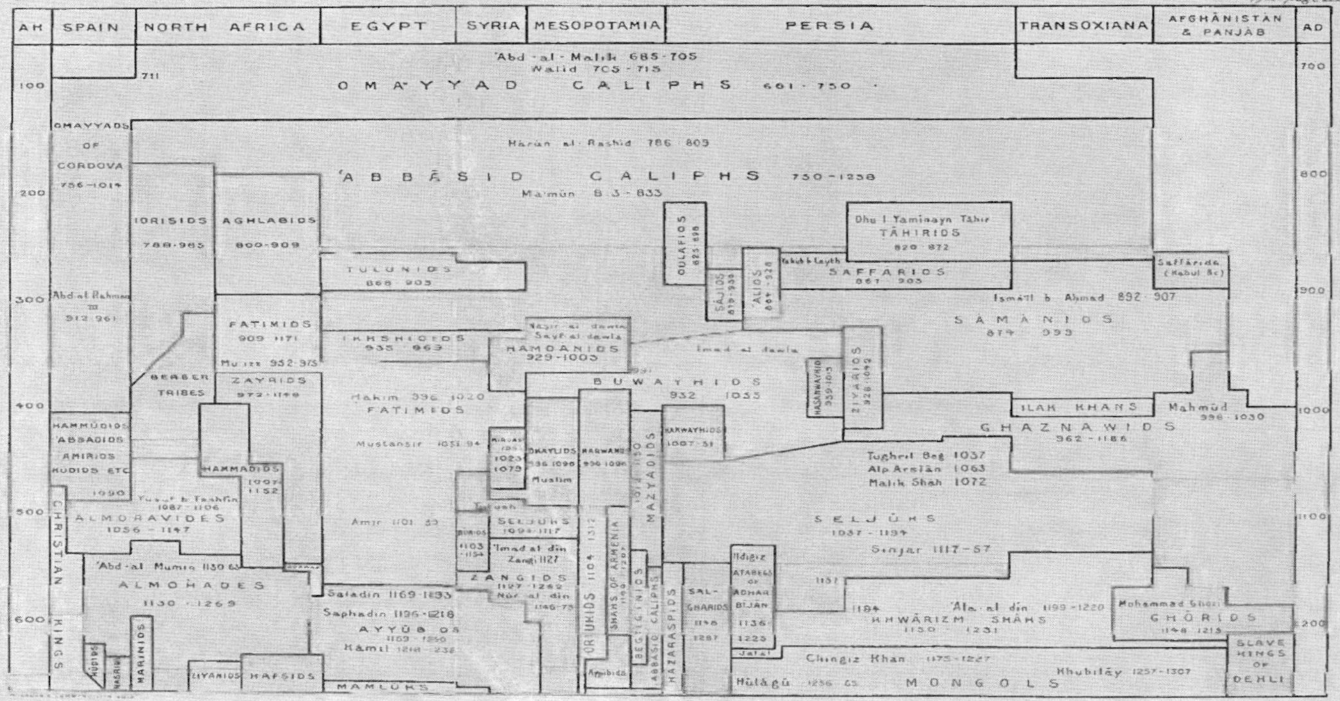

CONTENTS

I. THE CALIPHS

SÆC. VII–XIII

1. ORTHODOX
2. OMAYYADS
3. ʻABBĀSIDS

I. THE CALIPHS

SÆC. VII–XIII

On the death of the Prophet Moḥammad in A.D. 632, in the eleventh year after his Flight (Hijra, 622) from Mecca to Medīna, his father-in-law Abū-Bakr was elected head of the Muslims, with the title of *Khalīfa* or Caliph ('successor'). Three other Caliphs, 'Omar, 'Othmān, and 'Alī, were similarly elected in turn, without founding dynasties, and these first four successors are known as the Orthodox Caliphs (*Al-Khulafā Al-Rāshidūn*). On the murder of 'Alī in 661 (A.H. *40*), Mo'āwiya, a descendant of Omayya of the Prophet's tribe of the Ḳuraysh, assumed the Caliphate, and founded the dynasty of the *Omayyad Caliphs*, fourteen in number, whose capital was Damascus. In 750 (*132*) this dynasty was supplanted (except in Spain) by that of the *'Abbāsid Caliphs*, numbering thirty-seven, descended from 'Abbās, an uncle of the Prophet, and having Baghdād (founded 762, *145*) as their capital. The 'Abbāsid Caliphate at Baghdād was exterminated by the Mongol Hūlāgū in 1258 (*656*). A line of their descendants, the *'Abbāsid Caliphs of Egypt*, held a shadowy spiritual dignity at Cairo, until the last of the house was carried to Constantinople by the Ottoman Sulṭān Salīm I., after the conquest of Egypt in 1517, and surrendered his title of Caliph to the conqueror.

At the accession of the first Caliph, Abū-Bakr, the rule of Islām comprised no territory outside Arabia; but during his brief reign of two years the tide of Moḥammadan conquest had already begun to swell. In 633 (*12*) the Battle of the Chains, followed by other victories, admitted the Muslims into Chaldaea (-'Irāḳ -'Arabī), and gave them the city of -Hīra. In 634 (*13*) the Battle of the Yarmuk opened Syria to their arms; Damascus fell in 635 (*14*); Emesa, Antioch, and Jerusalem in 636; and the conquest of Caesarea completed the subjugation of Syria in 638 (*17*). Meanwhile the victory of Ḳādisīya in 635 (*14*) was followed by the conquest of Madā'in (Seleucia-Ctesiphon), the old double capital of Chaldaea, 637 (*16*); Mesopotamia was subdued, and the cities of -Basra and -Kūfa founded; and Khūzistān and Tustar were annexed in 638–40. The decisive Battle of Nahawand in 642 (*21*) put an end to the Sāsānid dynasty, and gave all Persia to the Muslims. By 661 (*41*) they were at Herāt, and soon carried their arms throughout Afghānistān and as far as the Indus, where they established a government in

Sind. In 674 (*54*) they occupied Bukhārā, and two years later Samarḳand, but these early raids in Transoxiana were not converted into settled conquests until 711 (*93*). On the East the Caliphate had reached its utmost limits in little more than forty years after the Muslims first led a campaign outside Arabia.

On the West their progress was slower. In 641 (*20*) Egypt was conquered, and by 647 (*26*) the Barbary coast was overrun up to the gates of Roman Carthage; but the wild Berber population was more difficult to subdue than the luxurious subjects of the Sāsānids of Persia or the Greeks of Syria and Egypt. Ḳayrawān was founded as the African capital in 670 (*50*); Carthage fell in 693 (*74*), and the Arabs pushed their arms as far as the Atlantic. From Tangier they crossed into Spain in 710 (*91*), and the conquest of the Gothic kingdom was complete on the fall of Toledo in 712. Southern France was overrun in 725, and in spite of Charles the Hammer's victory near Tours in 732 (*114*), the Muslims continued to hold Narbonne and to ravage Burgundy and the Dauphiné. Thus in the West the Caliphate attained its widest extent within a century after its commencement.

To the North, the Greeks retained Anatolia, which

never belonged to the Caliphate, but the Muslims invaded Armenia, and reached Erzerūm about 700. Cyprus had been annexed as early as 649 (*28*), and Constantinople was several times besieged from 670 (*50*) onwards.

Thus the empire of the Caliphs at its widest extended from the Atlantic to the Indus, and from the Caspian to the cataracts of the Nile. So vast a dominion could not long be held together. The first step towards its disintegration began in Spain, where 'Abd-a*l*-Raḥmān, a member of the suppressed Omayyad family, was acknowledged as an independent sovereign in 755 (*138*), and the 'Abbāsid Caliphate was renounced for ever. Thirty years later Idrīs, a great-grandson of the Caliph 'Alī, and therefore equally at variance with 'Abbāsids and Omayyads, founded an 'Alid dynasty in Morocco, with Tudgha for its capital, 788 (*172*). The rest of the North African coast was practically lost to the Caliphate when the Aghlabid governor established his authority at Ḳayrawān in 800 (*184*). In the following century, Egypt, together with Syria, attained independence under the rule of Ibn-Ṭūlūn, by the year 877 (*264*). It is true that after the collapse of the Ṭūlūnids, governors were again appointed over Syria and Egypt by the 'Abbāsid Caliphs for thirty years; but in 934 (*323*) -Ikhshīd founded his dynasty, and thenceforward no country west of the Euphrates ever recognized the temporal authority of the Caliphs of Baghdād, though their spiritual title was generally acknowledged on the coins and in the public prayer (*khuṭba*), except in Spain and Morocco.

In the East, the disintegration of the 'Abbāsid empire proceeded with equal rapidity. The famous general of -Ma'mūn, Ṭāhir Dhū-l-Yamīnayn, on being appointed Viceroy of the East in 819 (*204*), became to most intents independent; and his house, and the succeeding dynasties of the Ṣaffārids, Sāmānids, and Ghaznawids, whilst admitting the spiritual lordship of the Caliphs, reserved to themselves all the power and wealth of the eastern provinces of Persia and Transoxiana. From the middle of the ninth century the 'Abbāsids had fallen more and more under the baneful influence of mercenary Turkish bodyguards and servile *maires du palais*; and the absorption of the whole of their remaining territory by the Buwayhids, who occupied even the 'City of Peace,' Baghdād itself, in 945 (*334*), was little more than a change in their alien tyrants. From this date the Caliphs merely held a court, but governed no empire, until their extinction by the Mongols in 1258 (*656*). Occasionally, however, as in the Caliphate of -Nāṣir, they extended their authority outside the palace walls, and even ruled the whole province of Arabian -'Irāḳ (Chaldaea).

In classifying the dynasties which thus absorbed the 'Abbāsid empire, a geographical system is both natural and convenient. Beginning with the earliest secession, Spain, the dynasties of Andalusia and North Africa are placed first; those of Egypt and Syria come next; then follow the Persian and Transoxine dynasties; whilst those of India, which spread over a dominion never subdued to the Caliphate, are placed last. In dealing with the Persian and Syrian sections, however, the geographical arrangement is necessarily modified, since the wide sweep of the Seljūḳs and Mongols temporarily obliterated the older divisions and formed fresh starting points in the dynastic history. The relative positions, both geographical and chronological, of the various dynasties are shown in the table prefixed to the volume.

A.H.		A.D.
11—40	1. ORTHODOX CALIPHS	632—661
11	Abū-Bakr	632
13	'Omar	634
23	'Othmān	644
35	'Alī	656
—40		—661

[*Succeeded by Omayyads.*]

A.H.		A.H.
41—132	2. OMAYYAD CALIPHS	661—750
41	Mo'āwiya I	661
60	Yazīd I	680
64	Mo'āwiya II	683
64	Marwān I	683
65	'Abd-al-Malik	685
86	-Walīd	705
96	Sulaymān	715
99	'Omar	717
101	Yazīd II	720
105	Hishām	724
125	-Walīd II	743
126	Yazīd III	744
126	Ibrāhīm	744
127	Marwān II	744
—132		—750

[*'Abbāsids; Omayyads of Cordova*]

CONNEXION OF THE LINES OF CALIPHS

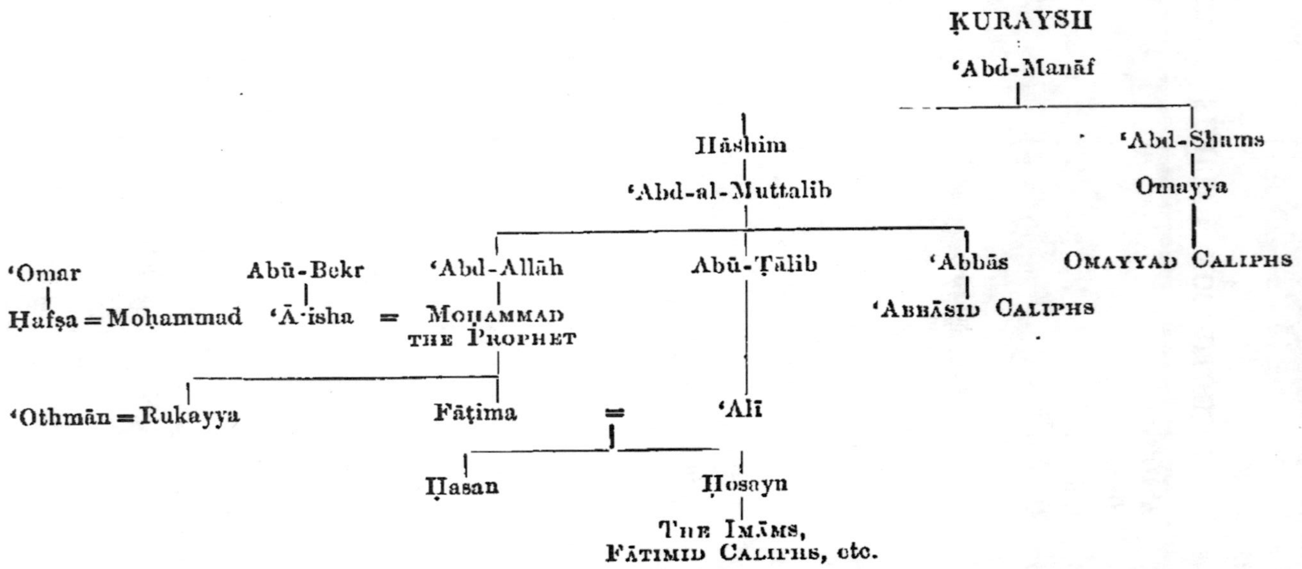

OMAYYAD CALIPHS

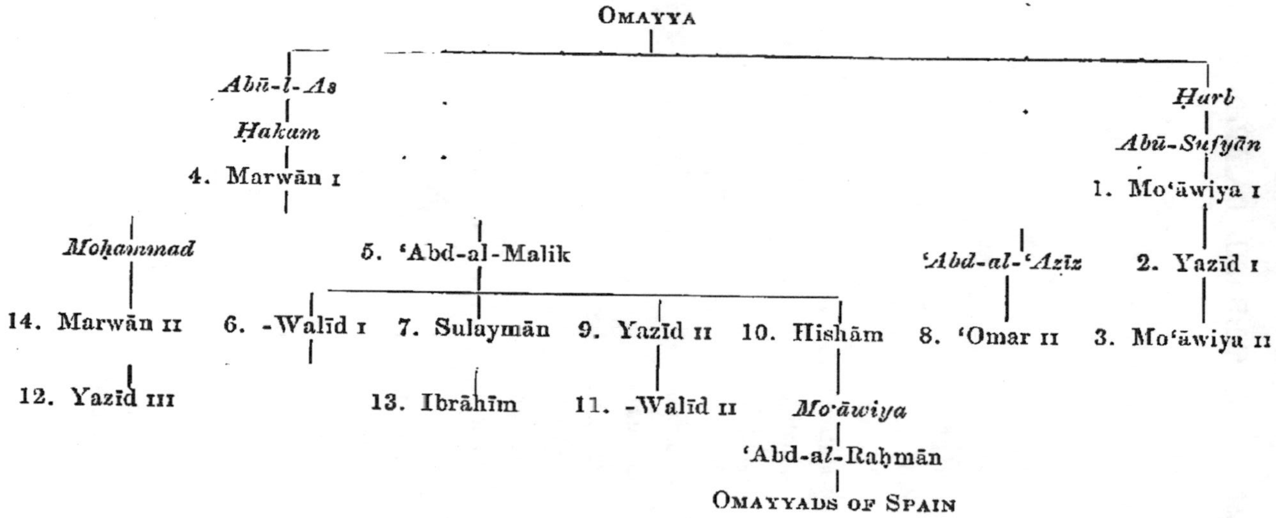

A.H.		A.D.
132—656	3. 'ABBĀSID CALIPHS	750—1258
132	-Saffāḥ	750
136	-Manṣūr	754
158	-Mahdī	775
169	-Hādī	785
170	-Rashīd	786
193	-Amīn	809
198	-Ma'mūn	813
218	-Mu'taṣim	833
227	-Wāthiḳ	842
232	-Mutawakkil	847
247	-Muntaṣir	861
248	-Musta'īn	862
251	-Mu'tazz	866
255	-Muhtadī	869
256	-Mu'tamid	870
279	-Mu'taḍid	892
289	-Muḳtafī	902
295	-Muḳtadir	908
320	-Ḳāhir	932
322	-Rāḍī	934
329	-Muttaḳī	940
333	-Mustakfī	944
334	-Muṭī'	946
363	-Ṭā'i'	974
381	-Ḳādir	991
422	-Ḳā'im	1031
467	-Muḳtadī	1075
487	-Mustaẓhir	1094
512	-Mustarshid	1118
529	-Rāshid	1135

530	-Muktafī	1136
555	-Mustanjid	1160
566	-Mustaḍi	1170
575	-Nāṣir	1180
622	-Ẓāhir	1225
623	-Mustanṣir	1226
640	-Musta'ṣim	1242
—656		—1258

[*Idrīsids, Aghlabids, Ṭūlūnids, Ṭāhirids, Ṣaffārids, Buwayhids, Ḥamdānids, Ghaznawids.*]

'ABBĀSID CALIPHS

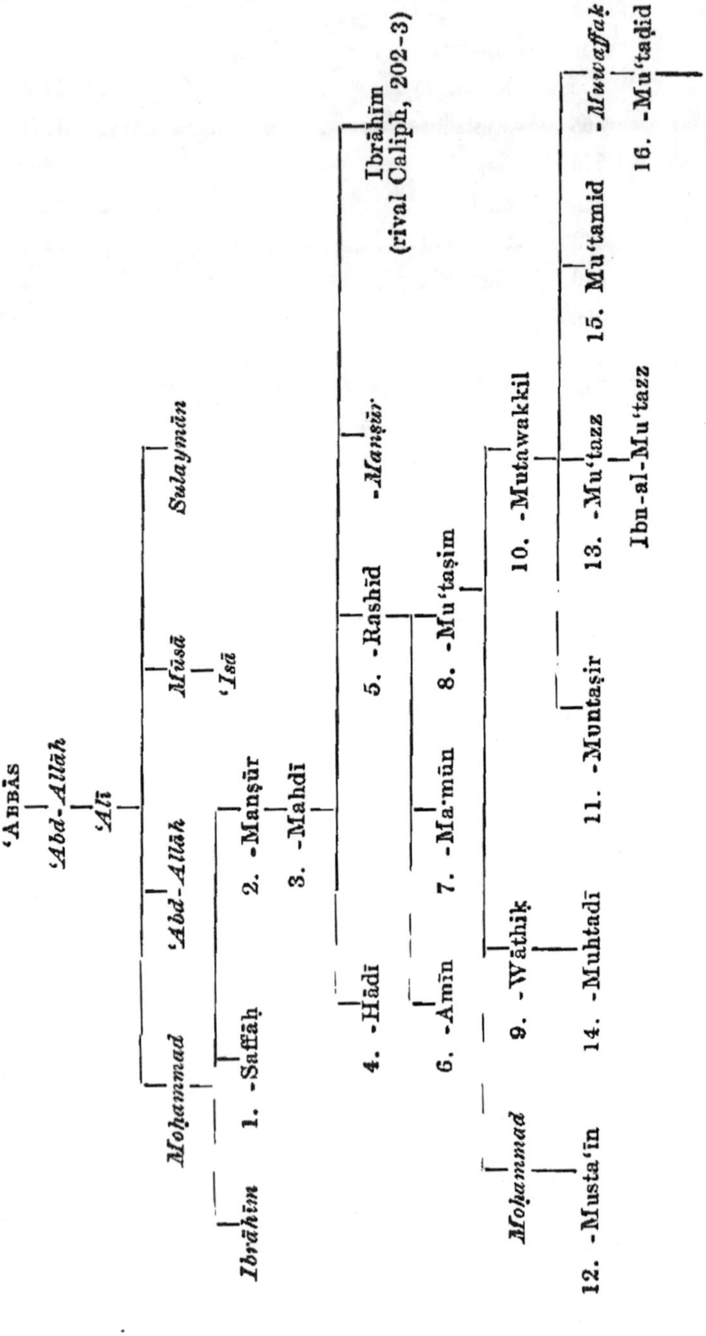

17. -Muktafī | 18. -Muktadir | 19. -Kāhir

22 -Mustakfī

20. -Rāḍī | 21. -Muttakī | 23. -Mutī'

24. -Ṭā·i'

25. -Kādir

26. -Kā·im

Jāhirat-al-dīn

27. -Muktadī

28. -Mustaẓhir

29. -Mustarshid | 31. -Muktafī

30. -Rāshid

32. -Mustanjid

33. -Mustaḍī

34. -Nāṣir

35. -Ẓāhir

36. -Mustanṣir | *-Mustanṣir 'Abbāsid Caliph of Egypt*

37. -Musta'ṣim

II. SPAIN

SÆC. VIII–XV

4. OMAYYADS OF CORDOVA

MINOR DYNASTIES

5. ḤAMMŪDIDS (MALAGA)

6. ḤAMMŪDIDS (ALGECIRAS)

7. 'ABBĀDIDS (SEVILLE)

8. ZAYRIDS (GRANADA)

9. JAHWARIDS (CORDOVA)

10. DHU-*L*-NŪNIDS (TOLEDO)

11. 'ĀMIRIDS (VALENCIA)

12. TOJIBIDS AND HŪDIDS (ZARAGOZA)

13. KINGS OF DENIA

ALMORAVIDES (*See NORTH AFRICA*)

ALMOHADES „ „ „

14. NAṢRIDS (GRANADA)

II. SPAIN

SÆC. VIII–XV

Spain was conquered by the Muslims in 710–12 (*91–3*), and ruled, like the other provinces of the Moḥammadan empire, by a series of governors appointed by the Omayyad Caliphs, until 756 (*138*). Among the few members of the Omayyad family who escaped from the general massacre which signalized the accession of the 'Abbāsids was 'Abd-*al*-Raḥmān, a grandson of Hishām, the tenth Omayyad Caliph. After some years of wandering, he took advantage of the disordered state of Spain, which was divided by the jealousies of the Berbers and the various Arab tribes, to offer himself as king. He met with an encouraging response, and landed in Andulasia at the close of 755. In the following year (*138*) he received the homage of most of Moḥammadan Spain, and successfully repelled an invasion of 'Abbāsid troops. His successors maintained themselves on the throne of Cordova with varying success against the encroachments of the Christians of the north, and the insurrections of the many factions among their own subjects, for two centuries and a half. They contented themselves with the titles of Amīr and Sulṭān, until 'Abd-al-Raḥmān III adopted that of Caliph in 929 (*317*). He was the greatest of the line, and not only exercised absolute sway over his subjects and kept the Christian kings of Leon, Castile and Navarre in check, but warded off the chief danger of Moorish Spain, invasion from Africa, and maintained his authority on the Mediterranean by powerful fleets. After his death, no great Omayyad carried on his work, but the famous minister and general, Almanzor (Al-Manṣūr), preserved the unity of the kingdom. After this, at the beginning of the eleventh century, Moorish Spain became a prey to factions and adventurers, and a number of petty dynasties arose, who are known in Spanish history as the *Reyes de Ṭaifas* or Party Kings. Most of these were absorbed by the most distinguished of their number, the cultured house of the 'Abbādids of Seville, who were the leaders of the Spanish Moors against the encroachments of the Christians, until they were forced to summon the *Almoravides* to their aid, and discovered that they had invited a master instead of an ally.

A.H.		A.D.
138—422	**4. OMAYYADS OF CORDOVA**	756—1031
138	'Abd-*al*-Raḥmān I	756
172	Hishâm I	788
180	-Ḥakam I	796
206	'Abd-*al*-Raḥmān II	822
238	Moḥammad I	852
273	-Mundhir	886
275	'Abd-Allāh	888
300	'Abd-*al*-Raḥmān III. (Al-Khalīfa *Al*-Nāṣir)	912
350	-Ḥakam II -Mustanṣir	961
366	Hishâm II -Mu'ayyad	976
399	Moḥammad II -Mahdī	1009
400	Sulaymān -Musta'īn	1009
400	Moḥammad II (again)	1010
400	Hishâm II (again)	1010
403	Sulaymān (again)	1013
407	*'Alī b. Ḥammūd* *	1016
408	'Abd-*al*-Raḥmān IV -Murtaḍā	1018
408	-*Ḳāsim b. Ḥammūd*	1018
412	*Yaḥyā b. 'Alī*	1021
413	-*Ḳāsim* (again)	1022
414	'Abd-*al*-Raḥmān V -Mustaẓhir	1023
414	Moḥammad III -Mustakfī	1024
416	*Yaḥyā* (again)	1025
418	Hishām III -Mu'tadd	1027
—422		—1031

[*Minor Dynasties*]

* Of the dynasty of Ḥammūdids. See Table 5.

OMAYYADS OF CORDOVA

- *Hishām, 10th Omayyad Caliph*
  - *Mo'āwiya*
    - 1. 'Abd-al-Raḥmān I
      - 2. Hishām I
        - 3. -Ḥakam I
          - 3. 'Abd-al-Raḥmān II
            - 5. Moḥammad I
              - 6. Mundhir
              - 7. 'Abd-Allāh
                - *Moḥammad*
                  - 8. 'Abd-al-Raḥmān III
                    - 9. -Ḥakam II
                      - 10. Hishām II
                    - *'Abd-al-Jabbār*
                      - *Hishām*
                        - 11. Moḥammad II
                        - 14. 'Abd-al-Raḥmān V
                    - *Sulaymān*
                      - *-Ḥakam*
                        - 12. Sulaymān
                    - *'Abd-al-Malik*
                      - *Moḥammad*
                        - 13. 'Abd-al-Raḥmān IV
                        - 16. Hishām III
                    - *'Obayd-Allāh*
                      - *'Abd-al-Raḥmān*
                        - 15. Moḥammad III

MINOR SPANISH DYNASTIES *

(REYES DE TAIFAS)

A.H.		A.D.
407–449	5. ḤAMMŪDIDS † (MALAGA)	1016–1057
407	ʻAlī -Nâṣir	1016
408	-Ḳāsim -Ma·mūn	1018
412	Yaḥyā Mu'tali	1021
413	-Ḳāsim (again)	1022
416	Yaḥyā (again)	1025
427	Idrīs I -Muta·ayyad	1035
431	Ḥasau -Mustanṣir	1039
434	Idrīs II -ʻÂlī	1042
438	Moḥammad I -Mahdī	1046
444	Idrīs III -Muwaffaḳ	1052
445	Idrīs II (again)	1053
446	Moḥammad II -Mustaʻlī	1054—
—449		1057

[*Almoravides*]

* In the tables and trees of these dynasties Codera's *Tratado de Numismática Arábigo-Española* (1879) has been generally followed: which see for lists of various petty rulers here omitted.

† The Hammūdids took the title of Caliph or 'Prince of the Faithful.'

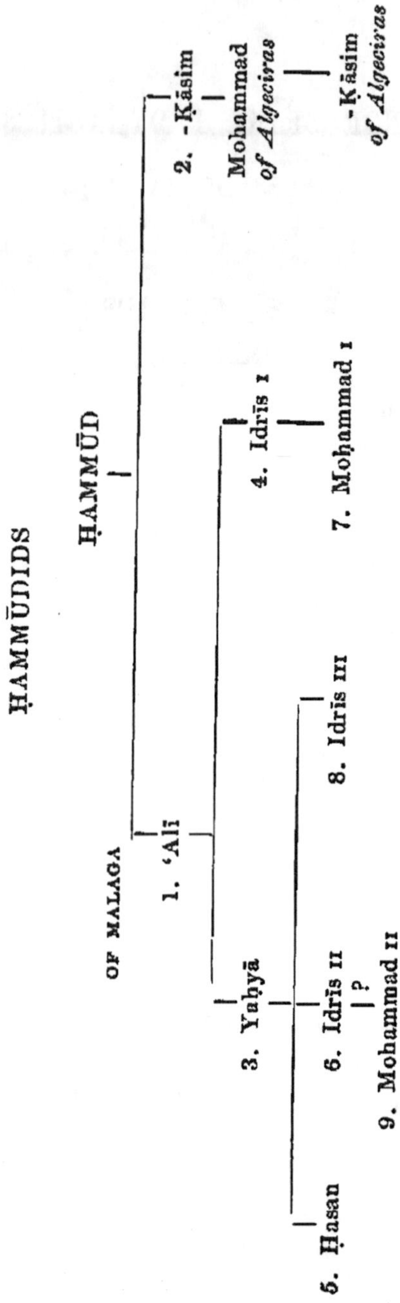
ḤAMMŪDIDS
OF MALAGA
ḤAMMŪD
1. ʻAlī
2. Ḳāsim
3. Yaḥyā
4. Idrīs I
Mohammad of Algeciras
5. Ḥasan
6. Idrīs II
7. Moḥammad I
8. Idrīs III
Ḳāsim of Algeciras
?
9. Mohammad II

A.H.		A.D.
431—450	**6. ḤAMMŪDIDS (ALGECIRAS)**	1039—1058
431	Moḥammad -Mahdī	1039
440	-Ḳāsim -Wāthiḳ	1048
—450		—1058
	[*'Abbādids of Seville*]	
414—484	**7. 'ABBĀDIDS (SEVILLE)**	1023—1091
414	Abū-l-Ḳāsim Moḥammad I. b. Ismā'īl . .	1023
434	Abū-'Amr 'Abbād -Mu'taḍid b. Moḥammad I .	1042
461—484	Abū-l-Ḳāsim Moḥammad II -Mu'tamid b. 'Abbād	1068—1091
	[*Almoravides*]	
403—483	**8. ZAYRIDS (GRANADA)**	1012—1090
403	Zāwī b. Zayrī	1012
410	Ḥabbūs	1019
430	Bādīs b. Ḥabbūs -Muẓaffar -Nāṣir . . .	1038
466	'Abd-Allāh b. Sayf-*al*-dawla Bulukkīn b. Bādīs .	1073
483	Tamīm b. Bulukkīn	1090
	[*Almoravides*]	
422—461	**9. JAHWARIDS (CORDOVA)**	1031—1068
422	Abū-l-Ḥazam Jahwar	1031
435	Abū-l-Walīd Moḥammad b. Jahwar . . .	1043
450—461	'Abd-al-Malik b. Moḥammad	1058—1068
	[*'Abbādids of Seville*]	
427—478	**10. DHU-*L*-NŪNIDS (TOLEDO)**	
427	Ismā'īl -Ẓāfir	1035
429	Yaḥyā -Ma'mūn b. Ismā'īl	1037
467—478	Yaḥyā -Ḳādir b. Ismā'īl b.-Ma'mūn . . .	1074—1085
	[*Alfonso VI of Leon*]	

A.H.		A.D.
412—478	11. 'ĀMIRIDS (VALENCIA)	1021—1085
412	'Abd-al-'Azīz -Manṣūr	1021
453	'Abd-al-Malik -Muẓaffar	1061
457	-*Ma'mūn of Toledo*	1065
467	-*Ḳādir* ,, ,, ...	1074
468	Abū-Bakr b. 'Abd-al-Malik	1075
478	-Ḳāḍī 'Othmān b. Abū-Bakr	1085
,,	-*Ḳādir of Toledo*	,,

[*Christians* (the *Cid*): then *Almoravides*]

410—536	12. TOJIBIDS & HŪDIDS (ZARAGOZA)	1019—1141
410	Mundhir -Manṣūr b. Yaḥyā -Tojibī	1019
414	Yaḥyā -Muẓaffar b. Mundhir	1023
420	Mundhir b. Yaḥyā	1029

431	Sulaymān -Musta'īn b. Hūd	1039
438	Aḥmad Sayf-*al*-dawla -Muḳtadir b. Sulaymān .	1046
474	Yūsuf -Mu'taman b. Aḥmad	1081
478	Aḥmad -Musta'īn b. Yūsuf	1085
503	'Abd-al-Malik 'Imād-*al*-dawla b. Aḥmad . .	1109
513—536	Aḥmad Sayf-*al*-dawla b. 'Abd-al-Malik . .	1119—1141

[*Christians*]

408—468	13. KINGS OF DENIA	1017—1075
408	Mujāhid b. Yūsuf	1017
436—468	'Alī Iḳbāl-*al*-dawla b. Mujāhid . . .	1044—1075

[*Hūdids of Zaragoza*]

In 1086 the *Almoravides* came to Spain, summoned by the 'Abbādids to help them against Alfonso of Leon. In 1090 they came again, and this time they conquered the whole of Moorish Spain, and made it a province of their African empire (see Table 19). Their successors in Africa, the *Almohades*, similarly annexed the Spanish province in 1145–50 (see Table 20). A few petty dynasties sprang up at Valencia and Murcia between these two invasions, and during the decline of the Almohades' power; but the only important line was that of the Naṣrids or Banū-Naṣr of Granada, whose cultivated Court and beautiful palace, Alhambra, for a time revived the splendour and distinction of Moorish Spain as it had been in the days of the great Caliph 'Abd-*al*-Raḥmān III. Their long struggle against the advancing Christians, however, ended in the fall of Granada before the assaults of Ferdinand and Isabella in 1492, and with the flight of Boabdil the last remnant of Moḥammadan rule vanished from the Peninsula.

A.H.		A.D.
629—897	14. NAṢRIDS (GRANADA)	1232—1492
629	Moḥammad I -Ghālib	1232
671	Moḥammad II -Faḳīh	1273
701	Moḥammad III	1302
708	Naṣr Abū-l-Juyūsh	1309
713	Ismā'īl I Abū-l-Walīd	1314
725	Moḥammad IV	1325
733	Yūsuf Abū-l-Ḥajjāj	1333
755	Moḥammad V -Ghānī	1354
760	Ismā'īl II	1359
761	Moḥammad VI Abū-Sa'īd	1360
763	Moḥammad V (again)	1362
793	Yūsuf II	1391
794	Moḥammad VII	1392
810	Yūsuf III Abū-l-Ḥajjāj -Nāṣir	1407
820	Moḥammad VIII -Mutamaṣṣik	1417
831	Moḥammad IX -Ṣaghīr	1427
833	Moḥammad VIII (again)	1429
835	Yūsuf IV	1432
835	Moḥammad VIII (third time)	1432
848	Moḥammad X	1444
849	Sa'd -Musta'īn	1445
850	Moḥammad X (again)	1446
857	Sa'd (again)	1453
866	'Alī Abū-l-Ḥasan	1461
887	Moḥammad XI (Boabdil)	1482
888	'Alī Abū-l-Ḥasan (again)	1483
890	Moḥammad XII (Zaghal)	1485
892 —897	Moḥammad XI (Boabdil, again)	1486 —1492

[*Ferdinand and Isabella of Castile*]

NAṢRIDS OF GRANADA

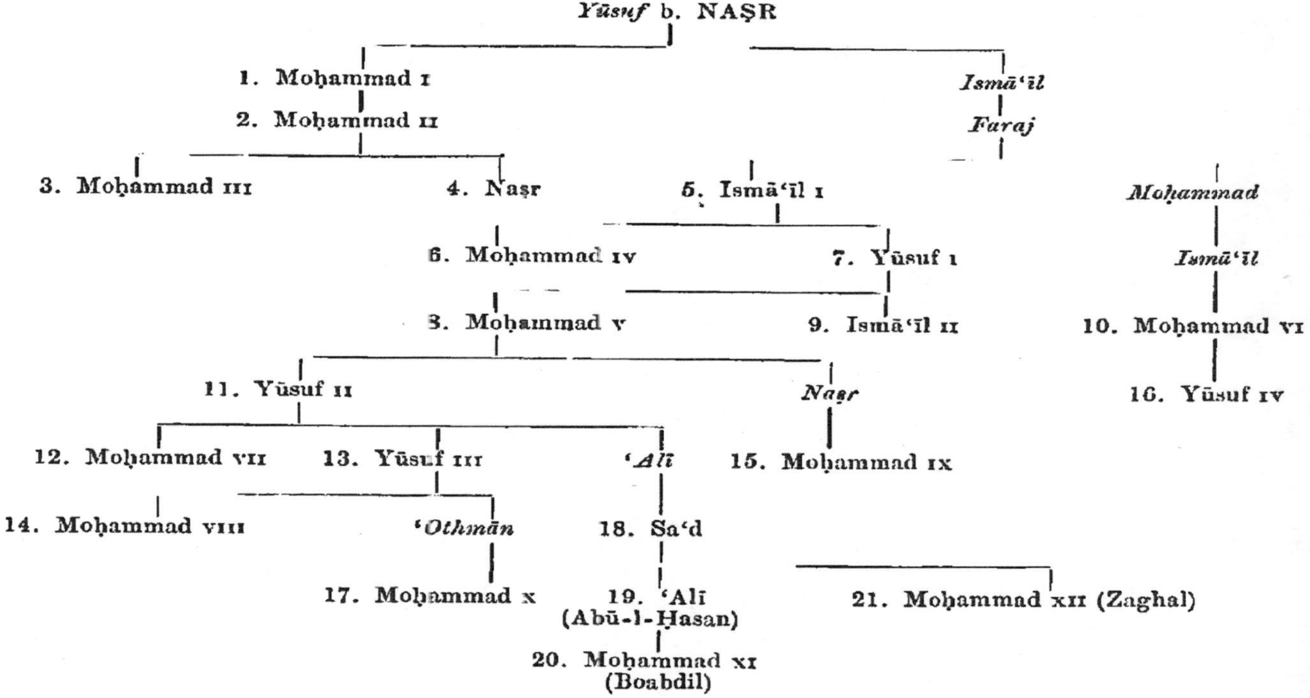

III. NORTH AFRICA

SÆC. VIII–XIX

15. IDRĪSIDS (MOROCCO)

16. AGHLABIDS (TUNIS, ETC.)

FĀṬIMIDS (*See EGYPT*)

17. ZAYRIDS (TUNIS)

18. ḤAMMĀDIDS (ALGIERS)

19. ALMORAVIDES (MOROCCO, ALGIERS, SPAIN)

20. ALMOHADES (NORTH AFRICA, SPAIN)

21. MARĪNIDS (MOROCCO)

22. ZIYĀNIDS (ALGIERS)

23. ḤAFṢIDS (TUNIS)

24. SHARĪFS (MOROCCO)

III. NORTH AFRICA

SÆC. VIII–XIX

The narrow strip of habitable land between the grea African desert and the Mediterranean Sea was always the nursery of schismatics. The superstitious and credulous Berbers offered a favourable soil for the germination of all varieties of Moḥammadan heresy. Any prophet who found himself without honour in his own country had only to go to the Berbers of North Africa to be sure of a welcome and an enthusiastic following; whilst the distance from the centre of the Caliphate and the natural turbulence and warlike character of the population predisposed the 'Abbāsids to ignore the disloyalty of provinces which profited them little and cost them ceaseless energy and expense to control. Hence the success of such strange developments of Islām as the Almoravides and Almohades, the establishment of 'Alid dynasties such as the Idrīsids and Fāṭimids, and in our own time the widespread authority of the Prophet -Sanūsī.

North Africa had been subdued by the Arabs with difficulty between the years 647 (*26*) and 700, and had since been ruled with varying success by the lieutenants of the Caliphs. So long as Yazīd b. Ḥātim, the popular and energetic governor of Ḳayrawān for the 'Abbāsids, lived, the tendency of the Berbers to foster rebellion and schism was held in check, but on his death in 787 (*170*) North Africa became a prey to anarchy, which was only suppressed by allowing the local dynasties, which then sprang up, to exercise independent authority. After the year 800 the 'Abbāsid Caliphs had no influence whatever west of the frontier of Egypt.

A.H.		A.D.
172—375	15. IDRĪSIDS	788—985

15. IDRĪSIDS (MOROCCO)

In the year 785 (*168*) an insurrection of the partisans of the family of ʿAlī took place at -Medīna. Among those who took part in it was Idrīs b. ʿAbd-Allāh b. Ḥasan b. Ḥasan b. ʿAlī b. Abū-Ṭālib. On the suppression of the revolt Idrīs fled to Egypt, and thence to Morocco where he founded an ʿAlid dynasty in the region about Ceuta. His coins bear the names of the towns of Tudgha and -Walīla. The Idrīsid dominions reached their greatest extent about 860, and gradually dwindled until the extinction of the dynasty in 985 (*375*). Some of the dates are not recorded by Ibn-Khaldūn.

172	Idrīs I	788
177	Idrīs II b. Idrīs I	793
213	Moḥammad b. Idrīs II	828
221	ʿAlī I b. Moḥammad	836
234	Yaḥyā I b. Moḥammad	849
	Yaḥyā II b. Yaḥyā	
	ʿAlī II b. ʿOmar b. Idrīs II	
	Yaḥyā III b. -Ḳāsim b. Idrīs II	
292	Yaḥyā IV b. Idrīs b. ʿOmar	904
310	-Ḥasan	922

[*Miknasa Berbers*]

A.H.		A.D.
184—296	16. AGHLABIDS (TUNIS, ETC.)	800—909

Ibrāhīm b. -Aghlab was governor of the province of Zāb for the Caliph at the time of confusion which followed upon the death of Yazīd the 'Abbāsid governor-general of 'Africa' (Afrīḳiya, *i.e.* Tunis) in 787 (*170*), and was appointed to the government of the whole African province by the Caliph Hārūn -Rashīd in 800 (*184*); but did not interfere with the authority of the Idrīsids in the far west. His dynasty was practically independent, and the Aghlabids seldom troubled to put the Caliphs' names on their coins in token even of spiritual suzerainty. They were not only enlightened and energetic rulers on land, but employed large fleets on the Mediterranean, harried the coasts of Italy, France, Corsica, and Sardinia, and conquered Sicily in 827–78; which island remained in Moḥammadan hands until the conquest by the Normans. The Aghlabid domination in Africa when at its best was indeed the period of the greatest ascendancy of the Arabs in the Mediterranean: their corsairs were the terror of the seas, and besides Sicily they took Malta and Sardinia, and even invaded the suburbs of Rome. The incapacity of the later Aghlabid princes, however, and the growth of sectarian disaffection under the fostering influence of the Shī'ite Idrīsids in the west, paved the way for the Fāṭimid triumph in 909 (*296*).

184	Ibrāhīm I	800
196	'Abd-Allāh I	811
201	Ziyādat-Allāh I	816
223	Abū-'Akāl -Aghlab	837
226	Moḥammad I	840
242	Aḥmad	856
249	Ziyādat-Allāh II	863
250	Moḥammad II	864
261	Ibrāhīm II	874
289	'Abd-Allāh II.	902
290	Ziyādat-Allāh III	903
—296		—909

[*Fāṭimids*]

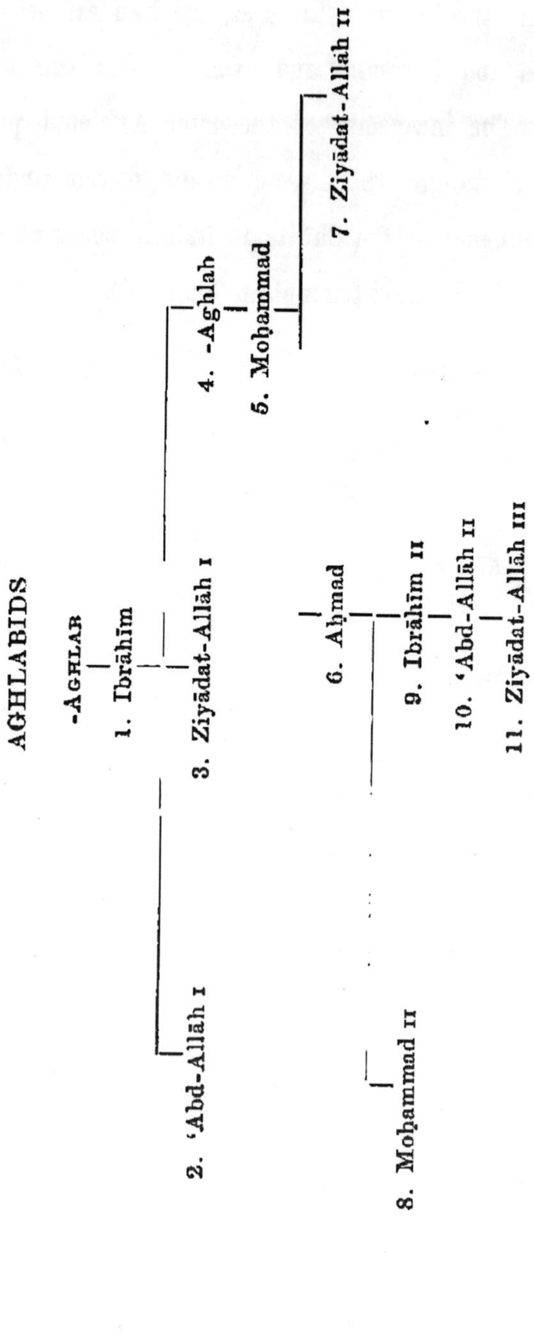
AGHLABIDS
-Aghlab
1. Ibrāhīm
2. 'Abd-Allāh I
3. Ziyādat-Allāh I
4. -Aghlab
5. Moḥammad
6. Aḥmad
7. Ziyādat-Allāh II
8. Moḥammad II
9. Ibrāhīm II
10. 'Abd-Allāh II
11. Ziyādat-Allāh III

The Aghlabids were succeeded by the *Fāṭimids*, who, however, belong more particularly to the series of Egyptian Dynasties (see Table 27). Their empire, which at one time included the whole north African coast from Egypt to the Atlantic, together with Sicily and Sardinia, became split up into various kingdoms as soon as their removal of their seat of government to Cairo in 972 (*362*) weakened their control of the more western provinces. Their lieutenant over Africa, Yūsuf Bulukkīn, chief of the Sanhaja Berbers, soon declared himself independent and founded the dynasty of the *Zayrids*, whilst another dynasty, the *Ḥammādids*, established themselves at Bougie (Bujāya) in Algeria and restricted the Zayrids' authority to little more than the province of Tunis. Further west in Morocco various tribes of Berbers, -Miknasa, Maghrawa, etc., acquired independence, and occupied the site of the Idrīsids' kingdom, but hardly attained to the dignity of dynasties. These were in turn subdued by the *Almoravides*, who also took a large part of the territory of the Ḥammādids of Algeria; but it was reserved for the *Almohades* to reign in the capitals of Ḥammād and Zayrī.

A.H.		A.D.
362—543	17. ZAYRIDS (TUNIS)	972—1148
362	Yūsuf Bulukkīn b. Zayrī	972
373	Manṣūr b. Yūsuf	983
386	Bādīs b. Manṣūr	996
406	-Mu'izz b. Bādīs	1015
453	Tamīm b. -Mu'izz	1061
501	Yaḥyā b. Tamīm	1107
509	'Alī b. Yaḥyā	1115
515	-Ḥasan b. 'Alī	1121
—543		—1148

[*Roger of Sicily; then Almohades*]

398—547	ḤAMMĀDIDS (ALGERIA)	1007—1152
398	Ḥammād	1007
419	-Ḳāïd b. Ḥammad	1028
446	Muḥassin b. -Ḳāïd	1054
447	Bulukkīn b. Moḥammad b. Ḥammād .	1055
454 ?	-Nāṣir b. 'Alnās b. Moḥammad . .	1062 ?
481	-Manṣūr b. -Nāṣir	1088
498	Bādīs	1104
500	-'Azīz	1106
?	Yaḥyā b. -'Azīz	——
—547		—1152

[*Almohades*]

A.H. A.D.

448–541 19. ALMORAVIDES (-MURĀBIṬS) 1056–1147

(MOROCCO, PART OF ALGERIA, SPAIN)

In the middle of the eleventh century the successes of the Christians in Spain, the energy of the Genoese and Pisans in recovering for Christendom the islands of Corsica and Sardinia, and the valour of the Normans in Southern Italy, had thoroughly humbled the power of the Muslims in the Mediterranean. The Fāṭimids of Egypt alone maintained the ancient prestige of the Saracens. The Zayrids of Tunis were incapable even of repressing the frequent revolts which disturbed their restricted dominion; and the rivalry between Zayrids, Ḥammādids, and Fāṭimids prevented any collective action against the Christians. It was time for a Moḥammadan revival, and among a people so easily excited to religious exaltation as the Berbers a revival was always possible if a prophet could be found. The prophet appeared among the tribe of Lamtuna in the person of 'Abd-Allāh b. Tāshfīn. This man preached a holy war for the glory of Islām, and the Berbers were not slow to follow him. His adherents called themselves *Al-Murābiṭīn*, which means literally 'pickets who have hobbled their horses on the enemy's frontier,' and hence 'Protagonists for the Faith.'

The Spaniards corrupted the name into Almoravides, and the French *marabout*, or devotee, is another perversion of it. The Almoravides acknowledged the supremacy of the 'Abbāsid Caliphs. The Lamtuna Berbers under 'Abd-Allāh were joined by the great clan of the Masmuda, and led by Abū-Bakr and his second cousin Yūsuf b. Tāshfīn, reduced Sijilmāsa and Aghmāt by 1068 (*460*), founded the city of Morocco (Marrākush), and in the course of the next fifteen years spread over Fez, Mequinez (Miknasa), Ceuta (Sabta), Tangier (Ṭanja), Salee, and the west of Morocco. In 1086 Yūsuf b. Tāshfīn, whose great qualities both as general and as administrator had secured the devotion of the Protagonists, was entreated by the 'Abbādids of Spain to come over and help them against the assaults of Alfonso VI. and Sancho of Aragon and the invincible valour of the Cid Campeador Rodrigo Diaz de Bivar. Yūsuf utterly crushed the Castilian army at the battle of Zallāka, or, as the Spaniards call it, Sacralias, near Badajoz, October 23, 1086; but he did not follow up his victory. Leaving 3000 Berbers to support the Andalusians he returned to Africa. But in 1090 the King of Seville again prayed him to come and help him against the Christians, and this time Yūsuf annexed the whole of Moorish Spain, with the exception of

Toledo, which remained in the possession of the Christians, and Zaragosa, where the Hūdids were suffered to subsist. The success of the Almoravides, however, was fleeting. Their hardy warriors soon became enervated in soft Andalusia, and offered no adequate resistance to the steady advance of the Christians. They made no attempt to recover the command of the Mediterranean, and were content to leave the Ḥammādids and Zayrids in possession of most of Algeria, Tunis, and Tripoli. The Almoravide dynasty had lasted less than a century when the fanatical rush of the *Almohades* swept over the whole of north Africa and southern Spain, and left no rival house standing.

A.H.		A.D.
448	Abū-Bakr	1056
480	Yūsuf	1087
500	'Alī	1106
537	Tāshfīn	1143
541	Ibrāhīm	1146
541	Isḥāḳ	1147

ALMORAVIDES

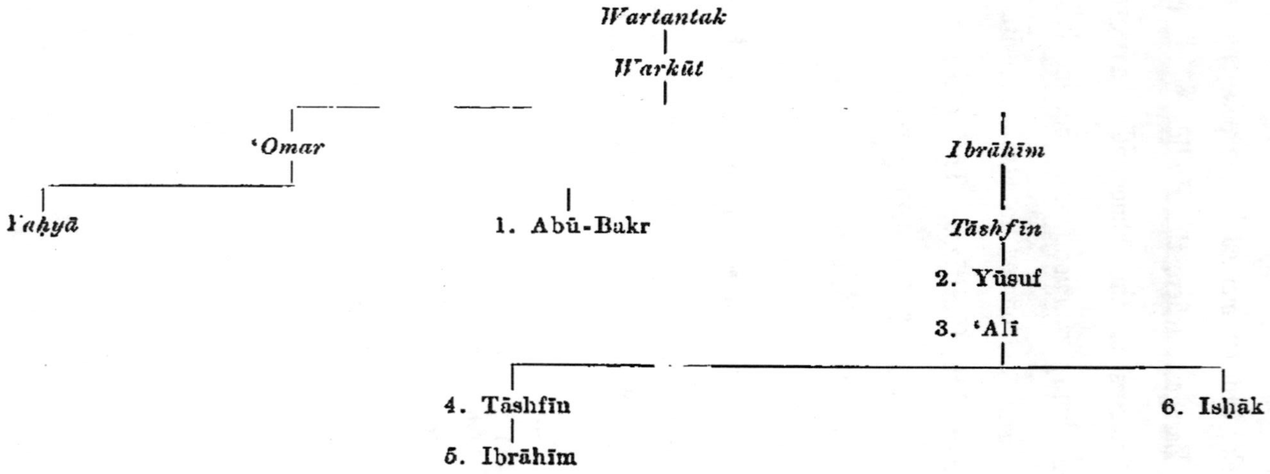

A.H.		A.D.
524–667	20. ALMOHADES (-MUWAḤḤIDS)	1130–1269

(ALL NORTH AFRICA)

The Muwaḥḥids (in Spanish, Almohades) or Unitarians were so called because their doctrine was a protest against the realistic anthropomorphism of orthodox Islām. Their prophet Abū-'Abd-Allāh Moḥammad b. Tūmart, a Berber of the Masmuda tribe, began to preach the doctrine of the Unity of God (-*Tawḥīd*) and took the symbolic title of the Mahdī, at the beginning of the 12th century. Dying in 1128 (*522*) he left the command of the Unitarians to his friend and general 'Abd-al-Mu'min, who formally accepted the chief authority over the Masmuda Muwaḥḥids in 1130. In 1140 (*534*) 'Abd-al-Mu'min began a long career of conquest. He annihilated the army of the Almoravides in 1144, captured Oran, Tilimsān, Fez, Ceuta, Aghmāt, and Salee in two years, and by the successful siege of Morocco in 1146 (*541*) put an end to the Almoravide dynasty. Meanwhile he had sent an army into Spain (1145) and in the course of five years reduced the whole Moorish part of the Peninsula to his sway. Master of Morocco and Spain, he next carried his conquests eastwards, and in 1152 (*547*) abolished the Ḥammūdid rule in Algeria; in 1158 (*553*) he drove the Norman successors of the Zayrids out of Tunis, and by the annexation of Tripoli united the whole coast from the frontier of Egypt to the Atlantic together with Moorish Spain under his sceptre. The Holy War with the Christians in Spain was the chief anxiety of his successors, and the disastrous defeat at Las Navas in 1235 (*632*) was the signal for the expulsion of the Almohades from the Peninsula, which was then divided between the ever-encroaching Christians and the local Moḥammadan dynasties, among whom the Naṣrids of Granada (Table 14) offered the most stubborn resistance to the enemy, and held out until the fall of their city in 1492 delivered the whole of Spain over to Ferdinand and Isabella the Catholic. The loss of Spain was quickly followed by the undermining of the Almohades' power in Africa. Tripoli had long before been annexed by Saladin (1172). Their lieutenants in Tunis, the *Ḥafṣids*, threw off their allegiance and founded an independent dynasty in 1228; whose example was followed by the *Ziyānids* of Tlemçen (Tilimsān) in western Algeria, in 1235; while, amidst the confusion created by many pretenders to the throne of Morocco, the chiefs of the mountain tribe of the *Marīnids* pushed their way to the front and put an end to the dynasty of the Almohades by the conquest of their capital, Morocco, in 1269 (*667*).

A.H.		A.D.
524	'Abd-al-Mu'min	1130
558	Abū-Ya'ḳūb Yūsuf I	1163
580	Abū-Yūsuf Ya'ḳūb -Mansūr . . .	1184
595	Moḥammad -Nāṣir	1199
611	Abū-Ya'ḳūb Yūsuf II -Mustanṣir . .	1214
620	'Abd-al-Wāḥid -Makhlū'	1223
621	Abū-Moḥammad 'Abd-Allāh -'Ādil .	1224
624	Yaḥyā -Mu'taṣim	1227
626	Abū-l-'Ulā Idrīs -Ma'mūn . . .	1229
630	'Abd-al-Wāḥid -Rashīd	1232
640	Abū-l-Ḥasan 'Alī -Sa'īd	1242
646	Abū-Ḥafṣ 'Omar -Murtaḍa	1248
665	Abū-l-'Ulā -Wāthiḳ	1266
—667		—1269

[*Marīnids, Ziyānids, Ḥafṣids*]

ALMOHADES

- *'Alī*
  - 1. 'Abd-al-Mu'min
    - 2. Abū-Ya'ḳūb Yūsuf I
      - 3. Abū-Yūsuf Ya'ḳūb -Manṣūr (dashed line)
        - 4. Mohammad -Nāṣir
          - 5. Abū-Ya'ḳūb Yūsuf II -Mustanṣir
          - 8. Yaḥyā -Mu'taṣim
        - 7. 'Abd-Allāh -'Ādil
        - 9. Idrīs -Ma'mūn
          - 10. 'Abd-al-Wāḥid -Rashīd
          - 11. Abu-l-Ḥasan 'Alī -Sa'īd
      - 6. 'Abd-al-Wāḥid -Makhlū'
      - *Isḥāḳ*
        - 12. 'Omar -Murtaḍa
    - *Abū-Ḥafṣ 'Omar*
      - *Moḥammad*
        - 13. Abū-l-'Ulā -Wāthiḳ

A.H. 625—941 | 21. ḤAFṢIDS | A.D. 1228—1534

21. ḤAFṢIDS (TUNIS)

A.H. 625—941 A.D. 1228—1534

The Ḥafṣids were at first lieutenants of the Almohades in their province of Tunis. The government passed from father to son, and the dynasty became independent. For three centuries the Ḥafṣids governed Tunis with justice and mildness, and cultivated friendly commercial relations with the trading republics of Italy. The Corsair Khayr-*al*-dīn Barbarossa conquered Tunis in the name of the Ottoman Sultan in 1534, and though the Emperor Charles v. restored the Ḥafṣid king in 1535 and placed a Spanish garrison at the Goletta of Tunis, the province remained chiefly in the hands of the Corsairs, who re-took Tunis itself in 1568 and the Goletta in 1574;* since when, it has been a province of the Ottoman Empire, but in 1881 became practically a possession of France. Tripoli, which had been taken from the kingdom of Tunis by the Spaniards in 1510, was added to the Ottoman Empire by the Corsairs in 1551.

* See my *Barbary Corsairs* (1890), ch. viii, xii, xiv, xv.

A.H.		A.D.
625	Abū-Zakaryā Yaḥyā I	1228
647	Abū-'Abd-Allāh Moḥammad I -Mustanṣir .	1249
675	Abū-Zakaryā Yaḥyā II	1277
678	Abū-Isḥāḳ Ibrāhīm I	1279
683	Abū-Ḥafṣ 'Omar I	1284
694	Abu-'Abd-Allāh Moḥammad II -Mustanṣir .	1295
709	Abu-Bakr I -Shadīd	1309
709	Abū-l-Baḳā Khālid I	1309
711	Abū-Yaḥyā Zakaryā	1311
717	Abu-Ḍarba Moḥammad III -Mustanṣir . .	1317
718	Abū-Yaḥyā Abū-Bakr II -Mutawakkil . .	1318
747	Abū-Ḥafṣ 'Omar II	1346
[747	*Marīnid occupation*	1346
750	Abū-l-'Abbās Aḥmad I -Faḍl . . .	1349
751	Abū-Isḥāḳ Ibrāhīm II -Mustanṣir . .	1350
770	Abū-l-Baḳā Khālid II	1368
772	Abu-l-'Abbās Aḥmad II -Mustanṣir . .	1370
796	Abū-Fāris 'Abd-al-'Azīz	1394
837	Moḥammad IV -Muntaṣir	1433
839	Abū-'Amr 'Othmān	1435
893	Abū-Zakaryā Yaḥyā III	1488
899	Abū-'Abd-Allāh Moḥammad V .	1493
932	-Ḥasan	1525
—941		—1534

[*Corsair Pashas, and Beys, under the Ottoman Sultans*]

A.H.		A.D.
633—796	22. ZIYĀNIDS	1235—1393

(ALGERIA)

The Ziyānids, lieutenants of the Almohades in Algeria, followed the example of their neighbours the Ḥafṣids to make themselves independent as soon as their masters began to grow feeble. Their capital was Tlemçen (Tilimsān). In their turn the Ziyānids succumbed to the power of the Marīnids of Morocco in 1393.

633	Yagmorasan b. Ziyān	1235
681	'Othmān I	1282
703	Abū-Ziyān I	1303
707	Abū-Ḥammū Mūsā I	1307
718	Abū-Tāshfīn 'Abd-al-Raḥmān I . .	1318
749	{ Abū-Sa'īd 'Othmān II . . . . . Abū-Thābit -Zaīm	1348
753	Abū-Ḥammū Mūsā II	1352
788	Abū-Tāshfīn 'Abd-al-Raḥmān II . .	1386
796	Abū-Ziyān II	1393

[*Marīnids of Morocco*]

HAFṢIDS

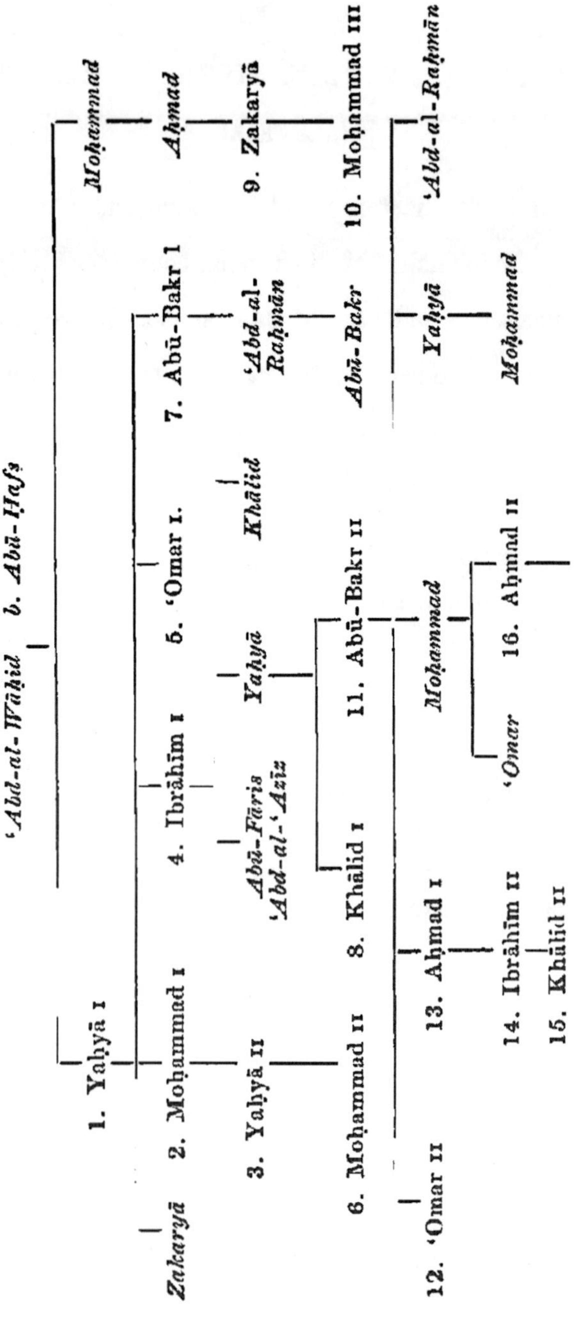

'Abd-al-Wāḥid b. Abū-Ḥafṣ
1. Yaḥyā I
Moḥammad
Zakaryā
2. Moḥammad I
4. Ibrāhīm I
5. 'Omar I.
7. Abū-Bakr I
Aḥmad
3. Yaḥyā II
Abū-Fāris
'Abd-al-'Azīz
Yaḥyā
Khālid
'Abd-al-Raḥmān
9. Zakaryā
6. Moḥammad II
8. Khālid I
11. Abū-Bakr II
Abū-Bakr
10. Moḥammad III
12. 'Omar II
13. Aḥmad I
Moḥammad
Yaḥyā
'Abd-al-Raḥmān
14. Ibrāhīm II
15. Khālid II
'Omar
16. Aḥmad II
Moḥammad

- 17. Abū-Fāris 'Abd-al-'Azīz
  - *Manṣūr*
    - 18. Moḥammad IV
      - 19. 'Othmān
        - *Mas'ūd*
          - 20. Yaḥyā III
          - *Ḥasan*
            - 21. Moḥammad V
              - 22. Ḥasan
                - Aḥmad
                - Moḥammad

ZIYĀNIDS

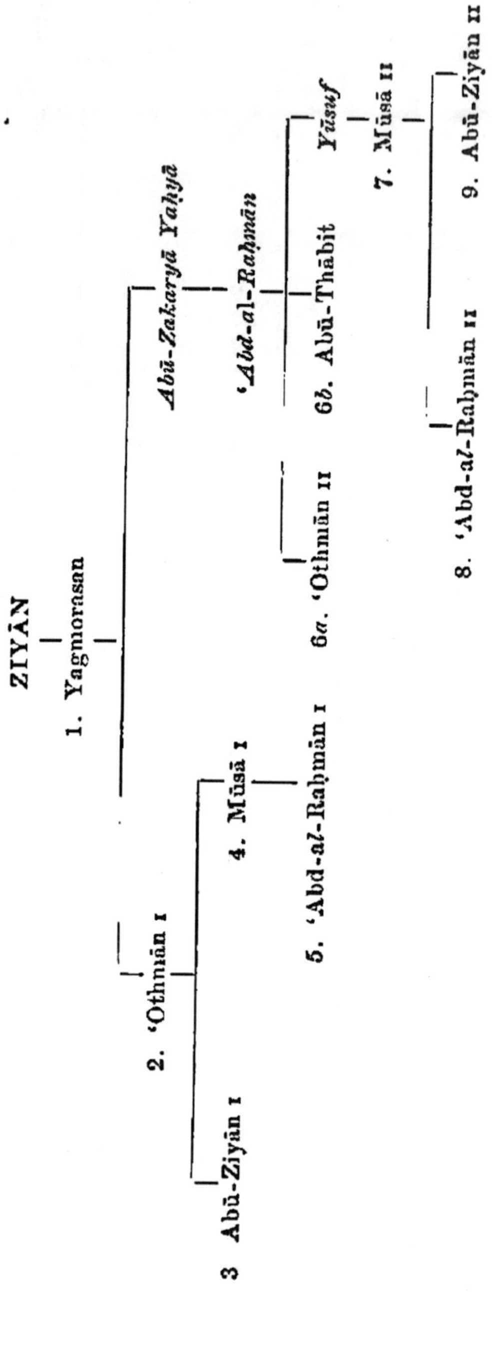
ZIYĀN
1. Yagmorasan
2. 'Othmān I
Abū-Zakaryā Yaḥyā
3 Abū-Ziyān I
4. Mūsā I
'Abd-al-Raḥmān
5. 'Abd-al-Raḥmān I
6a. 'Othmān II
6b. Abū-Thabit
Yūsuf
7. Mūsā II
8. 'Abd-al-Raḥmān II
9. Abū-Ziyān II

From the 16th to the present century the North African provinces of Algiers, Tunis, and Tripoli were in the possession, more or less nominal, of the *'Othmānlī* or Ottoman Sulṭāns of Turkey. The annexation of these provinces was due to the energy of the Barbary Corsairs. Previously to the arrival of Barbarossa, the Spaniards under Don Pedro Navarro had established several strong positions on the African coast, at the Peñon de Alger, Bougie (Bujāya), Oran (Wahrān), Tripoli, etc., with a view to overawing the petty pirates of Algiers. In 1509 Urūj Barbarossa, a Lesbian adventurer, occupied the island of Jarba, off the coast of Tripoli, and began his operations against the Spaniards. He took Jījil in 1514, Algiers in 1516, Tinnis and Tlemçen (Tilimsān) from the Marīnids in 1517; and in 1519 his brother Khayr-al-dīn Barbarossa was recognised by the Ottoman Sulṭān as Beglerbeg or Governor-General of the province of Algiers, which corresponded very nearly to the Algeria of to-day, though the Spaniards kept their hold on the fortress or Peñon de Alger until 1530 and held Oran till 1706. In 1534 Khayr-al-dīn took Tunis from the Ḥafṣids, but the city was retaken by the Emperor Charles v. in the following year, and not restored to the Corsairs of Algiers till 1568. It was again captured for the moment by Don John of Austria in 1573, but finally annexed by Ochiali (Ulūj 'Alī) in 1574. Meanwhile another Corsair, Dragut (Torghūd), reduced Tripoli to the authority of the Porte in 1551, and drove out the Knights of St. John, who had held it since their expulsion from Rhodes in 1522.

The three provinces of Algiers, Tunis, and Tripoli were thus annexed to the Turkish Empire in 1519, 1568, and 1551, respectively. Algiers was governed first by a series of twenty-six Pashas, appointed from Constantinople; but in 1671 the janissary garrison of Algiers elected a *Dey* from amongst themselves, whose power soon eclipsed that of the Pasha, and in 1710 the two offices were united in that of Dey, which subsisted until the French conquest in 1830. Tunis was governed until 1705 by *Deys* appointed by the Porte, after which the Turkish soldiery elected their own *Beys*, one of whom still affects to reign, though Tunis has been occupied by France since 1881. Tripoli is still a Turkish province governed by a Pasha appointed by the Sulṭān. Morocco alone of the North African provinces has never owned Christian rule, though the Spaniards held various forts on the coast, and still retain Ceuta; and the English once owned Tangier, but neglected to keep it.*

* See my *Barbary Corsairs* (1890).

A.H.		A.D.
591—875	23. MARĪNIDS	1195—1470

23. MARĪNIDS (MOROCCO)

The Marīnids traced their dynasty from 1195 (*591*), as rulers in the highlands of Morocco; but they did not succeed to the capital of the Almohades till 1269 (*667*). Soon after 1393 (*796*) they added to their kingdom the territory of the Ziyānids in western Algeria. They were superseded by their kinsmen the Wat'asids in 1470.

591	'Abd-al-Ḥaḳḳ	1195
614	'Othmān I	1217
637	Moḥammad I	1239
642	Abū-Yaḥyā Abū-Bakr	1244
656	Abū-Yūsuf Ya'ḳūb	1258
685	Abū-Ya'ḳūb Yūsuf	1286
706	Abū-Thābit 'Āmir	1306
708	Abū-*l*-Rabī' Sulaymān	1308
710	Abū-Sa'īd 'Othmān II	1310
731	Abū-l-Ḥasan 'Alī	1331
749	Abū-Aynān	1348
759	-Sa'īd	1358
760	Abū-Sālim Ibrāhīm	1359
762	Abū-'Omar Tāshfīn	1361
763	'Abd-al-Ḥalīm	1361
763	Abū-Ziyān Moḥammad II	1361
768	'Abd-al-'Azīz	1366

A.H.		A.D.
774	Moḥammad III -Sa‘īd	1372
776	Abū-l-‘Abbās Aḥmad -Mustanṣir ‘Abd-*al*-Raḥmān	1374
786	Mūsā	1384
786	-Muntaṣir	1384
788	Moḥammad IV -Wathiḳ	1386
789	Abū-l-‘Abbās Aḥmad -Mustanṣir (again)	1387
796	Abū-Fāris	1393
?	Fāris -Mutawakkil	?
811	Abū-Sa‘īd	1408
819	Sa‘īd Ya‘ḳūb	1416
827	‘Abd-Allāh	1424
875	Sharīf	1470

WAT‘ASIDS

A.H.		A.D.
875	Sa‘īd, Shaykh Wat‘as	1470
906	Moḥammad I b. Sa‘īd	1500
936	Aḥmad b. Moḥammad	1530
957	Moḥammad II b. Aḥmad	1550

[*Sharīfs of Morocco*]

MARĪNIDS

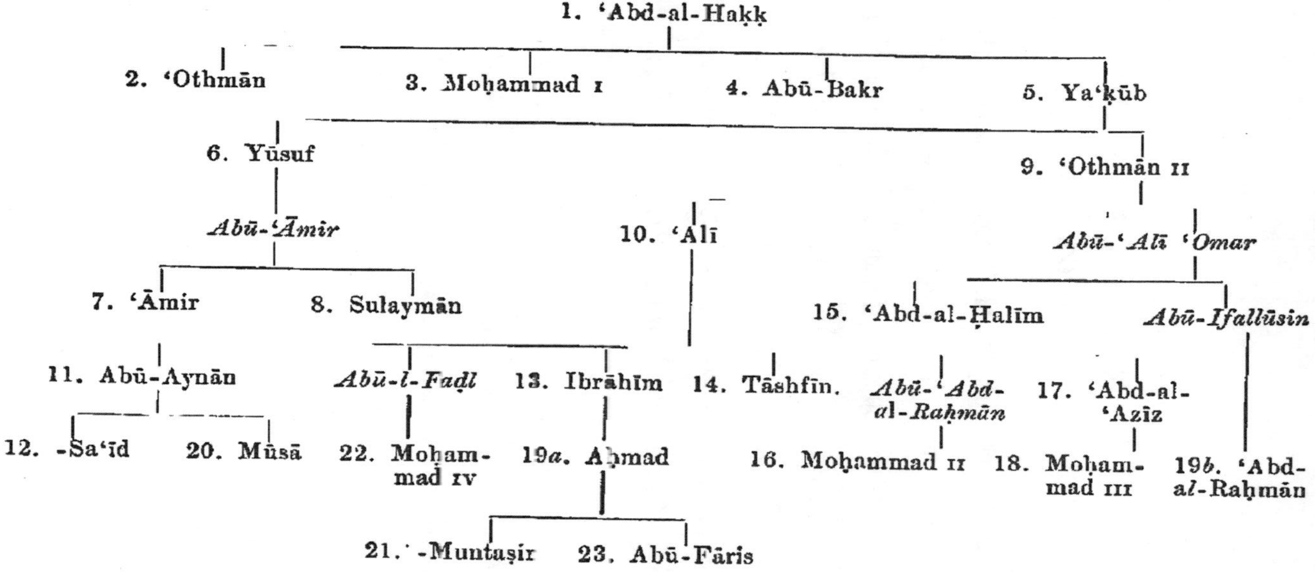
1. ‘Abd-al-Haḳḳ
2. ‘Othmān
3. Moḥammad I
4. Abū-Bakr
5. Ya‘ḳūb
6. Yūsuf
9. ‘Othmān II
Abū-‘Āmir
10. ‘Alī
Abū-‘Alī
‘Omar
7. ‘Āmir
8. Sulaymān
15. ‘Abd-al-Ḥalīm
Abū-Ifallūsin
11. Abū-Aynān
Abū-l-Faḍl
13. Ibrāhīm
14. Tāshfīn.
Abū-‘Abd-al-Raḥmān
17. ‘Abd-al-‘Azīz
12. -Sa‘īd
20. Mūsā
22. Moḥam-mad IV
19a. Aḥmad
16. Moḥammad II
18. Moḥam-mad III
19b. ‘Abd-al-Raḥmān
21. -Muntaṣir
23. Abū-Fāris

A.H.		A.D.
951–1311	24. SHARĪFS	1544–1893
reigning	(MOROCCO)	reigning

The title *Sharīf* (lit. 'noble') implies descent from the Prophet Moḥammad, from whom the Sharīfs of Morocco trace their lineage through Ḥasan the elder son of Fāṭima by 'Alī. The Sharīfs possessed themselves of Tarudant in 1515, and Morocco and Fez soon afterwards, but their formal assumption of sovereignty dates from 1544 (*951*). The series falls into two divisions, Ḥasanī and Filalī Sharīfs, and a period of anarchy for six years occurred between the two. Their boundaries have always remained much as they are in the present day, but there has frequently been a rival Sharīf at Fez in opposition to the Sharīf of Morocco. The Sharīfs claim to be inheritors of the title of Caliph and Prince of the Faithful.

A.H.		A.D.
951—1069	A. ḤASANĪ SHARĪFS	1544—1658
951	Moḥammad I -Shaykh	1544
965	ʻAbd-Allāh	1557
981	Moḥammad II	1573
983	Abū-Marwān ʻAbd-al-Malik I	1575
986	Abū-l-ʻAbbās Aḥmad I -Manṣoor	1578
1012	Shaykh, Abū-Fāris, Zaydān } rivals	1603
1016	Zaydān (alone)	1608
1038	Abū-Marwān ʻAbd-al-Malik II	1628
1040	Walīd	1630
1045	Moḥammad III	1635
1064	Aḥmad II	1654
—1069		—1658

1075—1311	B. FILALĪ SHARĪFS	1664—1893
1075	-Rashīd b. -Sharīf b. ʻAlī	1664
1083	Ismāʻīl -Samīn	1672
1139	Aḥmad -Dhahabī	1727
1141	ʻAbd-Allāh*	1729
1171	Moḥammad I	1757
1204	-Yazīd	1789
1206	Hishām	1792
1209	Sulaymān	1795
1238	ʻAbd-al-Raḥman	1822
1276	Moḥammad II	1859
1290	Ḥasan (now reigning)	1873

* Interrupted by ʻAlī b. Ismāʻīl, 1147-9; -Mustaḍī b. Ismāʻīl, 1151-3, and Zayn-al-ʻAbidīn, 1158.

ḤASANĪ SHARĪFS

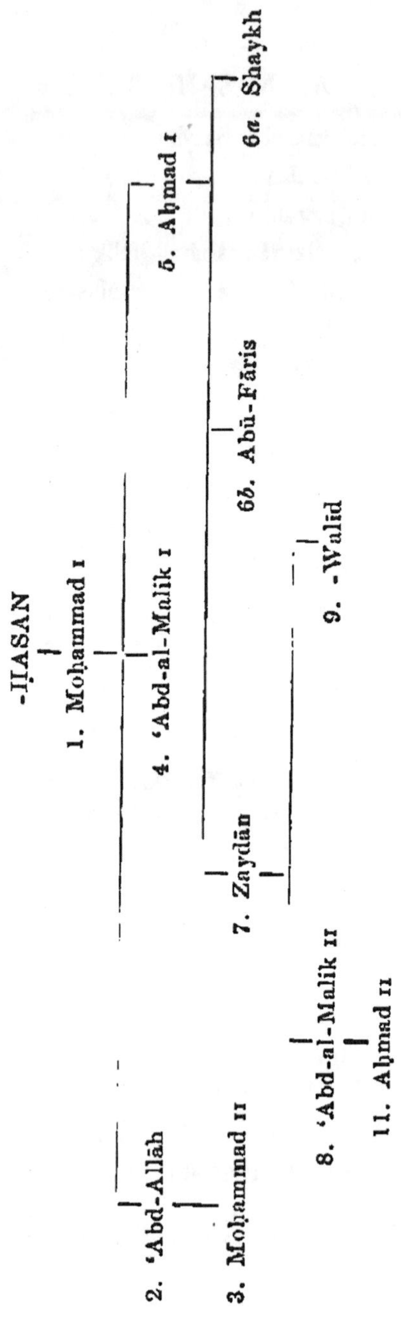

FILALĪ SHARĪFS

Sharīf b. 'Alī

1. -Rashīd
2. Ismā'īl
3. Aḥmad
4. 'Abd-Allāh
5. Moḥammad I
6. -Yazīd
7. Hishām
8. Sulaymān
9. 'Abd-al-Raḥmān
10. Moḥammad II
11. Ḥasan

IV. EGYPT AND SYRIA

SÆC. IX–XIX.

25. ṬŪLŪNIDS

26. IKHSHĪDIDS

27. FĀṬIMIDS

28. AYYŪBIDS

29. MAMLŪKS

'OTHMĀNLĪS (*See X*)

30. KHEDIVES

IV. EGYPT AND SYRIA

SÆC. IX—XIX

Egypt and Syria have generally formed one government in Moḥammadan history. Syria was conquered by the Arabs in 635–638 (*14–17*), and Egypt in 641 (*21*). From the time of the conquest to 868 (*254*) Egypt was ruled as a separate province by 98 governors appointed by the Omayyad and 'Abbāsid Caliphs; but the new governor in 868, Aḥmad b. Ṭūlūn, founded a dynasty which lasted 37 years. This was succeeded after an interval by the Ikhshīdids, who in turn gave place to the greatest of mediæval Egyptian dynasties, that of the Fāṭimid Caliphs. Under these last, however, Syria became the seat of independent dynasties (Mirdāsids, Būrids, Zangids), but was again united to Egypt by Saladin, the founder of the Ayyūbid dynasty, and so continued until both became separate provinces of the Ottoman Empire. In 1831 Ibrāhīm Pasha, eldest son of Moḥammad 'Alī, again joined Syria to the dominions of the ruler of Egypt, but it was restored to the Porte in 1841 by the intervention of the European Powers, and has ever since been a Turkish vilāyat.

A.H. 254—292 ṬŪLŪNIDS A.D. 868—905

Ṭūlūn was a Turkish slave, who was sent by the Sāmānid ruler of Bukhārā as a present to the Caliph -Ma'mūn, and attained high rank in the court at Baghdād and Surra-man-ra'ā. His son Aḥmad succeeded to his father's dignity in 240, and was appointed deputy-governor of Egypt in 868 (*254*), where he soon made himself practically independent. In 877 (*264*) he was allowed to incorporate Syria in his government, and the two countries remained in the possession of his dynasty until its extinction in 905 (*292*). The Ṭūlūnids were renowned for the wealth and luxury of their capital -Ḳaṭāi' (between -Fusṭāṭ and the later Cairo) and for their public works.

A.H.		A.D.
254	Aḥmad b. Ṭūlūn	868
270	Khumārawayh b. Aḥmad	883
282	Jaysh Abū-l-Asākir b. Khumārawayh	895
283	Hārūn b. Khumārawayh	896
292	Shaybān b. Aḥmad	904 —905

[*Governors under the 'Abbāsid Caliphs*]

A.H.		A.D.
323—358	**IKHSHĪDIDS**	935—969

After a brief interval, during which the governors of the 'Abbāsid Caliphs again held precarious sway in Egypt and Syria, Moḥammad -Ikhshīd established another quasi-independent dynasty. -Ikhshīd was the generic title of the rulers of Farghāna, beyond the Oxus, and Ṭughj, the father of Moḥammad, was the son of a Farghāna officer in the service of the Caliph of Baghdād. Ṭughj rose to be governor of Damascus, but was disgraced and died in prison. Moḥammad retrieved his father's misfortune and became in turn governor of Damascus in *318*, and in *321* governor of Egypt. He did not take over the office, however, till 935 (*323*). In 938 (*327*) he assumed the title of -Ikhshīd, and in 941 (*330*) Syria was added to his dominions, together with Mecca and Medīna in the following year.

A.H.		A.D.
323	Moḥammad -Ikhshīd b. Ṭughj . .	935
334	Abū-l-Ḳāsim Ūngūr b. -Ikhshīd . .	946
349	Abū-l-Ḥasan 'Alī b. -Ikhshīd . . .	960
355	Abū-l-Misk Kāfūr [a eunuch] . .	966
357	Abū-l-Fawāris Aḥmad b. 'Alī . . .	961
—358		—969

[*Fāṭimids*]

A.H.		A.D.
297—567	27. FĀṬIMIDS	909—1171

The Fāṭimids, like the Idrīsids, were (or pretended to be) descendants of Fāṭima the daughter of the Prophet (see the genealogical table, p. 72). The Idrīsids had prepared the way for them, and numerous *dā'īs* or missionaries had impregnated the Berbers with Shi'ite doctrine, until the task of the new Prophet 'Obayd-Allāh, who took the title of Al-Mahdī, and claimed to be Caliph and Prince of the Faithful, became simple: in 909 (*297*) he suppressed the effete remnant of the Aghlabids and soon made himself master of all North Africa, with the exception of the Idrīsid kingdom in Morocco. The Fāṭimid capital was the city of -Mahdīya (the 'Africa' of Froissart) near Tunis. Half a century later they added Egypt and Syria to their dominions. Jawhar the Fāṭimid general conquered the former country from the boy-king of the Ikhshīdid dynasty in 969 (*356*), and founded the fortified palace of -Ḳāhira, which developed into the city of Cairo. Southern Syria was taken at the same time, and Aleppo was incorporated in 991 (*381*) in the Fāṭimid Empire, which now stretched from the Syrian desert and the Orontes to the borders of Morocco. The removal of the seat of government from Ḳayruwān and -Mahdīya to Cairo, however, cost the Fāṭimids the loss of their western provinces (see p. 39); and the Normans gained Sicily in 1071, Malta in 1098, Tripoli in 1146 and -Mahdīya and Ḳayruwān in 1148: but the power of the Fāṭimid Caliphs in Egypt and Syria long continued undiminished and their wealth and commerce spread throughout the Mediterranean lands. Saladin supplanted the last Fāṭimid Caliph in 1171 (*567*).

A.H.		A.D.
297	-Mahdī Abū-Moḥammad 'Obayd-Allāh .	909
322	-Ḳāïm Abū-l-Ḳāsim Moḥammad . .	934
334	-Manṣūr Abū-Ṭāhir Ismā'īl . . .	945
341	-Mu'izz Abū-Tamīm Ma'add . . .	952
365	-'Azīz Abū-Manṣūr Nazār . . .	975
386	-Ḥākim Abū-'Alī -Manṣūr . . .	996
411	-Ẓāhir Abū-l-Ḥasan 'Alī . . .	1020
427	-Mustanṣir Abū-Tamīm Ma'add . .	1035
487	-Musta'lī Abū-l-Ḳāsim Aḥmad . .	1094
495	-Āmir Abū-'Alī -Manṣūr . . .	1101
524	-Ḥāfiẓ Abū-l-Maymūn 'Abd-al-Majīd .	1130
544	-Ẓāfir Abū-l-Manṣūr Ismā'īl . . .	1149
549	-Fāïz Abū-l-Ḳāsim 'Īsā. . . .	1154
555	-'Āḍid Abū-Moḥammad 'Abd-Allāh .	1160
—567		—1171

[*Ayyūbids*]

MOHAMMAD

1. *'Alī = Fāṭima*

The Seven Imāms of the Ismā'īlis / The 'Concealed Imāms' of the Ismā'īlis	The Twelve Imāms of the Imāmī Sect
2. *-Ḥasan* † 50	3. *Ḥosayn* † 61
	4. *'Alī Zayn-al-'ābidīn* † 94
	5. *Moḥammad -Bāḳir* † 113
	6. *Jā'far -Ṣādiḳ* † 148
7. *Ismā'īl* or 7 *Moḥammad*	7. *Mūsā -Ḳazam* † 183
Ismā'īl	8. *'Alī -Riḍā* † 202
Moḥammad	9. *Moḥammad -Jawād* † 220
Aḥmad	10. *'Alī -Hādī* † 254
'Abd-Allāh	11. *-Ḥasan -'Askarī* † 260
Aḥmad	12. *Moḥammad -Muntaẓar* disappeared about 260
-Ḥosayn	
'Abd-Allāh	

The Seven Imāms of the Ismā'īlis: 2. *-Ḥasan* to 7. *Ismā'īl* or 7 *Moḥammad*.

The 'Concealed Imāms' of the Ismā'īlis: *Ismā'īl* to *'Abd-Allāh*.

FĀṬIMIDS

1. -Mahdī
2. -Ḳāïm
3. -Manṣûr
4. -Mu'izz
5. -'Azīz
6. -Ḥākim
7. -Ẓāhir
8. -Mustanṣir
9. Musta'lī
10. -Amir

Moḥammad (son of 8. Mustanṣir)

11. -Ḥāfiẓ
12. -Ẓāfir
13. -Fāïz
14. -'Āḍid

A.H.		A.D.
564—648	28. AYYŪBIDS	1169—1250

Ṣalāḥ-al-dīn, or Saladin, the son of Ayyūb (Job), was of Kurdish extraction, and served under Nūr-al-dīn (Nouredin) Maḥmūd b. Zangī, who had lately made himself king of Syria (see IX.). By him Saladin and his uncle Shīrkūh were sent to Egypt, where a civil war invited interference. Friendly assistance developed into annexation, and after the death of Shīrkūh Saladin became virtual master of Egypt in 1169 (*564*), though the last Fāṭimid Caliph did not die till three years later. In the first month of 567 (Sept. 1171) Saladin caused the *Khutba* or public prayer to be said at Cairo in the name of the contemporary 'Abbāsid Caliph -Mustaḍī, instead of the Fāṭimid -'Āḍid, who lay on his death-bed. The change was effected without disturbance, and Egypt became once more Sunnite instead of Shī'ite. The Holy Cities of the Hijāz generally formed part of the dominion of the ruler of Egypt; and in 1173 (*569*) Saladin sent his brother Tūrān-Shāh to govern the Yaman (see

V.). Tripoli was taken from the Normans in 1172 (*568*). The death of his former master Nūr-*al*-dīn in the same year laid Syria open to invasion, and in 1174 (*570*) Saladin entered Damascus and swept over Syria (*570–572*) up to the Euphrates in spite of the opposition of the Zangids. He did not annex Aleppo until 1183 (*579*), after the death of Nūr-*al*-dīn's son, -Ṣāliḥ. He reduced -Mōṣil and made the various princes of Mesopotamia his vassals in 1185–6 (*581*). He was now master of the country from the Euphrates to the Nile, except where the Crusaders retained their strongholds. The battle of Hittīn, 4 July, 1187, destroyed the Christian kingdom of Jerusalem; the Holy City was occupied by Saladin within three months; and hardly a castle, save Tyre, held out against him. The fall of Jerusalem roused Europe to undertake the Third Crusade. Richard I. of England and Philip Augustus of France set out for the Holy Land in 1190, and joined in the siege of Acre in 1191. After a year and a half's fighting, peace was concluded in 1192 for three years without any advantage having been gained by the Crusaders. In March 1193 (*589*) Saladin died.

On his death, his brothers, sons, and nephews, divided the

various provinces of his wide kingdom, but one amongst them, his brother Sayf-al-dīn -'Ādil, the Saphadin of the Crusader chroniclers, gradually acquired the supreme authority. At first Saladin's sons naturally succeeded to their father's crowns in the various divisions of the kingdom:— -Afḍal at Damascus, -'Azīz at Cairo, -Ẓāhir at Aleppo. But in 1196 (*592*) -Afḍal was succeeded by -'Ādil at Damascus; in 1199 (*596*) -Manṣūr the successor of -'Azīz was supplanted by -'Ādil at Cairo; and Aleppo alone remained to the direct descendants of Saladin until 1260 (*648*).

Having acquired the sovereignty of Egypt and most of Syria in 1196–9, and appointed one of his sons to the government of Mesopotamia about 1200 (*597*), -'Ādil enjoyed the supreme authority in the Ayyūbid kingdom till his death in 1218 (*615*). His descendants carried on his rule in the several countries; and we find separate branches reigning in Egypt, Damascus, and Mesopotamia, all sprung from -'Ādil. Those who reigned at Ḥamāh, Emesa, and in the Yaman, were descended from other members of the Ayyūbid family.

In 1250 (*648*) the 'Ādilī Ayyūbids of Egypt, the chief branch of the family, who also frequently held Syria,

(To face p. 70)

AYYUBIDS

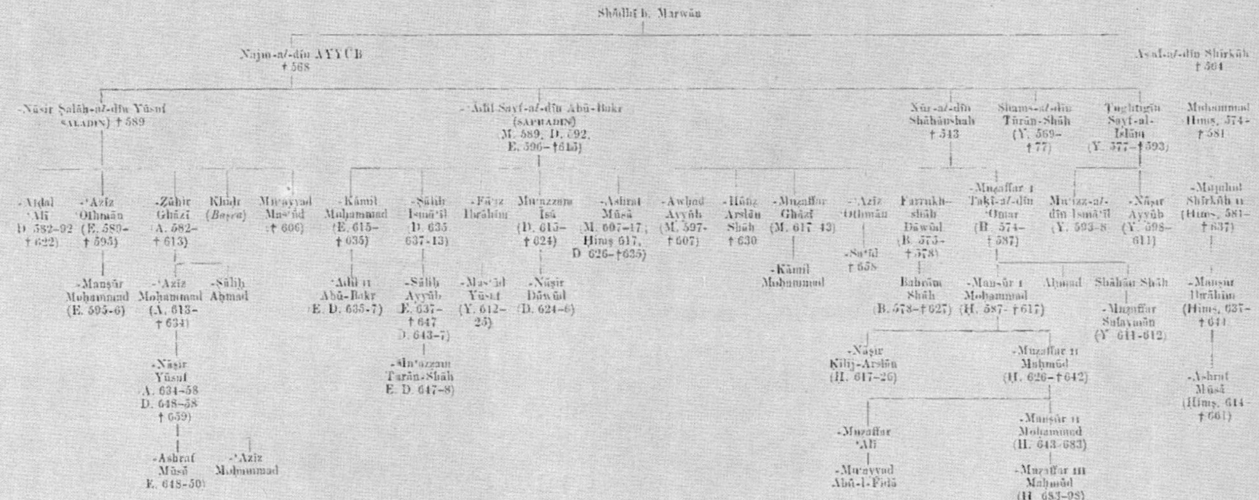

[A. = Aleppo; B. = Baʿalbakk; D. = Damascus; E. = Egypt; Ḥ. = Ḥamāh; M. = Mesopotamia; Y. = Yaman.]

made way for the Baḥrī Mamlūks or Slave Kings. The Damascus branch, after contesting the sovereignty of Syria with the Egyptian and Aleppo branches, was incorporated with Aleppo, and both were swept away in the Tatar avalanche of Chinghiz Khān in 1260 (*658*). The same fate had overtaken the Mesopotamian successors of -'Ādil in 1245 (*643*). The Mamlūks absorbed Emesa in 1262 (*661*). The Ayyūbids had given place to the Rasūlids in Arabia as early as 1228 (*625*). But at Hamāh a branch of the family of Saladin continued to rule with slight intermission until 1341 (*742*), and numbered in their line the well-known historian Abū-l-Fidā.

A. EGYPT

A.H.		A.D.
564	-Nāṣir Ṣalāḥ-*al*-dīn Yūsuf (*Saladin*)	1169
589	-'Azīz 'Imād-*al*-dīn 'Othmān	1193
595	-Manṣūr Moḥammad	1198
596	-'Ādil Sayf-*al*-dīn Abū-Bakr * (*Saphadin*)	1199
615	-Kāmil Moḥammad *	1218
635	-'Ādil II Sayf-*al*-dīn Abū-Bakr *	1238
637	-Ṣāliḥ Najm-*al*-dīn Ayyūb *	1240
647	-Mu'aẓẓam Tūrān-Shāh *	1249
648	-Ashraf Mūsā	1250
—650		—1252

[*Mamlūks*]

* These Sulṭāns also ruled at Damascus.

B. DAMASCUS

A.H.		A.D.
582	-Afḍal Nūr-al-dīn 'Alī	1186
592	-'Ādil Sayf-al-dīn Abū-Bakr (*see Egypt*) .	1196
615	-Mu'aẓẓam Sharaf-al-dīn 'Īsā . . .	1218
624	-Nāṣir Ṣalāḥ-al-dīn Dāwūd . . .	1227
626	-Ashraf Mūsā (*of Mesopotamia*) . .	1228
635	-Ṣāliḥ Ismā'īl.	1237
635	-Kāmil (*of Egypt*)	1237
635	-'Ādil (,,)	1238
637	-Ṣāliḥ (,,)	1240
637	-Ṣāliḥ Ismā'īl (restored)	1240
643	-Ṣāliḥ (*of Egypt*)	1245
647	-Mu'aẓẓam (*of Egypt*)	1249
648	-Nāṣir Ṣalāḥ-al-dīn Yūsuf (*of Aleppo*) .	1250
—658		—1260
	[*Tatars*]	

C. ALEPPO

582	-Ẓāhir Ghiyāth-al-dīn Ghāzī . . .	1186
613	-'Azīz Ghiyāth-al-dīn Moḥammad . .	1216
634	-Nāṣir Ṣalāḥ-al-dīn Yūsuf (*see Damascus*)	1236
—658		—1260
	[*Tatars*]	

D. MESOPOTAMIA

597?	-Awḥad Najm-al-dīn Ayyūb . . .	1200?
607	-Ashraf Muẓaffar-al-dīn Mūsā (*see Damascus*)	1210
628	-Muẓaffar Ghāzī	1230
—643		—1245
	[*Tatars*]	

A.H.		A.D.

E. ḤAMĀH

A.H.		A.D.
574	-Muẓaffar I Taḳi-al-dīn 'Omar . .	1178
587	-Manṣūr I Moḥammad	1191
617	-Nāṣir Ḳilij-Arslān.	1220
626	-Muẓaffar II Taḳī-al-dīn Maḥmūd . .	1229
642	-Manṣūr II Moḥammad	1244
683	-Muẓaffar III Maḥmūd	1284
—698		—1298

[*Governors under the Mamlūk Sulṭāns*]

A.H.		A.D.
710	-Mu'ayyad Abū-l-Fidā Ismā-'īl (*the historian*)	1310
733	-Afḍal Moḥammad	1332
—742		—1341

[*Mamlūks*]

F. EMESA (ḤIMṢ)

A.H.		A.D.
574	-Moḥammad b. Shīrkūh	1178
581	-Mujāhid Shīrkūh	1185
637	-Manṣūr Ibrāhīm	1239
644	-Ashraf Muẓaffar-al-dīn Mūsā . .	1245
—661		—1262

[*Mamlūks*]

G. ARABIA

A.H.		A.D.
569	-Mu'aẓẓam Tūrān-Shāh b. Ayyūb . .	1173
577	-Sayf-al-Islām Tughtakīn b. Ayyūb .	1181
593	-Mu'izz-al-dīn Ismā'īl	1196
598	-Nāṣir Ayyūb.	1201
611	-Muẓaffar Sulaymān	1214
612	-Mas'ūd Ṣalāḥ-al-din Yūsuf	1215
—625 or 626		—1228

[*Rasūlids*]

A.H. 650—922 29. MAMLŪK SULTĀNS A.D. 1252—1517

Mamlūk means 'owned,' and was generally applied to a white slave. The Mamlūk Sulṭāns of Egypt were Turkish and Circassian slaves, and had their origin in the purchased body-guard of the Ayyūbid Sulṭān -Ṣāliḥ Ayyūb. The first of their line was a woman, Queen Shajar-*al*-durr, widow of -Ṣāliḥ; but a representative of the Ayyūbid family (Mūsā) was accorded the nominal dignity of joint sovereignty for a few years. Then followed a succession of slave kings, divided into two dynasties, the Baḥrī ('of the River') and the Burjī ('of the Fort') who ruled Egypt and Syria down to the beginning of the 16th century. In spite of their short reigns and frequent civil wars and assassinations, they maintained as a rule a well-organized government, and Cairo is still full of proofs of their appreciation of art and their love of building.* Their warlike qualities were no less conspicuous in their successful resistance to the Crusaders, and to the Tatar hordes that overran Asia and menaced Egypt in the 13th century.

* See my *Cairo* (1892) chap. iii, and *Art of the Saracens of Egypt* (1886) chap. i.

A.H.		A.D.
648—792	**A. BAḤRĪ MAMLŪKS**	**1250—1390**
648	Shajar-al-durr	1250
648	-Mu'izz 'Izz-al-dīn Aybak	1250
655	-Manṣūr Nūr-al-dīn 'Alī	1257
657	-Muẓaffar Sayf-al-dīn Ḳuṭuz . . .	1259
658	-Ẓāhir Rukn-al-dīn Baybars -Bundukdārī .	1260
676	-Sa'īd Nāṣir-al-dīn Baraka Khān . . .	1277
678	-'Ādil Badr-al-dīn Salāmish . . .	1279
678	-Manṣūr Sayf-al-dīn Ḳalāūn . . .	1279
689	-Ashraf Ṣalāḥ-al-dīn Khalīl . . .	1290
693	-Nāṣir Nāṣir-al-dīn Moḥammad . . .	1293
694	-'Ādil Zayn-al-dīn Kitbughā . . .	1294
696	-Manṣūr Ḥusām-al-dīn Lājīn . . .	1296
698	-Nāṣir Moḥammad (again)	1298
708	-Muẓaffar Rukn-al-dīn Baybars -Jāshankīr .	1308
709	-Nāṣir Moḥammad (third time) . . .	1309
741	-Manṣūr Sayf-al-dīn Abū-Bakr . . .	1340
742	-Ashraf 'Alā-al-dīn Ḳūjūḳ	1341
742	-Nāṣir Shihāb-al-dīn Aḥmad . . .	1342
743	-Ṣāliḥ 'Imād-al-dīn Ismā'īl	1342
746	-Kāmil Sayf-al-dīn Sha'bān . . .	1345
747	-Muẓaffar Sayf-al-dīn Ḥājjī . . .	1346
748	-Nāṣir Nāṣir-al-dīn Ḥasan	1347
752	-Ṣāliḥ Ṣalāḥ-al-dīn Ṣāliḥ	1351
755	-Nāṣir Ḥasan (again)	1354
762	-Manṣūr Ṣalāḥ-al-dīn Moḥammad . .	1361
764	-Ashraf Nāṣir-al-dīn Sha'bān . . .	1363
778	-Manṣūr 'Alā-al-dīn 'Alī	1376
783	-Ṣāliḥ Ṣalāḥ-al-dīn Ḥājjī	1381
784	*Barḳūḳ* (see *Burjīs*)	1382
791	Ḥājjī again, with title of -Muẓaffar . .	1389
—792		—1390

[*Burjī Mamlūks*]

BAHRĪ MAMLŪKS

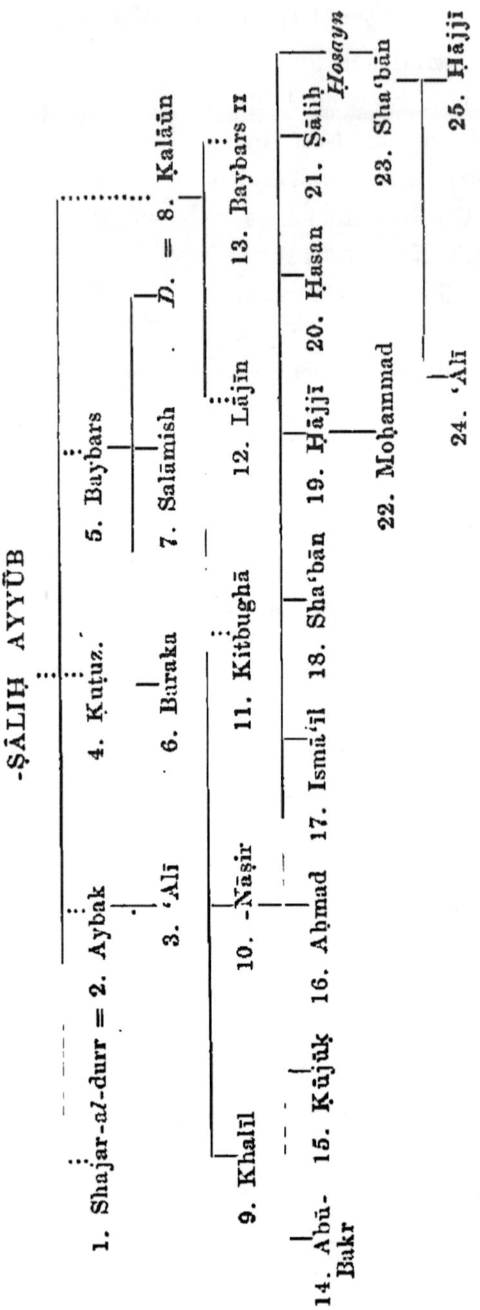

*** *Dotted* lines indicate the relation between master and slave.

A.H.		A.D.
784—922	B. BURJĪ MAMLŪKS	1382—1517
784	-Ẓāhir Sayf-al-dīn Barḳūḳ	1382
	[Interrupted by Ḥājjī 791-2.]	
801	-Nāṣir Nāṣir-al-dīn Faraj	1398
808	-Manṣūr 'Izz-al-dīn 'Abd-al-'Azīz . .	1405
809	-Nāṣir Faraj (again)	1406
815	-'Ādil -Musta'īn ('Abbāsid Caliph) . .	1412
815	-Mu'ayyad Shaykh	1412
824	-Muẓaffar Aḥmad	1421
824	-Ẓāhir Sayf-al-dīn Ṭaṭār	1421
824	-Ṣāliḥ Nāṣir-al-dīn Moḥammad . . .	1421
825	-Ashraf Sayf-al-dīn Bars-bey . . .	1422
842	-'Azīz Jamāl-al-dīn Yūsuf	1438
842	-Ẓāhir Sayf-al-dīn Jaḳmaḳ	1438
857	-Manṣūr Fakhr-al-dīn 'Othmān . . .	1453
857	-Ashraf Sayf-al-dīn Ināl	1453
865	-Mu'ayyad Shihāb-al-dīn Aḥmad . . .	1460
865	-Ẓāhir Sayf-al-dīn Khūshḳadam . . .	1461
872	-Ẓāhir Sayf-al-dīn Bilbey	1467
872	-Ẓāhir Timurbughā	1468
873	-Ashraf Sayf-al-dīn Ḳāït-Bey . . .	1468 —
901	-Nāṣir Moḥammad	1495
904	-Ẓāhir Ḳānsūh	1498
905	-Ashraf Jānbalāt	1499
906	-Ashraf Ḳānṣūh -Ghūri	1500
922	-Ashraf Tūmān-Bey	1516 —1517

[*Ottoman Sulṭāns.*]

As there are seldom more than two kings of a family in the above list a genealogical table is unnecessary.

A.H. 1220—1311 30. KHEDIVES A.D. 1805—1893

After the conquest by Salīm I in 1517 (*922*) Egypt remained for three centuries a Turkish Pāshālik, where, however, the authority of the Pasha sent from Constantinople was minimized by a council of Mamlūk Beys. The arrival of Napoleon in 1798 put an end to this divided system; but after the victories of England at Abū-kīr and Alexandria and the consequent retreat of the French in 1801, the old dissensions revived. In 1805, however, Moḥammad 'Alī, the commander of an Albanian regiment in the Turkish army of Egypt, after massacring a number of the Mamlūk chiefs, made himself master of Cairo. A second massacre in 1811 completed the work, and henceforward Egypt has been governed, in nominal subordination to the Porte, by the dynasty of Moḥammad 'Alī, whose fourth successor, Ismā'īl Pasha, in 1866, adopted the official title of Khedive. Syria was annexed in 1831, but restored to Turkey under pressure of England in 1841. The Sūdān was conquered in successive expeditions, down to the time of Ismā'īl, but abandoned after the death of General Gordon in 1885. The southern boundary of Egypt is now drawn near the second cataract of the Nile, and since the suppression of 'Arābī's military revolt by English troops in 1883, the administration of Egypt has been conducted under the advice of English officials.

A.H.		A.D.
1220	Moḥammad 'Alī	1805
1264	Ibrāhīm	1848
1264	'Abbās I	1848
1270	Sa'īd	1854
1280	Ismā'īl	1863
1300	Tawfīḳ	1882
1309	'Abbās II (regnant)	1892

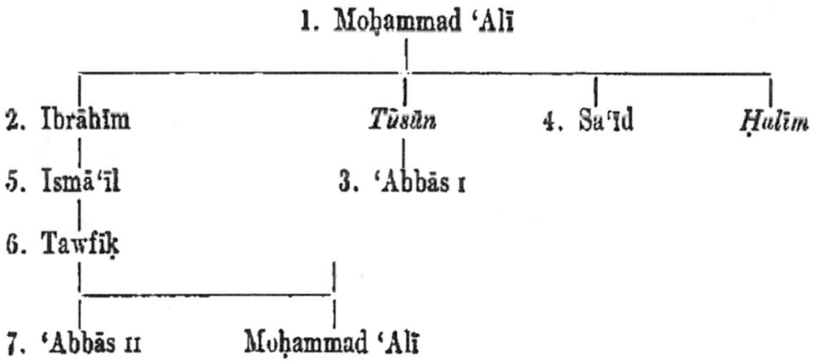

V. ARABIA FELIX (YAMAN)

SÆC. IX—XVIII

33. ZIYĀDIDS (ZABĪD)

34. YA'FURIDS (ṢAN'Ā, JANAD)

35. NAJĀḤIDS (ZABĪD)

36. ṢULAIḤIDS (ṢAN'Ā)

37. HAMDĀNIDS (ṢAN'Ā)

38. MAHDIDS (ZABĪD)

39. ZURAY'IDS ('ADEN)

AYYŪBIDS (*See EGYPT*)

40. RASŪLIDS (YAMAN)

41. ṬĀHIRIDS (YAMAN)

42. RASSID IMĀMS (SA'DA)

43. IMĀMS OF ṢAN'Ā

V. THE YAMAN

SEC. IX–XVIII

The history of Arabia after the Moḥammadan revolution bore a close resemblance to its pre-Islamic annals. The Arabs under the Caliphate were very like the Arabs of 'the Days of Ignorance,' a people of many disconnected tribes headed by chiefs, and many towns and districts governed by Shaykhs, who were sometimes under control, and at others asserted their independence and styled themselves Amīrs or Imāms. The Caliphs appointed a governor of the Yaman, and a sub-governor of Mecca or Medīna; but the outlying towns recognized chiefly the authority of their local Shaykhs. In the beginning of the third century of the Hijra, which saw the dismemberment of the great Islamic empire by the rise of powerful dynasties on its skirts, the governor of the Yaman followed the example of the Idrīsids and Aghlabids in North Africa; and about the time when the Ṭāhirids were amputating the right hand of the 'Abbāsid empire in Khurāsān, Moḥammad the *Ziyādid* established his authority at Zabīd, the city he had founded in the Tihāma, and thus inaugurated the rule of independent dynasties in Arabia, though the Caliphs still continued to appoint governors at intervals.

A.H.		A.D.
204—409	33. ZIYĀDIDS*	819—1018

33. ZIYĀDIDS*
(ZABĪD)

The Ziyādids, or Banū Ziyād, ruled at Zabīd for two centuries, and their kingdom included a considerable part of the Yaman. As their power waned, various independent rulers and dynasties sprang up: the *Ya'furids* established themselves at Ṣan'ā and Janad; Sulaymān b. Ṭarf subdued a wide territory bordering the northern coast of the Yaman, with 'Aththar for its capital; and the Carmathian 'Alī b. -Faḍl even plundered Zabīd itself shortly after 904 (*292*). Under the last Ziyādid, the government of their province fell entirely into the hands of a succession of slaves, until Najāḥ, an Abyssinian slave of Marjān, the last Ziyādid *Maire du palais*, substituted his own dynasty, the *Najāḥids*, at Zabīd in 1021 (*412*).

* The history of the Arabian dynasties may be read in H. C. Kay's comprehensive work *Yaman, its early mediæval history*, 1892, which includes a translation of the Arabic history of 'Omāra and other important and interesting materials.

A.H.		A.D.
204	Moḥammad b. 'Abd-Allāh b. Ziyād . .	819
245	Ibrāhīm b. Moḥammad	859
289	Ziyād b. Ibrahīm	901
291?	Abū-l-Jaysh Isḥāḳ b Ibrāhīm . . .	903?
371	'Abd-Allāh (*or* Ziyād, *or* Ibrāhīm) b Isḥāḳ .	981
—409		—1018

VEZĪRS

371	Rushd	981
c. 373	-Ḥosayn b Salāma	983
402	Marjān	1011
—412		—1021

Nafīs, 407—12

[*Najāḥids*]

A.H. 247—345 34. YA'FURIDS A.D. 861—956

(ṢAN'A AND JANAD)

247	Ya'fur b. 'Abd-*al*-Raḥmān	861
259	Moḥammad b Ya'fur	872
279	'Abd al-Ḳādir b. Aḥmad b. Ya'fur . .	892
279	Ibrāhīm b. Moḥammad	892
c. 285	As'ad b. Ibrāhīm	c. 898
288	*Rassid Imām -Hadī*	900
299	*Carmathian 'Ali b. -Faḍl*	911
303	As'ad *restored*	915
332	Moḥammad b. Ibrāhīm	943
352	'Abd-Allāh b. Kaḥṭān	963
—387		—997

[Dynasty becomes insignificant]

A.H.		A.D.
412—553	35. NAJĀḤIDS	1021—1158

(ZABĪD)

Najāḥ, the Abyssinian slave of the last Mayor of the Palace of the Ziyādid dynasty, ruled Zabīd till his death in 1060 (*452*); the town was then (*454*) seized by the Ṣulayḥids and formed part of their dominions until *473*, when the son of Najāḥ recovered it, though it changed hands between the two dynasties several times during his life (see p. 94). After 1089 (*482*) Zabīd remained continuously with the Najāḥids, until their dynasty (which had fallen, like the Ziyādids, under the influence of vezīrs) gave place to the *Mahdids* in 1059 (*554*).

A.H.		A.D.
412	-Mu'ayyad Najāḥ (+452)	1021
454	*'Alī -Dā'ī, Ṣulayḥid*	1062
473	Sa'īd -Aḥwal b. Najāḥ	1080
482	Jayyāsh b. Najāḥ	1089
498	-Fātik I b. Jayyāsh	1104
503	-Manṣūr b. -Fātik	1109
c. 517	-Fātik II b. -Manṣūr	c. 1123
531	-Fātik III b. Moḥammad b. -Mansūr . .	1136
—554		—1159

[*Mahdids.*]

NAJAḤIDS

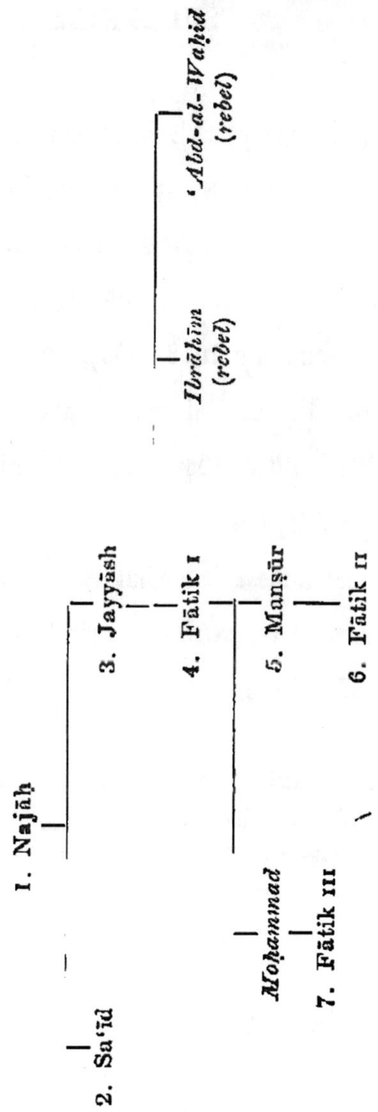
1. Najāḥ
2. Sa'īd
3. Jayyāsh
4. Fātik I
5. Manṣūr
6. Fātik II
Moḥammad
7. Fātik III
Ibrāhīm (rebel)
'Abd-al-Wāḥid (rebel)

A.H. 429—495 36. ṢULAYḤIDS A.D. 1037—1101

(ṢAN'Ā)

The *dā'ī* (missionary) 'Alī b. Moḥammad, founder of the Shī'ite dynasty of the Ṣulayḥids, or Banū Sulayḥ, made himself independent at Masār in 1037 (*429*), annexed Zabīd after the death of Najāḥ, in 1062 (*454*), conquered Ṣan'ā and all the Yaman by 1063 (*455*), and took possession of Mecca *455-6*. His capital was Ṣan'ā; but he also held Zabīd until his death in 1080 (*473*), and his son -Mukarram recovered it in *475*, but lost it in *479*, took it again about 1088 (*481*), and almost immediately lost it for the last time. In *480* -Mukarram removed his capital from Ṣan'ā to Dhū-Jibla in Mikhlāf Ja'far.

A.H.		A.D.
429	Abū-Kāmil 'Alī b. Moḥammad	1037
473	-Mukarram Aḥmad	1080
484	-Manṣūr Abū-Himyar Sabā	1091
—492		—1098

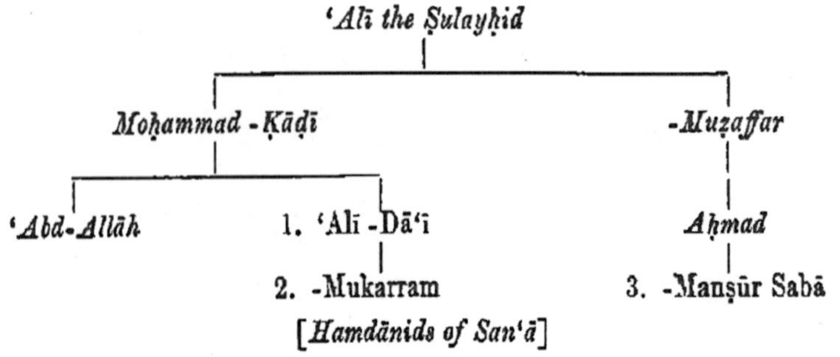

A.H. 492—569 | 37. HAMDĀNIDS | A.D. 1098—1173

37. HAMDĀNIDS

(ṢAN'Ā)

The various branches of the Banū Hamdān were descended from the tribes of Ḥāshid and Bakīl, which held a high rank among the Yaman Arabs, and occupied the country about Ṣan'ā and Sa'da. They supplied rulers to Ṣan'ā after the Ṣulayḥids for three quarters of a century, up to the Ayyūbid invasion.

A.H.		A.D.
492	Ḥātim b. -Ghashīm	1098
502	'Abd-Allāh b. Ḥātim	1108
504	Ma'n b. Ḥātim	1110
c. 510	Hishām b. -Ḳubbayt	*c.* 1116
	-Ḥamās b. -Ḳubbayt	
	Ḥātim b. -Ḥamās	
545	Ḥātim b. Aḥmad	1150
556	'Alī -Waḥīd b. Ḥātim	1160
—569		—1173

[*Ayyūbids.*]

A.H.		A.D.
554—569	38. MAHDIDS	1159—1173

38. MAHDIDS

(ZABĪD)

The Mahdids, or Banū-l-Mahdī, succeeded the Najāḥids at Zabīd. 'Alī b. -Mahdī was a devotee and prophet in the Tihāma, who acquired a following whom he named -Anṣār and Muhājirūn, or Helpers and Refugees (after the example of Moḥammad), and eventually 1150 (*545*) began to occupy forts and subdue the country, till at length he was able to attack and conquer Zabīd 1159 (*554*). His successors held the Tihāma, together with some districts and towns beyond, until the Ayyūbid conquest.

A.H.		A.D.
554	'Alī b. -Mahdī	1159
554	-Mahdī b. 'Alī	1159
558	'Abd-al-Nabī b. 'Alī	1162
—569		—1173

[*Ayyūbids.*]

A.H. 476—569 | 39. ZURAY'IDS ('ADEN) | A.D. 1083—1173

The two sons of -Karam, 'Abbās and Mas'ūd, were appointed joint governors of 'Aden in 1083 (*476*) by the Ṣulayḥid -Mukarram, and the joint system of government continued for several generations. The 'Aden princes Abū-Su'ūd and Abū-Gharāt asserted their independence of the king of Ṣan'ā, but were not always able to maintain it. The dynasty was, next to the Ṣulayḥids, the most important in the Yaman, and survived till the Ayyūbid conquest.*

-Karam

BANŪ MAS'ŪD

476 1. Mas'ūd 1083

2. Abu-l-Gharāt

3. Moḥammad

4. 'Alī 533 *dep.* 1138

BANŪ ZURAY'

476 i. 'Abbās 1083

c. 508 ii. Zuray' *c.* 1114

iii. Abū-Su'ūd

iv. Sabā

533 v. 'Alī -A'azz -Murtaḍā 1138

534 vi. Moḥammad 1139

548 vii. 'Imrān 1153

560—569 viii. Moḥammad Abū-Su'ūd Manṣūr 1164—1173

(*infants under vezīr* Yāsir b. Bilāl)

[*Ayyūbids*]

* The list is taken from H. C. Kay's *Yaman* (Edw. Arnold, 1892), p. 307.

A.H.		A.D.
569—625	**AYYŪBIDS (YAMAN)**	1173—1228

·The Ayyūbid conquest in 1173 (*569*) is the great crisis in the mediæval history of Arabia. The kinsmen of Saladin swept over the Yaman and overturned its dynasties with the same uncompromising thoroughness as they displayed in Egypt, Syria, and Mesopotamia. The Hamdānids of Ṣan'ā, the Mahdids of Zabīd, and the Zuray'ids of 'Aden, were alike suppressed by the Kurdish conqueror Tūrān Shāh, son of Ayyūb, and for half a century, 1173–1227 (*569-625*) the Yaman remained in the hands of the great family which ruled Egypt and Syria. The list of the Ayyūbids of Arabia has already been given (p. 79) in connexion with the leading branch of Egypt, but is here repeated for convenience.

A.H.		A.D.
569	-Mu'aẓẓam Tūrān -Shāh	1173
577	Sayf-al-Islām Tughtigīn	1181
593	Mu'izz-*al*-dīn Ismā'īl	1196
598	-Nāṣir Ayyūb	1201
611	-Muẓaffar Sulaymān	1214
612	-Mus'ūd Yūsuf	1215
—625		—1228

[*Rasūlids*]

A.H.		A.D.
626—858	40. RASŪLIDS	1229—1454

40. RASŪLIDS (YAMAN)

The Rasūlids succeeded the Ayyūbids in the government of all the Yaman, from Ḥaḍramawt to Mecca, and their power was maintained for over two centuries. They took their name from an envoy (*rasūl*) of the 'Abbāsid caliph, whose son, 'Alī b. Rasūl, was appointed governor of Mecca by the last Ayyūbid Sulṭān of Arabia, -Mas'ūd, in 1222 (*619*). On the death of Mas'ud in 1228 (*625*) 'Alī's son Nūr-al-dīn 'Omar established his authority over the Yaman.

626	-Manṣūr 'Omar b. 'Alī	1229
647?	-Muẓaffar Yūsuf	1249?
694	-Ashraf 'Omar	1295
696	-Mu'ayyad Dāwūd	1297
721	-Mujāhid 'Alī	1321
764	-Afḍal -'Abbās	1363
778	-Ashraf Ismā'īl I	1376
803	-Nāṣir Aḥmad	1400
829	-Manṣūr 'Abd-Allāh	1426
830	-Ashraf Ismā'īl II	1427
831	-Ẓāhir Yaḥyā	1428
842	-Ashraf Ismā'īl III	1438
845	-Muẓaffar Yūsuf	1441

Rival claimants:

846	-Mufaḍḍal Moḥammad . .	1442
846	-Nāṣir 'Abd-Allāh . . .	1442
854-8	-Mas'ūd	1450-4
855	-Mu'ayyad -Ḥosayn . .	1451

[*Ṭāhirids.*]

RASŪLIDS

- RASŪL
  - ‘Alī
    - 1. -Manṣūr ‘Omar
      - 2. -Muẓaffar Yūsuf
        - 3. -Ashraf ‘Omar
        - 4. -Mu·ayyad Dāwūd
          - 5. -Mujāhid ‘Alī
            - 6. -Afḍal -‘Abbās
              - 7. -Ashraf Ismā‘īl I
                - 8. -Nāṣir Aḥmad
                  - 9. -Manṣūr ‘Abd-Allāh
                  - 10. -Ashraf Ismā‘īl II
                    - *‘Omar*
                      - 13. -Muẓaffar Yūsuf
                - 11. -Ẓāhir Yaḥyā
                  - 12. -Ashraf Ismā‘īl III

A.H.
850—923

41. ṬĀHIRIDS

(YAMAN)

The Ṭāhirids, or Banū Ṭāhir, succeeded to the Yaman on the break-up of the Rasūlids, and maintained their authority until the conquest of Arabia by the last but one of the *Mamlūk Sulṭāns* of Egypt, Ḳānsūh -Ghūrī. The *'Othmānlī Turks* then occupied the country, thus made ready for their rule, in 1517 (*923*), but were forced to abandon it in 1633, in favour of the native Imāms.

A.H.		A.D.
850	Ẓāfir Ṣalāḥ-al-dīn 'Āmir I (*Zabīd*, †870) . -Mujāhid Shams-al-dīn 'Alī (*'Aden*, †883) .	1446
883	-Manṣūr Ṭāj-al-dīn 'Abd-al-Wahhāb . .	1478
894	-Ẓāfir Ṣalāḥ-al-dīn 'Āmir	1488
—923		—1517

ṬĀHIR

1*a*. -Ẓāfir I — 1*b*. -Mujāhid — *Dāwūd*

Dāwūd → 2. -Manṣūr → 3. -Ẓāfir II

[*Mamlūks; 'Othmānlīs*]

A.H.		A.D.
280—*c.* 700	42. RASSID IMĀMS	893—*c.* 1300

(SA'DA)

A line of Imāms of the Zaydite sect of the Shī'ites was founded at Sa'da in the Yaman by -Hādī Yaḥyā, grandson of -Ḳāsim -Rassi, a schismatic of the time of -Ma'mūn the 'Abbāsid Caliph, and lasted down to the present day. The series is confused and the dates often uncertain, but the following list and genealogical table give the results of the latest researches.*

† 246	-Ḳāsim -Rassi Tarjumān-al-dīn	† 860
280	-Hādī-ilā-l-ḥaḳḳ Yāḥyā	893
298	-Murtaḍā Abū-l-Ḳāsim Moḥammad . .	910
301	-Nāṣir Aḥmad	913
324	-Ḳāsim -Mukhtār	935
	Yūsuf -Dā'ī	
	-Ḳāsim -Manṣūr	
393	-Mahdī -Ḥosayn † 404	1003
426	Abū-Hāshim -Ḥasan	1035
430	*-Nāṣir Abū-l-Fatḥ -Daylamī* . . .	1038
532	-Mutawakkil Aḥmad † 566	1137
593	-Manṣūr 'Abd-Allāh † 614	1196
{ 614-23	-Nāṣir 'Izz-al-dīn Moḥammad . . .	1217-1226
{ 614	-Hādī Najm-al-dīn Yaḥyā	1217
623?	-Mahdī Aḥmad b. -Ḥosayn	1226?
656	-Mutawakkil Shams-al-dīn Aḥmad . .	1258
c. 680	-Muntaṣir Dāwūd	1281

* See H. C. Kay's *Yaman*, 1892, for further details.

To face p. 102.)

RASSID IMĀMS

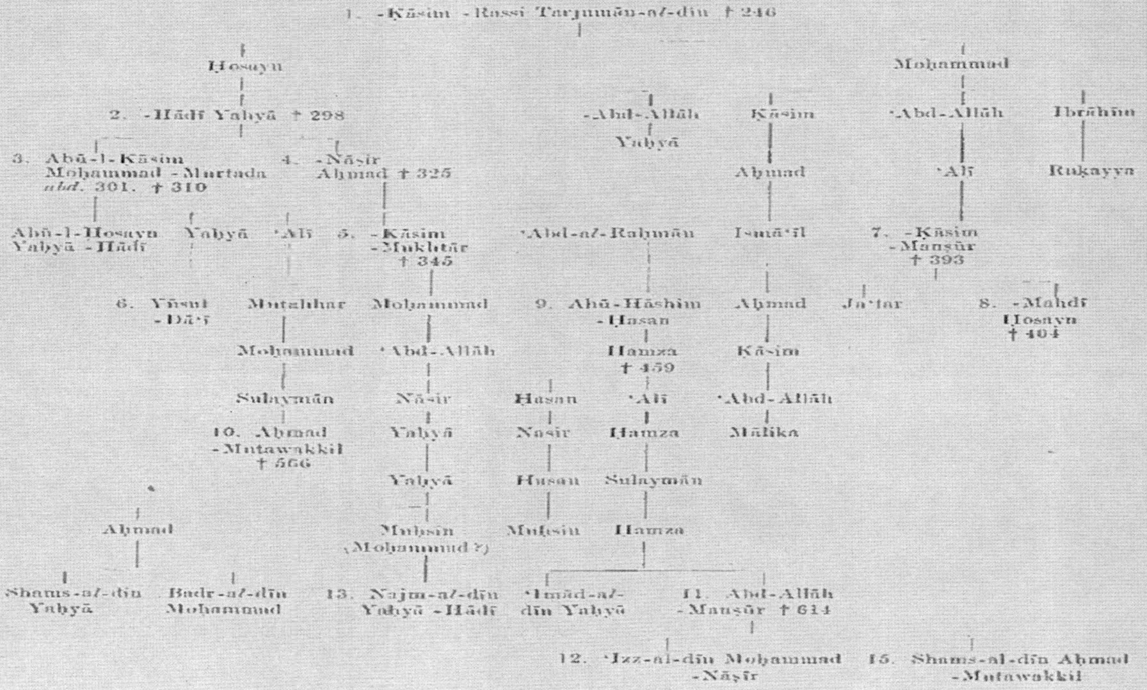

A.H.		A.D.
c. 1000—	**43. IMĀMS OF SAN'Ā**	c. 1591—

The preceding Imāms had their chief seat at Sa'da, but they frequently succeeded in taking Ṣan'ā. It was not, however, until the expulsion of the 'Othmānlī Turks in 1633 (*1043*) that Ṣan'ā became the permanent capital of the Imāmate of the Yaman. The Imāms who ruled there are generally distinguished by the title of Imāms of Ṣan'ā, but they were really only a continuation of the previous line of Sa'da, since their founder was -Ḳāsim -Manṣūr, a descendant of Yūsuf -Dā'ī, great-grandson of -Hādī Yaḥya, the founder of the Rassid Imāmate. The following list, chiefly after Niebuhr, is incomplete, for representatives of the same family still possess authority in the Yaman.

A.H.		A.D.
c. 1000	-Ḳāsim -Manṣūr	c. 1591
1029	-Mu'ayyad Moḥammad	1620
1054	-Mutawakkil Ismā'īl	1644
1087	-Majīd Moḥammad	1676
	-Mahdī Aḥmad	
1093	-Hādī Moḥammad	1682
1095	-Mahdī Moḥammad	1684
1126	-Naṣir Moḥammad	1714
1128	-Mutawakkil -Ḳāsim	1716
1139	-Manṣūr -Ḥosayn	1726
1139	-Hadī -Majīd Moḥammad	1726
1140	-Manṣūr (*restored*)	1727
1160	-Mahdī -'Abbās	1747
c. 1190	-Manṣūr	c. 1776

VI. SYRIA AND MESOPOTAMIA

(ARAB PERIOD)

SÆC. X—XII

VI. SYRIA AND MESOPOTAMIA

(ARAB PERIOD)

SÆC. X–XII.

In classifying the Moḥammadan dynasties of Asia, the purely geographical system adopted for Africa must be modified, in order to present the various groups of dynasties in historical sequence. These dynasties fall naturally into the following divisions:—VI. The Arab dynastics of Syria and Mesopotamia previous to the invasion of the Seljūḳ Turks; VII. The Persian and Transoxine dynastics before the Seljūḳs; VIII. The Seljūḳ family in all its ramifications; IX. The dynasties founded by officers who had served in the Seljūḳ armies, and subsisting between the decay of the Seljūḳ power and the invasion of the Mongols; X. The western successors of the Seljūḳs, especially the 'Othmānlī Turks; XI. The Mongol family of Chingiz Khān in all its branches; XII. The dynasties which sprang up in Persia on the decline of the Mongol power; XIII. The dynastics which sprang from Tīmūr

(Tamerlane) in Transoxiana on the decay of the older branch of the Mongols; XIV. The dynasties of India (including Afghānistān).

In this arrangement the geographical progress from west to east is still generally preserved. We have first Syria and Mesopotamia down to the great sweep of the Seljūḳ invasion; then Persia and Transoxiana to the same epoch. The Seljūḳs and their officers and successors in the west follow. A new power, that of the Mongols, then comes to sweep away for a time all these lesser dynasties, save the 'Othmānlīs. The Mongols in turn grow weak, and their Persian supplanters, notably the several dynasties of Shāhs, to the present day, are placed next. Further north and east, the Mongols were continued in a new line, that of Tīmūr; and the dynasties sprung from this renowned chief, together with their Uzbeg successors in Transoxiana, are brought down to the present day. Still moving eastward, we arrive at India, and begin the series of Moḥammadan dynasties of Hindūstān with their historical source, the Ghaznawids of Afghānistān, and carry them down to the fall of the Mogul Empire and the establishment of British supremacy in India.

The first of these groups is formed of the dynasties founded by Arab tribes in Syria and Mesopotamia. The geographical division is not arbitrary, for the mountains of Kurdistān and the Zagros range form a natural boundary between Persia and Mesopotamia, which, at least in the earlier centuries of Moḥammadan history, was seldom over-stepped. The Buwayhids indeed combined lower Mesopotamia with their Persian empire, but as a rule a dynasty which ruled in Diyār-Bakr or -Jazīra did not extend its sway beyond the mountains to the east, though it frequently spread into Syria. The first group is not only distinct geographically; it is also an ethnological class. With the exception of the Marwānids, who were Kurds, the dynasties classed in this group were all pure Arabs. The Arab tribes which had migrated from their native deserts northwards into Syria and Mesopotamia had always been a political power with which the Caliphs had to reckon, and on the rapid decay of the central authority at Baghdād the various clans which roamed the Syrian desert and the valley of the Euphrates began to form permanent settlements, to occupy towns and forts, and found dynasties. Thus the Taghlib tribe furnished the *Ḥamdānid* dynasty in -Mōṣil, Aleppo, and other cities;

the Banū Kilāb set the *Mīrdāsids* on the throne of Aleppo; the *Banū 'Oḳayl* established their rule in Diyār-Bakr and -Jazīra (Mesopotamia) and part of -'Irāḳ (Chaldaea); and the Banū Asad set up the powerful *Mazyadid* dynasty at -Ḥilla. Yet while they exercised authority over cities, districts, and even whole provinces, these Arab chiefs did not abandon their national life, but for the most part continued to dwell in tents with their tribesmen, and wander as the needs of their flocks or their predatory instincts suggested.

A.H.		A.D.
317—394	44. ḤAMDĀNIDS	929—1003

(-MŌṢIL, ALEPPO, ETC.)

The Ḥamdānid family, descended from the Arab tribe of Taghlib, had settled in the neighbourhood of -Mōṣil, and Ḥamdān b. Ḥamdūn had taken a prominent part in the political events of that city as early as 873 (*260*). In 894 (*281*) Moḥammad b. Ḥamdān was in possession of Māridīn, but was expelled by the Caliph -Mu'taḍid; in 904 (*292*) Abū-l-Hayjā 'Abd-Allāh b. Ḥamdān was appointed governor of -Mōṣil and its dependencies; and from this time the power of the Ḥamdānids greatly increased. In 919 (*307*) Ibrāhīm b. Ḥamdān was made governor of Diyār-Rabī'a, where he was succeeded by his brother Dāwūd in 921 (*309*); Sa'īd b. Ḥamdān became governor of Nahāwand in 924 (*312*), and several other members of the family received appointments. 'Abd-Allāh made his son -Ḥasan his lieutenant at -Mōṣil, which, with an interval, (*317—319*), the latter held, together with Diyār-Rabī'a, and Diyār-Bakr, until his deposition by his son Abū-Taghlib in 968 (*358*). In 941 (*330*) he was given the title of Nāṣir-*al*-dawla by the Caliph; and at the same time his brother 'Alī was named Sayf-*al*-dawla.

The latter, after governing Wāsiṭ, took Aleppo from the Ikhshīdids in 944 (*333*), and won a great reputation in his wars against the Greeks. The Ḥamdānids were Shī'ites, and Sayf-*al*-dawla paid homage to the Fāṭimid Caliphs. After the deaths of these two brothers, the power of the dynasty rapidly declined. The ***Fāṭimids*** absorbed the dominions of Sayf-*al*-dawla's grandsons in Syria, and the ***Buwayhids*** ousted Abū-Taghlib from Mesopotamia in 977–9 (*367–9*). The recovery of -Mōṣil by his brothers -Ḥosayn and Abū-Ṭāhir was but a temporary and brief revival.

I. OF -MŌṢIL

317	Nāṣir-*al*-dawla Abū-Moḥammad -Ḥasan	929
358 —369	'Uddat-*al*-dawla Abū-Taghlib -Ghaḍanfir	968 —979
371	Abū-Ṭāhir Ibrāhīm	981
—380	Abū-'Abd-Allāh -Ḥosayn . . .	—991

[*Buwayhids, 'Oḳaylids*]

II. OF ALEPPO

333	Sayf-*al*-dawla Abū-l-Ḥasan 'Alī . .	944
356	Sa'd-*al*-dawla Abū-l-Ma'ālī Sharīf .	967
381	Sa'īd-*al*-dawla Abū-l-Faḍā'il Sa'īd .	991
392	Abū-l-Ḥasan 'Alī.	1001
394	Abū-l-Ma'ālī Sharīf	1003

[*Fāṭimids*]

ḤAMDANIDS

ḤAMDAN

- Abū-l-ʻUlā Saʻīd (*Nahāwand*, 312; -*Mōṣil*, 317-19) † 323
  - *Abū-l-Farās* † 357
  - -*Ḥosayn* † 338
- Ibrāhīm (*Diyār-Rabīʻa*, 307-8)
- Dāwūd (*Diyār-Rabīʻa*, 309)
- Abū-l-Hayjā ʻAbd-Allāh (-*Mōṣil*, 292) † 317
  - (OF -MŌṢIL) 1. Nāṣir-al-dawla
    - 2. Abū-Taghlib † 369
    - 3a. -Ḥosayn
    - 3b. Abū-Ṭāhir Ibrāhīm † 380
    - Abū-l-Barakāt † 358
  - (OF ALEPPO) i. Sayf-al-dawla
    - ii. Saʻd-al-dawla
      - iii. Saʻīd-al-dawla
        - iva. ʻAlī
        - ivb. Sharīf

A.H.		A.D.
414—472	45. MIRDĀSIDS	1023—1079

(ALEPPO)

Asad-*al*-dawla Abū-'Alī Ṣāliḥ b. Mirdās, of the Arab tribe of the Banū Kilāb, raided the neighbourhood of Aleppo (Ḥalab) with his Bedouins as early as 1011; and in 1023 (*414*) the inhabitants revolted against the Fāṭimid governor, and delivered the city to Ṣāliḥ, who ruled Aleppo until killed in a battle with the Egyptians in 1029 (*420*). His son Shibl-*al*-dawla Naṣr succeeded him, but was also killed by the Fāṭimid army in 1037 (*429*), and it was not until five years later that another son, Mu'izz-*al*-dawla Tamāl, who had governed -Raḥba, recovered Aleppo from the Egyptians. In 1057 (*449*) Tamāl again abandoned Aleppo to Egypt, whilst his brother 'Aṭīya occupied -Raḥba. This fresh Fāṭimid rule was terminated in 1060 (*452*) by the conquest of the city by Rashīd-*al*-dawla, son of Shibl-*al*-dawla; but he was expelled in the following year by his uncle Mu'izz-*al*-dawla, who died in *454*, and bequeathed Aleppo to his brother 'Aṭīya. Rashīd-*al*-dawla, however, recovered the city in the same year, and 'Aṭīya seized -Raḳḳa, whence he was expelled by the 'Oḳaylid Muslim b. Ḳuraysh in 1070 (*463*). Rashīd-*al*-dawla was succeeded in *468* by his son Jalāl-*al*-dawla, who took Manbij from the Greeks, and whose brother Sābiḳ (or Shabīb) held Aleppo until its conquest by the 'Oḳaylid Muslim in 1079 (*472*).*

414	Ṣāliḥ b. Mirdās	1023
420	Shibl-*al*-dawla Abū -Kāmil Naṣr	1029
429	*Fāṭimids*	1037
434	Mu'izz-*al*-dawla Abū 'Ulwān Tamāl	1042
449	*Fāṭimids*	1057
452	Rashīd-*al*-dawla Maḥmūd	1060
453	Mu'izz-*al*-dawla *restored*	1061
454	Abū-Du'āba 'Aṭīya	1062
454	Rashīd-*al*-dawla *restored*	1062
468	Jalāl-*al*-dawla (Ṣamṣām-*al*-dawla) Naṣr	1075
468	Abū-l-Faḍā'il Sābiḳ	1076
—472		—1079

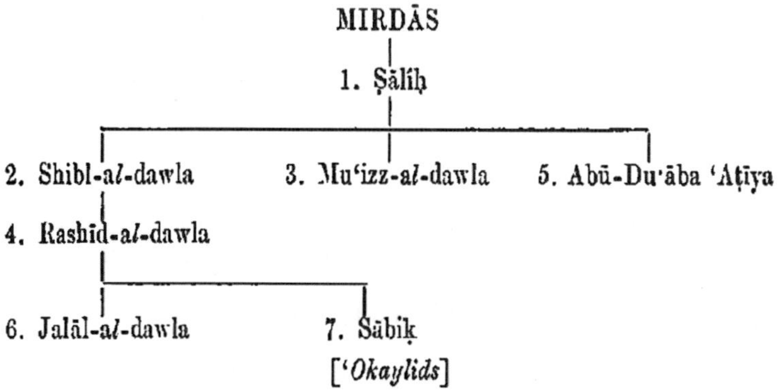

* See H. Sauvaire, *A Dinar of Salih ebn Merdas of Aleppo* (*Numismatic Chronicle*, 1873).

A.H.		A.D.
386–489	46. ‘OḲAYLIDS	996–1096

46. ‘OḲAYLIDS (-MŌṢIL, ETC.)

The Banū ‘Oḳayl, or ‘Oḳaylids, a very large Arab clan, formed one of the five divisions of the Banū Ka‘b, of the Modarite tribes of Arabia; and after their adoption of Islām their sub-clans spread over parts of Syria, -‘Irāḳ, and even North Africa and Andalusia. In the early days of the ‘Abbāsid Caliphate, -‘Irāḳ was full of ‘Oḳaylids. The Banū Muntafiḳ, one of their sub-clans, migrated to the marshy country about -Baṣra, called the Baṭīḥa or Baṭā·iḥ (‘The Swamps’), under the family of Ma‘rūf; the Banū Khafāja for centuries occupied themselves in looting caravans in the deserts of -‘Irāḳ, as late as 1327; while the Banū ‘Obāda inhabited, with the Banū Muntafiḳ, the country between -Kūfa, Wāsiṭ, and -Baṣra, and eventually furnished the line of ‘Oḳaylid princes of -Mōṣil. In the fourth century of the Hijra, the ‘Oḳaylids of Syria and -‘Irāḳ were tributary to the powerful Arab dynasty of Ḥamdānids, but on the fall of these princes, the ‘Oḳaylids attained independent sovereignty. Abū-Dhawwād Moḥammad was granted by the last of the Ḥamdānids the cities of Naṣībīn and Balad in 989 (*379*), to which he added -Mōṣil in *380*, but

To face p. 116)

'OKAYLIDS

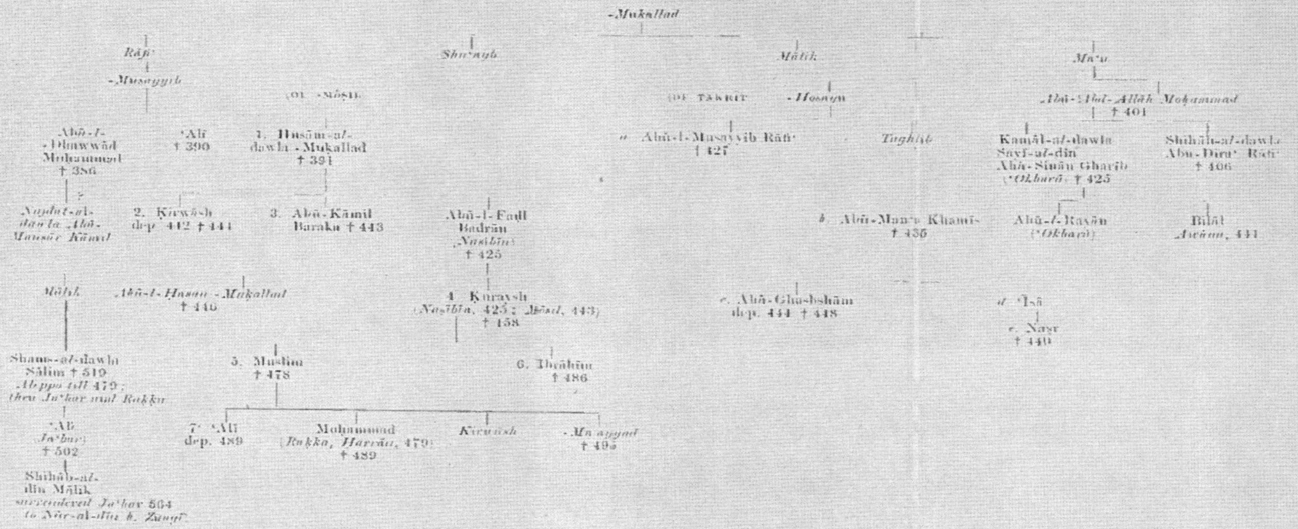

[Muḥyī-al-dīn Abū-l-Ḥārith Muhārish, descended from Shu'ayb b. -Mukallad, governed 'Āna and Ḥadītha, and was succeeded, 499, by his son Sulaymān, who died in 528. Muḥammad, descended from Mālik b. -Mukallad, governed Hīt in 496. See H. C. Kay, *Notes on the History of the Banū 'Okayl*, *J.R.A.S.*]

was expelled by the Buwayhids in *381*. His brother Muḳallad was more successful; he took -Mōṣil in 996 (*386*), and was confirmed in the government, together with -Kūfa, -Ḳaṣr, and -Jāmi'ān, by Bahā-*al*-dawla the Buwayhid, on condition of tribute; to which were presently added -Anbār, -Madā'in, and Daḳūḳā. In the time of Muslim b. Ḳuraysh, the dominions of the 'Oḳaylid of -Mōṣil extended from the neighbourhood of Baghdād to Aleppo. On his death, the principality speedily decayed in power, and -Mōṣil, its capital, was conquered by a Turkish adventurer, Ḳawām-*al*-dawla Karbuḳā in 1096, (*489*), and merged in the Seljūḳ empire. Other branches, or individual chiefs, of the 'Oḳaylids, who governed various small towns in Syria and Mesopotamia, are indicated in the genealogical table. After the destruction of their power in Mesopotamia the 'Oḳaylids returned to their old camping grounds in -Baḥrayn.

386	Ḥusām-*al*-dawla -Muḳallad	996
391	Mu'tamid-*al*-dawla Ḳirwāsh	1000
442	Za'īm-*al*-dawla Abū-Kāmil Baraka . .	1050
443	'Alam-*al*-dīn Abū-l-Ma'ālī Ḳuraysh . .	1051
453	Sharaf-*al*-dawla Abū-l-Makārim Muslim .	1061
478	Ibrāhīm	1085
486	'Alī	1093
—489	[*Seljūḳs*]	—1096

A.H. 380—489 | **47. MARWĀNIDS** | A.D. 990—1096

(DIYĀR-BAKR)

On the death of Bād, governor of Ḥiṣn Kayfā, in 990 (*380*) his sister's son, Abū-'Alī b. Marwān, a Kurd by race, succeeded to his dominions, which included the chief towns of Diyār-Bakr, such as Āmid, Arzan, Mayyāfāriķīn, and Kayfā. His successor paid homage to the Fāṭimid Caliph of Egypt, and was rewarded with the government of Aleppo, as the Caliph's officer, for a time, in succession to the expelled Ḥamdānids. The Marwānids also acknowledged the suzerainty of the Buwayhids; but vanished upon the invasion of the Seljūķs.

A.H.	Ruler	A.D.
380	Abū-'Alī -Ḥasan	990
387	Mumahhid-al-dawla Abū-Manṣūr	997
402	Naṣr-al-dawla Abū-Naṣr Aḥmad	1011
453	Niẓām-al-dawla Naṣr	1061
472	Manṣūr	1079
—489		—1096

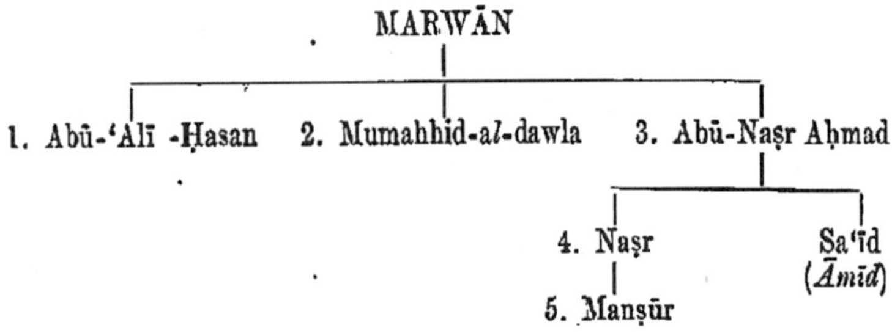

[*Seljūķs*]

A.H.		A.D.
403—545	48. MAZYADIDS	1012—1150

48. MAZYADIDS
(-ḤILLA)

The Banū Mazyad, a tribe of the Banū Asad, after leaving Arabia, spread over the deserts to -Ḳādisīya on the left bank of the Tigris. The fourth of the dynasty, Ṣadaḳa, built his new capital of -Ḥilla on the site of the town of -Jāmi'ān in 1101 (*495*), and the beauty of its buildings and extent of its trade were long celebrated. Ṣadaḳa is one of the great heroes of Arab history, extolled by poets and chroniclers. The dynasty declined after his death, and in 1162 (*558*) the Caliph -Mustanjid attacked the tribes of the Banū Asad in -'Irāḳ, and killed 4000 of their fighting men, so that they disappeared from the Euphrates country. The Banū Muntafiḳ of the Batiḥa succeeded to part of their territory; the Zangids replaced them in power.

403	Sanad-a*l*-dawla 'Alī I	1012
408	Nūr-a*l*-dawla Dubays I	1017
474	Bahā-a*l*-dawla Abū-Kāmil Manṣūr	1081
479	Sayf-a*l*-dawla Ṣadaḳa I	1086
501	Nūr-a*l*-dawla Dubays II	1107
529	Ṣadaḳa II	1134
532	Moḥammad	1137
540	'Alī II	1145
—545		—1150

[*Zangids*]

MAZYAD -ASADĪ

1. Sanad-*al*-dawla 'Alī I
† 408

Abū-l-Ḥasan -Mukallad

Abū-l-Ghanā·im Moḥammad
† 401

-Ḥasan Abū-'Abd-Allāh

2. Nūr-*al*-dawla Dubays I
† 474

Abū-Kawām
Thābit

3. Bahā-*al*-dawla Abū-Kāmil Manṣūr
† 479

4. Sayf-*al*-dawla Abū-l -Ḥasan Ṣadaka
† 501

5. Nūr-*al*-dawla
Dubays II † 529

Tāj-al-Mulūk Abū-*l*-Najm
Badrān †502

Abū-Kāmil Manṣūr

6. Ṣadaka II
† 532

7. Moḥammad
dep. 540

8. 'Alī II

VII. PERSIA AND TRANSOXIANA

(PERSIAN PERIOD)

SÆC. IX–XI

49. DULAFIDS (KURDISTĀN)

50. SĀJIDS (ADHARBĪJĀN)

51. 'ALIDS (ṬABARISTĀN)

52. ṬĀHIRIDS (KHURĀSĀN)

53. ṢAFFĀRIDS (PERSIA)

54. SĀMĀNIDS (TRANSOXIANA AND PERSIA)

55. ĪLAK KHĀNS (TURKISTĀN)

56. ZIYĀRIDS (JURJĀN)

57. ḤASANWAYHIDS (KURDISTĀN)

58. BUWAYHIDS (SOUTHERN PERSIA AND -'IRĀḲ)

59. KĀKWAYHIDS (KURDISTĀN)

VII. PERSIA AND TRANSOXIANA

(PERSIAN PERIOD)

SÆC. IX–XI

The following group of dynasties ruling in Persia and the province of *Mā-warā*-l-*nahr* (' Beyond the River' Oxus), or Transoxiana, up to the inroad of the Seljūḳs, belongs to the period of Persian revival. The Caliph -Ma·mūn, whose mother was a Persian slave, attained to the Caliphate, and dethroned his brother -Amīn, by the aid of Persian troops raised in Ḳhurāsān; his power was maintained by his Persian adherents; and his policy was unlimited conciliation of Persian national aspirations. The result was a revival of Persian influences at the expense of the old Arab polity, and the consequent weakening of the State. The great officers, governors, and generals, in the provinces began to acquire a dangerous degree of power, which -Ma·mūn and his successors in the Caliphate were unable to curb, and various Persian dynasties, professing a merely nominal dependence upon the Caliphs, sprang up, just as the Arab tribes of Mesopotamia further west asserted their authority against the decrepit Caliphate. Some dynasties, such as the Buwayhids, were not even orthodox, but professed the Shī'ite tenets, which have always been popular in Persia, as they are at this day. Although the period is characteristically Persian, it is not to be assumed that all the dynasts were Persians by race. Abū-Dulaf, for example, was an Arab, Ḥasanwayh a Kurd, whilst the Īlak Khāns were Turks. The chief dynasties, however, were of Persian origin.

A.H.		A.D.
c. 210—*c.* 285	**49. DULAFIDS**	*c.* 825—*c.* 898

(KURDISTĀN)

Abū-Dulaf -'Ijlī was an officer of the Caliph -Amīn, and received the government of Hamadhān, in which he was succeeded by his son 'Abd-al-'Azīz and his grandsons. 'Omar b. 'Abd-al-'Azīz increased his dominions by the acquisition of Iṣpahān and Nahāwand in 281. They were succeeded by other governors of the Caliphs.

c. 210	Abū-Dulaf -Ḳāsim b. Idrīs -'Ijlī	*c.* 825
228	'Abd-al-'Azīz	842
260	Dulaf	873
265	Aḥmad	878
280	'Omar	893
—*c.* 285		—*c.* 898

1. ABŪ-DULAF

2. 'Abd-al-'Azīz

3. Dulaf — 4. Aḥmad — 5. 'Omar — *Ḥārith Abū-Laylā* † 284

['*Abbāsid Governors*]

A.H.		A.D.
266—*c.* 318	50. SĀJIDS	879—*c.* 930

50. SĀJIDS

(ADHARBĪJAN)

Abū-*l*-Sāj Dīvdād was governor of -Kūfa and -Ahwāz at the time of his death, 879 (*266*). At that date his son Moḥammad was governor of the Hijāz; but was transferred to -Anbār in *269*; and then to Adharbījān in *276*, to which was added Armenia in 898 (*285*). On his death his brother Yūsuf, who had been Wālī of Mecca in 884 (*271*), succeeded to the government of Armenia and Adharbījān, setting aside Moḥammad's son Dīvdād. Yūsuf invaded -Rayy in 918 (*306*) and was imprisoned by the Caliph in the following year, but was restored to his appointments in 922 (*310*). He annexed -Rayy in *311*, and waged war upon the Carmathians. In 931 (*319*) the government of Adharbījān was vested in Mufliḥ, a freedman of Yūsuf's.

266	Abū-*l*-Sāj Dīvdād *died*	879
276	Moḥammad -Afshīn b. Dīvdād .	889
288	Yūsuf b Dīvdād	900
315	Abū-l-Musāfir -Fatḥ b. Moḥammad	927
—*c.* 318		—*c.* 930

[*'Abbāsid Governors*]

A.H. 250—316 | A.D. 864—928

51. 'ALIDS

(ṬABARISTĀN)

The branch of 'Alid, or Zaydite, Imāms who ruled at Sa'da in the Yaman has already been noticed (p. 102). Other members of the same family, descendants of either -Ḥasan or -Ḥosayn, the grandsons of the prophet Moḥammad, long maintained their rights to the Imāmate or Caliphate in the provinces bordering the southern shore of the Caspian, Daylam, Ṭabaristān, and Gīlān. A list of merely spiritual pontiffs, or sporadic rebels, is beyond the prêsent purpose, but in 864 (*250*) the 'Alids gained possession of Ṭabaristān, became a power, struck coins, and held the province for sixty-four years, until expelled by the *Sāmānids*. After this event, several rival houses of 'Alids continued to maintain themselves in Gīlān and Daylam, and at least one of them, Abū-l-Faḍl Ja'far -Thā'ir fī-llāh, exercised the royal privilege of coinage.

250	-Ḥasan b. Zayd	864
270	Moḥammad b. Zayd	883
287	*Sāmānid government*	900
301	-Nāṣir Ḥasan b. 'Alī -Utrūsh	913
304	-Ḥasan b. -Ḳāsim	916
—316		—928

[*Sāmānids*; *Ziyārids*.]

A.H.		A.D.
205--259	52. ṬĀHIRIDS (KHURĀSĀN)	820—872

Ṭāhir Dhū-l-Yamīnayn ('Ambidexter'), the celebrated general of -Ma'mūn, descended from a Persian slave, was appointed by that Caliph to the government of Khurāsān in 820 (*205*), where he and his dynasty became practically independent, though holding their authority by patent of the Caliphs and with express acknowledgment of vassalage. They did not attempt to extend their power much beyond the borders of their province, and after half a century collapsed tamely before the attack of Ya'ḳūb b. Layth the *Ṣaffārid*.

205	Ṭāhir Dhū-l-Yamīnayn	820
207	Ṭalḥa	822
213	'Abd-Allāh	828
230	Ṭāhir II	844
248	Moḥammad	862
—259		—872

1. Ṭāhir Dhū-l-Yamīnayn
- 2. Ṭalḥa
- 3. 'Abd-Allāh
  - *Mus'ab*
  - 4. Ṭāhir II
    - 5. Moḥammad
      - [*Ṣaffārids*]
    - *Ḥosayn*
  - *Sulaymān*
- *'Ali*

A.H.		A.D.
254—290	53. ṢAFFĀRIDS	867—903

53. ṢAFFĀRIDS

(PERSIA)

Ya'ḳūb, the son of -Layth the Ṣaffār ('Coppersmith'), was by a freak of fortune promoted from the leadership of a band of outlaws to a post of trust at the Court of the Caliph's governor of the province of Sijistān (Sīstān, or Nīmrūz), whom he eventually succeeded, sometime before 868 (*255*). By that year he had annexed Herāt and occupied Fārs, including the capital Shīrāz, to which he soon added Balkh and Tukhāristān, and in 872 (*259*) took Khurāsān from the Ṭāhirids. After an expedition in Ṭabaristān, where he defeated Ḥasan b. Zayd the 'Alid, he openly revolted against the Caliph -Mu'tamid, and advanced through Shīrāz and -Ahwāz upon Baghdād; but was routed by the Caliph's brother -Muwaffaḳ, and died in 878 (*265*). His brother and successor 'Amr was confirmed in the governments of Khurāsān, Fārs, Kurdistān, and Sijistān. The Caliph, however, distrusting 'Amr's increasing power, induced Ismā'īl the *Sāmānid* to attack him in 900 (*287*), when the

Ṣaffārid was defeated and made prisoner. His grandson Ṭāhir succeeded him in Sijistān, but, endeavouring to re-establish the power of his house in Fārs, was imprisoned 903 (*290*). Two other members of the family vainly sought to recover its lost territory. In *296* Sijistān was granted to the Sāmānids, but the Ṣaffārids continued for nearly a century to aim at the possession of this province, and several of them succeeded in holding it for a time.*

254	Ya'ḳūb b. -Layth	868
265	'Amr b. -Layth	878
287	Ṭāhir b. Moḥammad b. 'Amr	900
—290		—903

[*Sāmānids*]

* See H. Sauvaire, *Sur un fels Saffâride inédit de la Collection de M. Ch. de l'Écluse* (*Numismatic Chronicle*, 1881) for an account of the later Ṣaffārids of Sijistān.

A.H.		A.D.
261—389	54. SĀMĀNIDS	874—999

(TRANSOXIANA AND PERSIA)

Sāmān, a Persian noble of Balkh, being aided by Asad b. 'Abd-Allāh, the governor of Khurāsān, renounced Zoroastrianism, embraced Islām, and named his son Asad after his protector. Asad's four sons all distinguished themselves in the service of the Caliph -Ma'mūn, and were rewarded about 819 (*204*) with provincial governments: Nūḥ had Samarḳand; Aḥmad, Farghāna; Yaḥyā, -Shāsh; and Ilyās, Herāt. Aḥmad took the lead among his brothers, and not only succeeded Nūḥ at Samarḳand, but incorporated Kāshghar in his dominions. His second son Ismā'īl took Khurāsān from the Ṣaffārids in 903 (*290*), defeated Moḥammad b. Zayd the 'Alid of Ṭabaristān, and brought under his sway the whole territory from the Great Desert to the Persian Gulf, and from the borders of India to near Baghdād. His power was most firmly established in Transoxiana, where Bukhārā and Samarḳand became the centre of civilisation, learning, art, and scholarship for a large part of the Moḥammadan world. His successors were weakened by rebellions in Khurāsān and Sijistān and by the growing power of the *Buwayhids*. In half a century they were restricted to little more than Transoxiana and Khurāsān, whilst the real power fell more and more into the hands of the Turkish slaves with whom they filled their Court. One of these, Alptigīn, founded the dynasty of the *Ghaznawids*, which in 994 (*384*) succeeded to the Sāmānid territory south of the Oxus. North of the river their power was curtailed by the *Īlak Khāns* of Turkistān, who had acquired the leadership of the Turkish tribes from Farghāna to the borders of China, and after invading Transoxiana and taking Bukhārā in 990 (*380*), finally put an end to the Sāmānid dynasty in 999 (*389*); though Ibrāhīm -Muntaṣir continued to fight for the throne till 1104 (*395*).

A.H.		A.D.
261	Naṣr I b. Aḥmad	874
279	Ismā'īl b. Aḥmad	892
295	Aḥmad b. Ismā'īl	907
301	Naṣr II b. Aḥmad	913
331	Nūḥ I b. Naṣr	942
343	'Abd-al-Malik I b. Nūḥ	954
350	Manṣūr I b. Nūḥ	961
366	Nūḥ II b. Manṣūr	976
387	Manṣūr II b. Nūḥ II	997
389	'Abd-al-Malik II b. Nūḥ II	999

[*Khāns of Turkistān; Ghaznawids*]

SĀMĀNIDS

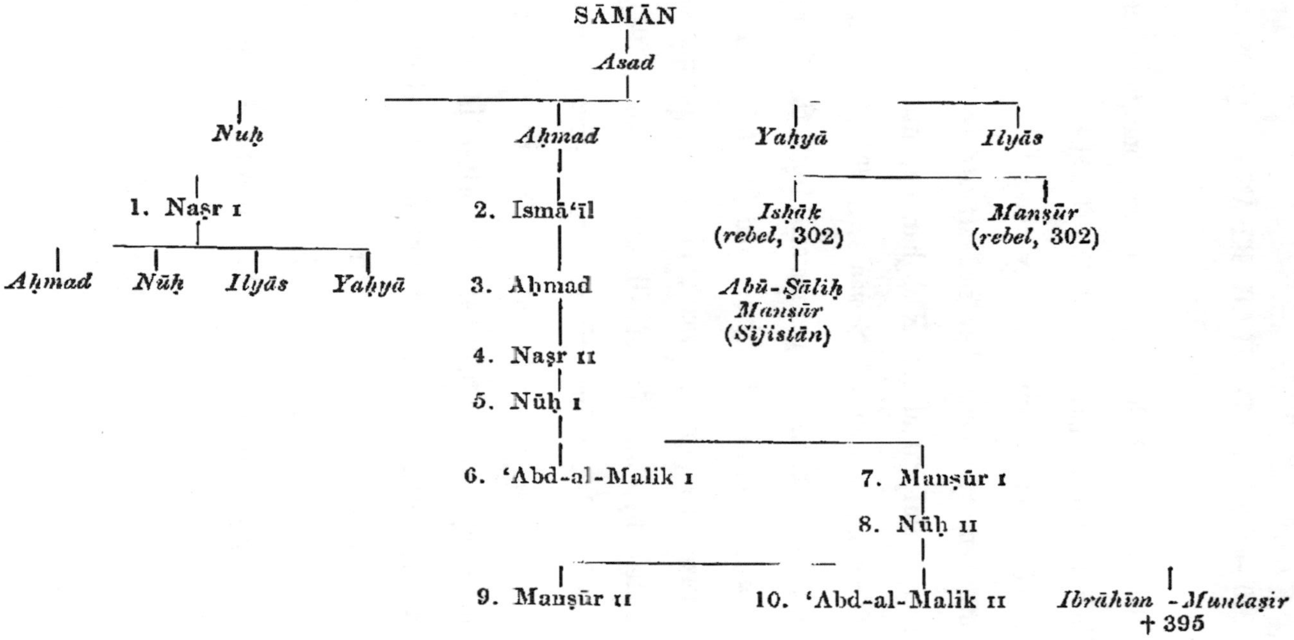
SĀMĀN
Asad
Nuḥ
Aḥmad
Yaḥyā
Ilyās
1. Naṣr I
2. Ismā'īl
Isḥāḳ (*rebel*, 302)
Manṣūr (*rebel*, 302)
Aḥmad
Nūḥ
Ilyās
Yaḥyā
3. Aḥmad
Abū-Ṣāliḥ Manṣūr (*Sijistān*)
4. Naṣr II
5. Nūḥ I
6. 'Abd-al-Malik I
7. Manṣūr I
8. Nūḥ II
9. Manṣūr II
10. 'Abd-al-Malik II
Ibrāhīm -Muntaṣir † 395

A.H.		A.D.
c. 320—*c.* 560	55. ĪLAK KHĀNS OF TURKISTĀN	*c.* 932—*c.* 1165

The history of these Khāns is very meagrely recorded. They appear to have united the Turkish tribes east of Farghāna under their authority towards the end of the tenth century, when they had already become Muslims. Their capital was at first Kāshghar, but after the conquest of Transoxiana from the Sāmānids in 999 (*389*) Īlak Naṣr ruled his tribesmen, who roamed from the Caspian as far as the borders of China, from Bukhārā. An attempt to seize the provinces south of the Oxus was signally defeated by Maḥmūd of Ghazna in 1007 (*398*), and henceforward the Īlak Khāns were restricted to Transoxiana, Kāshghar, and Eastern Tartary. Under their rule, many tribes established themselves in Transoxiana and were afterwards pressed forward into Persia: such as the celebrated Turkomān tribe of the *Seljūḳs*. The succession and chronology of the Khāns of Turkistān are exceedingly uncertain, and the following list is merely tentative.*

* From Dorn, *Inventaire des Monnaies de l'Institut des langues orientales du Ministère des Affaires Étrangères*, Appendice (*Petersburg*, 1881).

	'Abd-al-Ḳarīm Satuḳ
	Mūsā b. Satuḳ
† 383—4	Shihāb-a*l*-dawla Hārūn Bughrā Khān b. Sulaymān
c. 389—400	Abū-l-Ḥosayn Naṣr I b. 'Alī
c. 401—407	Ḳuṭb-a*l*-dawla Abū-Naṣr Aḥmad I b. 'Alī
c. 403—408	Sharaf-a*l*-dīn Ṭughān Khān b. 'Alī
	Abū-l-Muẓaffar Arslān Khān I b. 'Alī
† 423	Yūsuf Ḳadr Khān I
c. 421—425	Sharaf-a*l*-dawla Abū-Shujā' Arslān Khān II
c. 425—435	Maḥmūd I Bughrā Khān

In the West

	Chaghratigīn
c. 440—460	Abū-l-Muẓaffar 'Imād-a*l*-dawla Ibrāhīm Tufghāj or Tafḳāj Khān b. Naṣr
† 472	Shams-al-Mulk Naṣr II b. Tafḳāj
	Khiḍr Khān b. Tafḳāj
† 488	Aḥmad Khān II b. Khiḍr
† 490-5	Maḥmūd Khān II
† 495	Ḳādr Khān II b. 'Omar b. Aḥmad
	Maḥmūd Arslān Khān III b. Sulaymān
	Abū-l-Ma'ālī Ḥasan Tigīn b. 'Alī
	Rukn-a*l*-dīn Maḥmūd Khān III b. Arslān
c. 558	Ḳilij Tafghāj Khān b. Moḥammad
	Jalāl-a*l*-dīn 'Alī Gūrkān b. Ḥasan Tigīn

In the East.

439—55	Ṭughril Khān b. Yūsuf Ḳadr Khān
455	Ṭighril Tigīn b. Ṭughril
455?—496	Hārūn Bughrā Khān b. Yūsuf Ḳadr Khān
	Nūr-a*l*-dawla Aḥmad b. Arslān Khān

A.H.		A.D.
316—434	56. ZIYĀRIDS	928—1042

(JURJĀN)

The southern shore of the Caspian had never been well affected to the Caliphate, and the followers of 'Alī had repeatedly established their heterodox power in these regions (see p. 127); nor were the Sāmānids more successful than the Caliphs in maintaining their authority there. Taking advantage of this, Mardāwīj b. Ziyār, descended from a long line of princes, made himself independent in Ṭabaristān and Jurjān, and even occupied Iṣpahān and Hamadhān, and pushed his forces as far as Ḥulwān, on the Mesopotamian frontier, between the years 928—931 (*316—319*). He was the patron of the Buwayhids, and gave 'Alī b. Buwayh his first appointment as governor of Karaj. Mardāwīj held his dominions as titular vassal of the 'Abbāsid Caliph: his brother and successor Washmagīr paid nominal homage to the Sāmānids as well. After the rise of the *Buwayhids* in 932 (*320*), the authority of the Ziyārids scarcely extended beyond the borders of Jurjān and Ṭabaristān;

and Ḳābūs was even exiled for 18 years (*371—389*) by the Buwayhid Mu'ayyid-*al*-dawla. On his return, however, he recovered Gīlān as well as his former provinces, in which his sons succeeded him, until dispossessed by the *Ghaznawids*.

316	Mardāwīj b. Ziyār	928
323	Ẓahīr-*al*-dawla Abū-Manṣūr Washmagīr .	935
356	Bīstūn	967
366	Shams-al-Ma'ālī Ḳābūs	976
403	Falak-al-Ma'ālī Manuchahr	1012
420	Anūshīrwān (Dārā?)	1029
—434		—1042

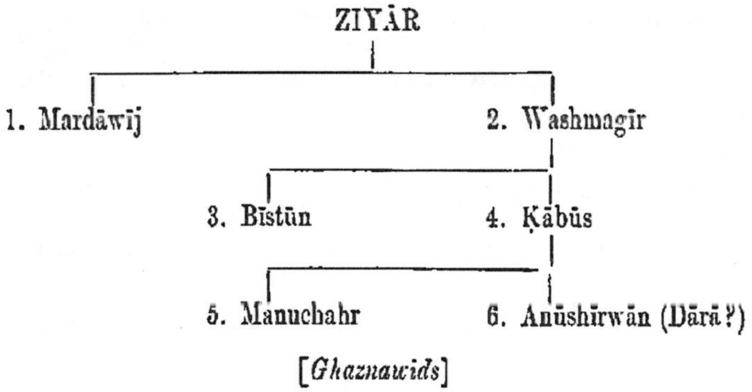

A.H.		A.D.
c. 348–406	57. ḤASANWAYHIDS	c. 959–1015

57. ḤASANWAYHIDS (KURDISTĀN)

Ḥasanwayh b. -Ḥosayn -Barzikānī was the chief of one of the Kurdish tribes which, like the Marwānids, began to make themselves prominent in the tenth century; before the middle of which he had possessed himself of a large part of Kurdistān, including the towns of Dīnawār, Hamadhān, Nahāwand, the fortress of Sarmāj, etc. His power was so considerable that the Buwayhids did not disturb him, and at his death 'Aḍud-*al*-dawla of that dynasty, after annexing his dominions, appointed Badr b. Ḥasanwayh as governor over his late father's province. Badr still further enhanced the dignity and authority of his family, and was decorated by the Caliph with the title of Nāṣir-*al*-dawla. His grandson Ẓāhir, who succeeded him in 1014 (*405*), only kept his position for a year, after which he was expelled by Shams-*al*-dawla the *Buwayhid*, and was shortly afterwards killed.

c. 348	Ḥasanwayh b. -Ḥosayn	c. 959
369	Nāṣir-*al*-dīn Abū-*l*-Najm Badr b. Ḥasanwayh	979
405	Ẓāhir b. Hilāl († 405) b. Badr . . .	1014
—406		—1015

[*Buwayhids*]

A.H.		A.D.
320–447	58. BUWAYHIDS	932—1055

(SOUTHERN PERSIA AND 'IRĀḲ)

Buwayh, reputed to be a descendant of the ancient Kings of Persia, was the chief of a warlike clan of the highlanders of Daylam, and like most of his countrymen had taken part in the frequent wars which disturbed the provinces bordering on the Caspian. Like them, also, he had transferred his services from the Sāmānids to the rising chieftain Mardāwīj the Ziyārid about 930 (*318*), and his eldest son 'Alī ('Imād-al-dawla) had been granted by Mardāwīj the government of Karaj. 'Alī, with the help of troops from Daylam and Gīlān, soon extended his authority southwards, occupied Iṣpahān for a time, and annexed Arrajān 932 (*320*) and Nubandijān (*321*), whilst his brother Ḥasan (Rukn-al-dawla) drove the Arab garrison out of Kāzirūn. The two brothers then pushed on to the eastward, and joined by the third, Aḥmad (Mu'izz-al-dawla), seized Shīrāz (*322*). The Caliph was forced to recognize them as his lieutenants, and when Mu'izz-al-dawla, working his way westward from Kirmān, and reducing the province of -Ahwāz (or Khūzistān), entered Baghdād itself in 945 (*334*), the Caliph -Mustakfī not only bestowed the honorific titles of 'Imād, Rukn, and Mu'izz *al*-dawla on the three brethren, but granted Mu'izz the rank and style of *Amīr-al-Umarā*, or Premier Noble, a dignity which was held by many subsequent members of the family. It is a mistake to say that they were ever given the title of *Sulṭān*, for they never styled themselves so on their coinage, but used the titles *Amīr* and *Malik*. Their authority, nevertheless, was as absolute as any Sulṭān's in Baghdād, and the Caliphs were their abject puppets, though treated with outward homage, in spite of the Buwayhids' Shī'ite proclivities. How the brothers and their descendants divided Persia and -'Irāḳ among themselves is shown in the following tables, as well as the intricate history of the dynasty permits. Division among the princes encouraged aggression, and the wide dominions of the Buwayhids fell peacemeal to the *Ghaznawids*, *Kākwayhids*, and *Seljūḳs*.

I. OF FĀRS

320	'Imād-*al*-dawla Abū-l-Ḥasan 'Alī . .	932
338*	'Aḍud-*al*-dawla Abū-Shujā' Khusrū . .	949
372*	Sharaf-*al*-dawla Abū-l-Fawāris Shīr Zayd .	982
379	Ṣamṣām-*al*-dawla Abū-Kālinjār -Marzubān .	989
388*	*Bahā-al-dawla* (of -'Irāḳ)	998
403*	Sulṭān-*al*-dawla Abū-Shujā' . . .	1012
415*	'Imād-*al*-dīn Abū-Kālinjār -Marzubān .	1024
440*	Abū-Naṣr Khusrū Fīrūz -Raḥīm . . .	1048
—447		—1055

* Also ruling -'Irāḳ, etc., see next list.

II. OF -'IRĀḲ, -AHWĀZ, AND KIRMĀN

320	Mu'izz-*al*-dawla Abū-l-Ḥosayn Aḥmad. .	932
356	'Izz-*al*-dawla Bakhtiyār	967
367	*Aḍud-al-dawla (of Fārs)*	977
372	*Sharaf-al-dawla (of Fārs)*	982
379	Bahā-*al*-dawla Abū-Naṣr Fīrūz . . .	989
403	*Sulṭān-al-dawla (of Fārs)*	1012

DIVIDED PROVINCES:

-'IRĀḲ

411	Musharrif-*al*-dawla	1020
416	Jalāl-*al*-dawla	1025
435	*'Imad-al-dīn (of Fārs)*	1043
440	*Abū-Naṣr Khusrū Fīrūz (of Fārs)* . .	1048
—447		—1055

KIRMĀN

403	Ḳawām-*al*-dawla Abū-l-Fawāris . . .	1012
419	*'Imād-al-dīn (of Fārs)*	1028
440	Abū-Manṣūr Fullād Sattūn	1048
—448		—1056

III. OF -RAYY, HAMADHĀN, AND IṢPAHĀN

320	Rukn-al-dawla Abū-'Ali Ḥasan . . .	932
366-	Mu'ayyid-al-dawla Abū-Manṣūr (*Iṣpahān only*)	976
—373		—983
366	Fakhr-al-dawla Abū-l-Ḥasan 'Alī (*adding Iṣpahān* 373)	976
387	Majd-al-dawla Abū-Ṭālib Rustam (*deposed by Maḥmūd of Ghazna*)	997
—420		—1029
387	Shams-al-dawla Abū-Ṭāhir (*Hamadhān only*)	997
c. 412	Samā-al-dawla Abū-l-Ḥasan (*deposed by Ibn-Kākwayh*)	*c.* 1021
—414		—1023

[*Kākwayhids; Ghaznawids; Seljūks*]

GEOGRAPHICAL DISTRIBUTION OF THE BUWAYHIDS

FĀRS	KIRMĀN, -ʿAHWAZ, -ʿIRĀḲ	-RAYY, HAMADHĀN	IṢPAHĀN
320 ʿImād-al-dawla	320. Muʿizz-al-dawla	320 Rukn-al-dawla	
338 ʿAḍud-al-dawla			
	356 ʿIzz-al-dawla		
		366 Fakhr-al-dawla	366 Mu·ayyid-al-dawla
	367 (ʿAḍud)		
372 Sharaf-al-dawla		373	
379 Ṣamṣām-al-dawla	379 Bahā-al-dawla		
		387 Shams-al-dawla	387 Majd-al-dawla
388 (Bahā)			
			398 (*Kākwayhids*)
403 Sulṭān-al-dawla	(KIRMĀN) 403 Ḳawām-al-d.		
	411 Musharrif-al-d.		
		412 Sumā-al-dawla	
		414 (*Kākwayhids*)	
415 ʿImād-al-dīn	416 Jalāl-al-d.		
	419 (ʿImād)		420 (*Ghaznawids*)
	435		
440 Khusrū Fīrūz —447 (*Seljūḳs*)	440 Fullād — Sattūn 448		

BUWAYHIDS

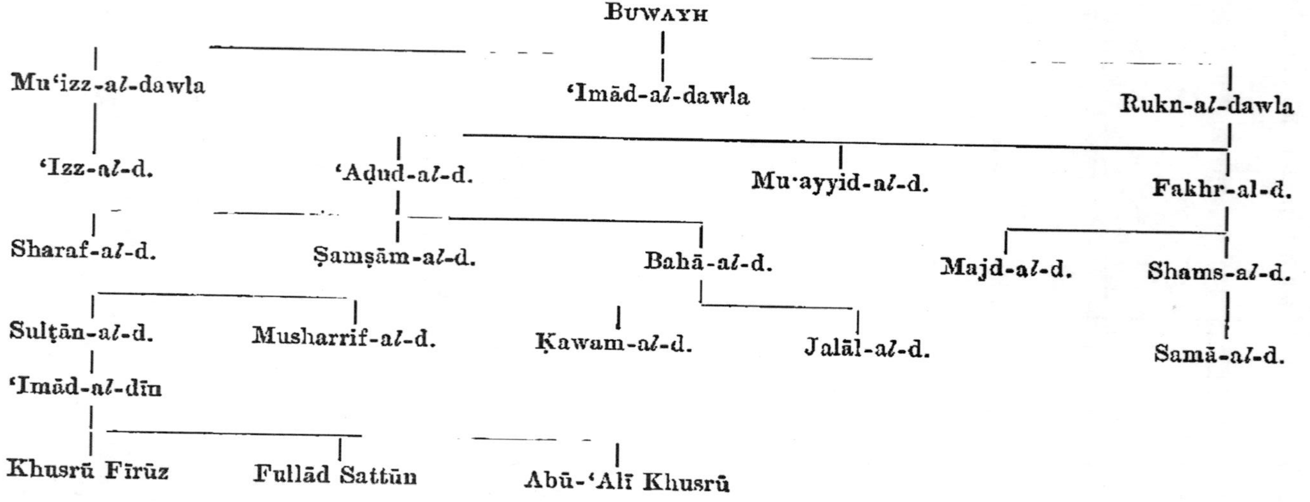
Buwayh
Mu'izz-al-dawla
'Imād-al-dawla
Rukn-al-dawla
'Izz-al-d.
'Aḍud-al-d.
Mu·ayyid-al-d.
Fakhr-al-d.
Sharaf-al-d.
Ṣamṣām-al-d.
Bahā-al-d.
Majd-al-d.
Shams-al-d.
Sulṭān-al-d.
Musharrif-al-d.
Ḳawam-al-d.
Jalāl-al-d.
Samā-al-d.
'Imād-al-dīn
Khusrū Fīrūz
Fullād Sattūn
Abū-'Alī Khusrū

A.H.		A.D.
398—443	59. KĀKWAYHIDS (KURDISTĀN)	1007—1051

Moḥammad b. Dushmanzār, known as Ibn-Kākwayh, was first cousin to Majd-*al*-dawla the Buwayhid, of Hamadhān, whose dominions he annexed by the deposition of Samā-*al*-dawla in 1023 (*414*). He had previously taken Iṣpahān in 1007 (*398*). The family continued to rule in Iṣpahān, Hamadhān, Yazd, Nahāwand, etc., until their conquest by the *Seljūḳ* Ṭughril Beg in 1051 (*443*).

A.H.		A.D.
398	‘Alā-*al*-dawla Abū-Ja‘far Moḥammad . .	1007
433	Ẓahīr-*al*-dīn Abū-Manṣūr Farāmarz . .	1041
—443		—1051

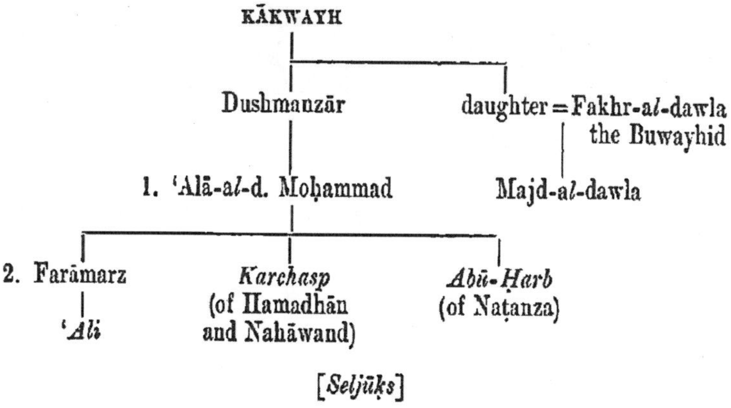

VIII. THE SELJŪḲS

SÆC. XI–XII

60. A GREAT SELJŪḲS OF PERSIA

B SELJŪḲS OF KIRMĀN

C SELJŪḲS OF SYRIA

D SELJŪḲS OF -'IRĀḲ

E SELJŪḲS OF -RŪM

60A. DĀNISHMANDIDS (CAPPADOCIA)

A.H. A.D.

429—700 60. THE SELJŪḲS 1037—1300

(WESTERN ASIA)

The advent of the Seljūḳian Turks forms a notable epoch in Moḥammadan history. At the time of their appearance the Empire of the Caliphate had vanished. What had once been a realm united under a sole Moḥammadan ruler was now a collection of scattered dynasties, not one of which, save perhaps the Fāṭimids of Egypt (and they were schismatics) was capable of imperial sway. Spain and Africa, including the important province of Egypt, had long been lost to the Caliphs of Baghdād; northern Syria and Mesopotamia were in the hands of turbulent Arab chiefs, some of whom had founded dynasties; Persia was split up into the numerous governments of the Buwayhid princes (whose Shī'ite opinions left little respect for the puppet Caliphs of their time), or was held by sundry insignificant dynasts, each ready to attack the other and thus contribute to the general weakness. The prevalence of schism increased the disunion of the various provinces of the vanished Empire. A drastic remedy was needed, and it was found in the invasion of the Turks. These rude nomads, unspoilt by town life and civilised indifference to religion, embraced Islām with all the fervour of their uncouth souls. They came to the rescue of a dying State, and revived it. They swarmed over Persia, Mesopotamia, Syria, and Asia Minor, devastating the country, and exterminating every dynasty that existed there; and, as the result, they once more reunited Moḥammadan Asia, from the western frontier of Afghānistān to the Mediterranean, under one sovereign; they put a new life into the expiring zeal of the Muslims, drove back the re-encroaching Byzantines, and bred up a generation of fanatical Moḥammadan warriors, to whom, more than to anything else, the Crusaders owed their repeated failure. This it is that gives the Seljūḳs so important a place in Moḥammadan history.

The Seljūḳs, or Saljūḳids, were the descendants of Seljūḳ b. Yakāk, a Turkomān chieftain in the service of one of the Khāns of Turkistān. Seljūḳ migrated from the Kirghiz steppes with all his clan to Jand in the province of Bukhārā, where he and his people enthusiastically embraced Islām. He and his sons and grandsons took part in the wars between the Sāmānids, the Ilak Khāns, and Maḥmūd of Ghazna, and the brothers Ṭughril Beg and Chagar Beg eventually became strong enough to venture upon the invasion of Khurāsān at the head of their wild Turkomān tribes, and after several victories over the Ghaznawid armies succeeded in taking the chief cities. In 1037 (*429*) the public prayer was said in the name of Chagar Beg Dāwūd, 'King of Kings,' in the mosques of Merv, while his brother Ṭughril Beg was similarly proclaimed in Nayshāpūr. Balkh, Jurjān, Ṭabaristān, and Khwārizm were speedily annexed; the Jibāl, Hamadhān, Dīnawār, Ḥulwān, -Rayy, and Iṣpahān followed (*433—7*), and in 1055 (*447*) Ṭughril Beg entered Baghdād itself, and had his name proclaimed as Sulṭān in the city of the Caliph.

Other Turkish tribes came to swell their armies, and the whole of western Asia, from the borders of Afghānistān to the frontier of the Greek Empire in Asia Minor and of the Fāṭimid Caliphate of Egypt, became united under the rule of the Seljūḳs before 1077 (*470*).

Ṭughril Beg, Alp-Arslān, and Malik Shāh held supreme sway over the whole of this vast Empire, but after the death of the last, civil war sprang up between the brothers Bargiyāruḳ and Moḥammad, and separate branches of the Seljūḳ family attained virtual independence in different parts of the widely scattered dominions, although the main line still preserved a nominal suzerainty down to the death of Sinjar, the last 'Great Seljūḳ' (whose rule was almost confined to Khurāsān) in 1157 (*552*). The Seljūḳs of Kirmān, of -'Irāḳ, of Syria, and of -Rūm or Asia Minor, were the chief sub-divisions of the family, but individual members of it ruled in Adharbījān, Tukhāristān, and other provinces. In the East, the Seljūḳ empire succumbed before the attack of the Khwārizm Shāh; in Adharbījān, Fārs, Mesopotamia, and Diyār-Bakr it was supplanted by dynasties founded by Seljūḳ officers, or Atābegs, but in -Rūm it survived until the beginning of the power of the 'Othmānlī Turks in 1300.

(To face p. 157)

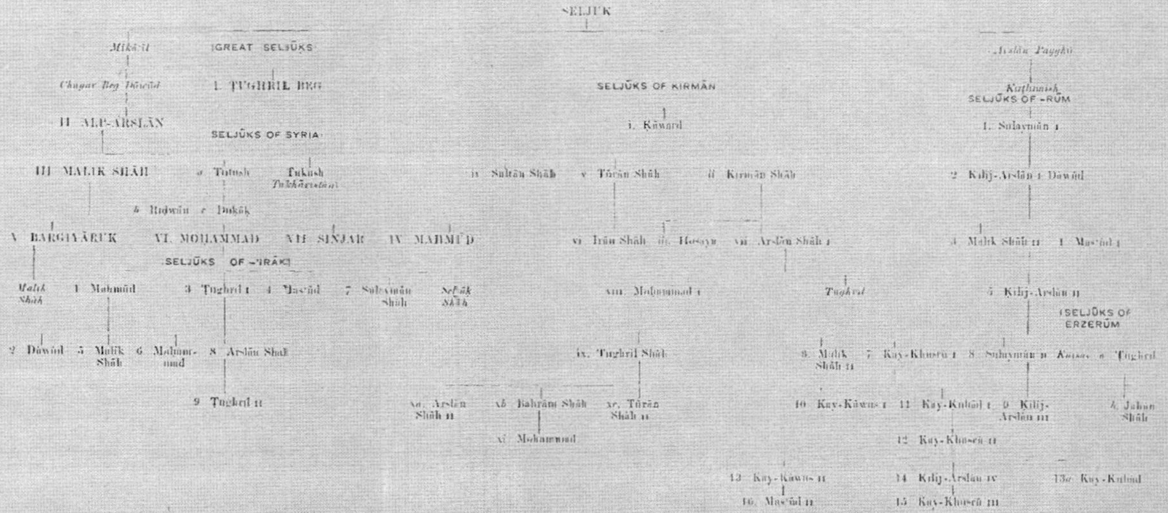
SELJUK
Mikā'il
(GREAT SELJŪKS)
Chagar Beg Dāwūd
I. ṬUGHRIL BEG
II. ALP-ARSLĀN
SELJŪKS OF SYRIA
III. MALIK SHĀH
a Tutush
Tukush
b Ridwān
c Dukāk
V. BARGIYĀRUK
VI. MOḤAMMAD
VII. SINJAR
IV. MAḤMŪD
SELJŪKS OF 'IRĀḲ
Malik Shāh
1 Maḥmūd
3 Ṭughril I
4 Mas'ūd
7 Sulaymān Shāh
Seljūk Shāh
2 Dāwūd
5 Malik Shāh
6 Moḥammad
8 Arslān Shāh
9 Ṭughril II
SELJŪKS OF KIRMĀN
i. Ḳāward
ii. Sulṭān Shāh
v. Tūrān Shāh
iii. Kirmān Shāh
vi. Īrān Shāh
iv. Ḥosayn
vii. Arslān Shāh I
viii. Moḥammad I
Ṭughril
ix. Ṭughril Shāh
xa. Arslān Shāh II
xb. Bahrām Shāh
xc. Tūrān Shāh II
xi. Moḥammad
Arslān Payghū
Ḳutlumish
SELJŪKS OF RŪM
1. Sulaymān I
2 Ḳilij-Arslān I
Dāwūd
3 Malik Shāh II
4 Mas'ūd I
5 Ḳilij-Arslān II
(SELJŪKS OF ERZERŪM)
6. Malik Shāh II
7 Kay-Khusrū I
8 Sulaymān II
Ṭughril
10 Kay-Kāwus I
11 Kay-Ḳubād I
9 Ḳilij-Arslān III
Jahān Shāh
12 Kay-Khusrū II
13 Kay-Kāwus II
14 Ḳilij-Arslān IV
13a Kay-Ḳubād
16. Mas'ūd II
15 Kay-Khusrū III

A.H.		A.D.
429—552	A. GREAT SELJŪḲS	1037—1157
429	Rukn-a*l*-dīn Abū-Ṭālib Ṭughril Beg . .	1037
455	‘Aḍud-a*l*-dīn Abū-Shujā‘ Alp-Arslān . .	1063
465	Jalāl-a*l*-dīn Abū-l-Fatḥ Malik Shāh . .	1072
485	Nāṣir-a*l*-dīn Maḥmūd	1092
487	Rukn-a*l*-dīn Abū-l-Muẓaffar Bargiyāruḳ .	1094
498	Malik Shāh II	1104
498*	Ghiyāth-a*l*-dīn Abū-Shujā‘ Moḥammad .	1104
511†	Mu‘izz-a*l*-dīn Abū-l-Ḥārith Sinjar . .	1117
—552		—1157
	[*Shāhs of Khwārizm*]	

433—583	B. SELJŪḲS OF KIRMĀN	1041—1187
433	‘Imād-a*l*-dīn Ḳarā-Arslān Ḳāward Beg .	1041
465	Kirmān Shāh	1072
467	Ḥosayn	1074
467	Rukn-a*l*-dīn Sulṭān Shāh	1074
477	Tūrān Shāh.	1084
490	Irān Shāh	1097
494	Arslān Shāh	1100
536	Mughīth-a*l*-dīn Moḥammad I	1141
551	Muḥyī-a*l*-dīn Ṭughril Shāh	1156
563	{ Bahrām Shāh Arslān II Shāh Turkān Shāh } (rivals)	1167
583	Moḥammad II	1187
	[*Ghuzz Turkomāns*]	

* Moḥammad had been at open war with Bargiyāruḳ for many years before the latter's death.

† Sinjar had been governor of Khurāsān for twenty years before his accession as Great Seljūḳ.

A.H.		A.D.
487—511	C. SELJŪḲS OF SYRIA	1094—1117
487	Tutush b. Alp-Arslān	1094
488	Riḍwān b. Tutush (*at Aleppo*) . . .	1095
	(Duḳāḳ b Tutush *at Damascus* 488–497)	
507	Alp-Arslān -Akhras b. Riḍwān . . .	1113
508	Sulṭān Shāh b. Riḍwān	1114
—511	-	—1117

[*Būrids, Ortuḳids*]

A.H.		A.D.
511—590	D. SELJŪḲS OF -'IRĀḲ AND KURDISTĀN	1117—1194
511	Mughith-al-dīn Maḥmūd	1117
525	Ghiyāth-al-dīn Dāwūd.	1131
526	Ṭughril I	1132
527	Ghiyāth-al-dīn Mas'ūd	1133
547	Mu'īn-al-dīn Malik Shāh	1152
548	Moḥammad	1153
554	Sulaymān Shāh	1159
556	Arslān Shāh	1161
573	Ṭughril II	1177
—590		—1194

[*Shāhs of Khwārizm*]

A.H.		A.D.
470—700	E. SELJŪḲS OF RŪM (ASIA MINOR)	1077—1300
470	Sulaymān I b. Ḳuṭlumish	1077
479	*Interregnum*	1086
485	Ḳilij-Arslān Dāwūd	1092
500	Malik Shāh I	1106
510	Mas'ūd I	1116
551*	'Izz-al-dīn Ḳilij-Arslān II	1156
584	Ḳuṭb-al-dīn Malik Shāh II	1188
588	Ghiyāth-al-dīn Kay-Khusrū I	1192
597	Rukn-al-dīn Sulaymān II	1200
600	Ḳilij-Arslān III	1203
601	Kay-Khusrū I *restored*	1204
607	'Izz-al-dīn Kay-Kāwus I	1210
616	'Alā-al-dīn Kay-Ḳubād I	1219
634	Ghiyāth-al-dīn Kay-Khusrū II	1236
643	'Izz-al-dīn Kay-Kāwus II †	1245
655	Rukn-al-dīn Ḳilij-Arslān IV.	1257
666	Ghiyāth-al-dīn Kay-Khusrū III	1267
682	Ghiyāth-al-dīn Mas'ūd II ‡	1283
696	'Alā-al-dīn Kay-Ḳubād II	1296
—700		—1300

[*Mongols, 'Othmānlī Turks, etc.*]

* Ḳilij-Arslān survived till 588, but divided his dominions among his sons some years earlier.

† In conjunction with his brothers Ḳilij-Arslān III and Kay-Ḳubād.

‡ Mas'ūd was allowed by the Mongol Abāgā to govern Sīwās, Arzanjān and Erzerūm, from the death of his father Kay-Kāwus in 677, during the nominal sovereignty of his cousin Kay-Khusrū III, whom he succeeded in 682. Mas'ūd appears to have been restored to his kingdom on the deposition of his nephew Kay-Ḳubād in 700, and to have reigned for four years; but the last four Seljūḳs were merely governors under the Mongols of Persia.

A.H. A.D.

c 490–560 60A. DĀNISHMANDIDS c 1097–1165

(SĪWĀS, CAESAREA, MALATĪA)

Whilst the Seljūḳs were extending their empire in Asia Minor, another Turkish chief, Gumishtigīn, son of Dānishmand, established his power in Cappodocia over the cities of Sīwās (Sebaste), Ḳayṣarīya (Caesarea), and Malaṭīya (Melitene), near which last place he inflicted a sanguinary defeat upon the Franks. His successors played a distinguished part in the wars of the Crusades, but the dynasty was soon absorbed in its greater Seljūḳ neighbour.

A.H.		A.D.
	Moḥammad I Gumishtigīn b. Tilū Dānishmand	
499	Ghāzī b. Gumishtigīn	1105
529	Moḥammad II. b. Ghāzī	1134
537	Dhū-*l*-Nūn b. Moḥammad II . . .	1142
	Yaghi (*or* Ya'ḳūb) Arslān b. Ghāzī	
560	Ibrāhīm b. Moḥammad II	1165

[*Seljūḳs of -Rūm*]

IX. THE ATĀBEGS

(SELJŪḲ OFFICERS)

SÆC. XII—XIII

IX. THE ATÂBEGS

(SELJŪḲ OFFICERS)

SÆC. XII–XIII

The Seljūḳ Empire was a military power, and the army on which it depended was commanded by Turkish slaves. Free men could not be trusted with the highest commands or the rule of distant provinces; it was necessary to rely on the fidelity of purchased slaves brought up at the court in close relations with the Seljūḳ princes. Every Seljūḳ had a following of mamlūks, generally brought from Kipchak, who filled the chief offices of the court and camp, and eventually won their manumission by hard service. The inevitable result of this system was the supplanting of the senile master by the virile slave. As the Seljūḳs grew weak and their empire broke up into sub-divisions, their mamlūks, who had fought their battles for them, became the guardians or regents (Atābegs) of their youthful heirs, and speedily exchanged the delegated function for the privileges of sovereignty. In this way Ṭughtigīn, a mamlūk of the Seljūḳ Tutush, was appointed Atābeg over his youthful heir Duḳāḳ, and on his death assumed full sovereign powers at Damascus. 'Imād-*al*-dīn Zangī, founder of the Atābegs of -Mōṣil and Aleppo, etc., was the son of a slave of the third Seljūḳ Sulṭān Malik Shāh; the Adharbījān Atābegs sprang from a Kipchak mamlūk of Mas'ūd the Seljūḳ Sulṭān of -'Irāḳ; Anushtigīn, ancestor of the Khwārizm Shāhs, was cupbearer to Sulṭān Malik Shāh; Ortuḳ and Salghar, founders of dynasties in Diyār-Bakr and Fārs, were Seljūḳ officers; and the Begtigīnids, Hazāraspids, and Ḳutlugh Khâns were officers of the slaves of the Seljūḳs. In the twelfth century the whole Seljūḳ empire, save Anatolia, was in the hands of these captains of their hosts, who form a distinct group of dynasties.

A.H.		A.D.
497—549	61. BŪRIDS	1103—1154

(ATĀBEGS OF DAMASCUS)

Ṭughtigīn—one of the numerous officers who held command in the Seljūḳ armies, became Atābegs or regents of the younger Seljūḳ princes, and eventually usurped their power—was an enfranchised mamlūk of Sulṭān Tutush, and afterwards, 1095 (*488*), was appointed Atābeg of his son Duḳāḳ, the Seljūḳ prince of Damascus, whom he succeeded.

A.H.		A.D.
497	Sayf-al-Islām Ẓahīr-*al*-dīn Ṭughtigīn . .	1103
522	Tāj-al-Mulūk Būrī	1128
526	Shams-al-Mulūk Ismā'īl	1132
529	Shihāb-*al*-dīn Maḥmūd	1134
533	Jamāl-*al*-dīn Moḥammad	1138
534	Mujīr-*al*-dīn Abaḳ (or Anaz, † 564) . .	1139
—519		—1154

[*Zangids*]

1. Ṭughtigīn

2. Būrī — 3. Ismā'īl — 4. Maḥmūd — 5. Moḥammad

6. Abaḳ

A.H. 521–648 | 62. ZANGIDS | A.D. 1127–1250

62. ZANGIDS

(ATĀBEGS OF MESOPOTAMIA AND SYRIA)

The Atābeg 'Imād-al-dīn Zangī was the son of Āḳsunḳur the Ḥājib (chamberlain), a Turkish slave of Malik Shāh, and from 1085 to 1094 (*478–487*) lieutenant of Tutush at Aleppo, against whom he rebelled, and was slain. Zangī was appointed governor of -'Irāḳ, including Baghdād, in 1127 (*521*), and in the same year annexed -Mōṣil, Sinjār, -Jazīra and Ḥarrān, and then Aleppo (*522*) and other Syrian cities. He especially distinguished himself as the champion of the Muslims against the Crusaders, and was the true forerunner of Saladin. On his death his dominions were divided between his sons Nūr-al-dīn Maḥmūd, another famous anti-crusader, who held Syria, and Sayf-al-dīn Ghāzī, who ruled in -Mōṣil and Mesopotamia. In the next generation the Syrian branch died out; but a new offshoot had been established at Sinjār; whilst a fourth sub-dynasty sprang up somewhat later at -Jazīra. The Sinjār line gave place to the Ayyūbids in 1221 (*618*); the others came under the rule of Lu·lu·, the slave and vezīr of the last of the -Mōṣil Zangids, until all were absorbed in the empire of the *Mongols*.

A.H.		A.D.
521—631	A. ATĀBEGS OF -MŌṢIL	1127—1234
521	'Imād-*al*-dīn Zangī (*with Aleppo*) . .	1127
541	Sayf-*al*-dīn Ghāzī I	1146
544	Ḳutb-*al*-dīn Mōdūd	1149
565	Sayf-*al*-dīn Ghāzī II	1169
576	'Izz-*al*-dīn Mas'ūd I	1180
589	Nūr-*al*-dīn Arslān Shāh I	1193
607	'Izz-*al*-dīn Mas'ūd II	1210
615	Nūr-*al*-dīn Arslān Shāh II	1218
616	Nāṣir-*al*-dīn Maḥmūd	1219
631	Badr-*al*-dīn Lu·lu·	1233
657	Ismā'īl b. Lu·lu·	1259
—660	[*Mongols*]	—1262
541—577	B. ATĀBEGS OF SYRIA	1146—1181
541	Nūr-*al*-dīn Maḥmūd b. Zangī	1146
569	-Ṣāliḥ Ismā'īl	1173
—577		—1181
	[*Atābegs of -Mōṣil and Sinjār*, 577; *then Ayyūbids*, 579]	
566—617	C. ATĀBEGS OF SINJĀR	1170—1220
566	'Imād-*al*-dīn Zangī b. Mōdūd	1170
594	Ḳuṭb-*al*-dīn Moḥammad	1197
616	'Imād-*al*-dīn Shāhānshāh	1219
616	Maḥmūd (*or* 'Omar)	1219
—617	[*Ayyūbids*]	—1220
576—648	D. ATĀBEGS OF -JAZĪRA	1180—1250
576	Mu'izz-*al*-dīn Sinjār Shāh	1180
605	Mu'izz-*al*-dīn Maḥmūd	1208
6*xx*	-Mas'ūd	12*xx*
—648	[*Ayyūbids*]	—1250

ZANGIDS

I. ZANGĪ b. Āḳsunḳur

(*A. Atābegs of -Mōṣil*) (*B. Atābegs of Syria*)

II. Ghāzī I — III. Mōdūd — i. Maḥmūd

(*C. Atābegs of Sinjār*)

IV. Ghāzī II — V. Mas'ūd I — 1. Zangī — ii. Ismā'īl

(*D. Atābegs of -Jazīra*)

a. Sinjār Shāh — VI. Arslān Shāh I — 2. Moḥammad

b. Maḥmūd — VII. Mas'ūd II — 3. Shāhānshāh — 4. Maḥmūd

c. -Mas'ūd — VIII. Arslān Shāh II — IX. Maḥmūd

Badr-*al*-dīn Lu'lu' (vezīr of IX)
(-*Mōṣil*, *Sinjār*, -*Jazīra* 637–660)

-Ṣāliḥ Ismā'īl (-*Mōṣil*, 657–60) — -Sa'īd (*Aleppo*, 658) — -Muẓaffar 'Alā-*al*-dīn 'Alī (*Sinjār*, 657–8) — Sayf-*al*-dīn (-*Jazīra*, 657–8) — -Mujāhid

A.H.		A.D.
539—630	63. BEGTIGĪNIDS	1144—1232

(ATĀBEGS OF ARBELA, ETC.)

In 1144 (*539*) 'Imād-*al*-dīn Zangī appointed one of his Turkish officers, Zayn-*al*-dīn 'Alī Kūchuk b. Begtigīn, to be his viceroy at -Mōṣil, and in 1149 (*544*) placed Sinjār and afterwards Ḥarrān, Takrit, Irbil (Arbela), etc., under his authority. On Zayn-*al*-dīn's death at Irbil in 1167 (*563*), his elder son Muẓaffar-*al*-dīn Kūkburī fled to Ḥarrān, whilst Irbil passed to the younger son Zayn-*al*-dīn Yūsuf, under the tutorship of the Amīr Mujāhid-*al*-dīn Ḳā·imāz. On Yūsuf's death in 1190 (*586*), Saladin, who then exercised supreme influence over Syria and Mesopotamia, appointed Muẓaffar-*al*-dīn Kūkburī as his brother's successor at Irbil and Shahrazūr, but gave his former governments of Ḥarrān, -Ruhā (Edessa) and Sumaysāṭ to his own nephew Taḳī-*al*-dīn 'Omar. Kūkburī died in 1232 (*630*), and being without sons bequeathed Irbil to the 'Abbāsid Caliph.

539	Zayn-*al*-dīn 'Alī Kūchuk b. Begtigīn . .	1144
563	Zayn-*al*-dīn Yūsuf b. 'Alī (at Irbil) † 586 .	1167
563	Muẓaffar-*al*-dīn Kūkburī b. 'Alī (at Ḥarrān) .	1167
586	,, ,, ,, ,, ,, (at Irbil)	1190
—630		—1232

[*'Abbāsids; then Mongols*]

A.H.		A.D.
495—712	64. ORTUḲIDS	1101—1312

64. ORTUḲIDS

(DIYĀR-BAKR)

Ortuḳ b. Aksab, the founder of this dynasty, was a Turkomān officer in the Seljūḳ armies, and was appointed governor of Jerusalem when the Holy City was conquered by his commander Tutush the Seljūḳ Sulṭān of Damascus. Ortuḳ's sons Sukmān and Īl-Ghāzī, both famous in the wars with the Latin princes of Palestine succeeded to their father's post in 1091 (*484*), until the city was annexed by the Fāṭimid Caliph in 1096 (*489*), when they retired to Edessa (-Ruhā) and -'Irāḳ respectively. In 1101 (*495*) Īl-Ghāzī was appointed prefect of Baghdād by the Seljūḳ Sulṭān Moḥammad, and in the same year Sukmān was made governor of Ḥiṣn Kayfā in Diyār-Bakr, to which he added Māridīn a year or two later. In 1108 (*502*), however, Māridīn was transferred to his brother Īl-Ghāzī, and henceforward there were two collateral lines of Ortuḳids, at Kayfā and at Māridīn. The Kayfā branch, after the warlike exploits of Sukmān against Baldwin and Jocelin, settled down into tranquil obscurity, hastened to pay homage to Saladīn, when his power became threatening, and were rewarded with the addition of the city of Āmid to their territory in 1183 (*579*), until their line was suppressed by the *Ayyūbid* -Kāmil in 1231 (*629*). A minor branch of the Kayfā family governed Khartapirt (Quart-Pierre) in Diyār-Bakr from 1127 (*521*) to 1223 (*620*). Īl-Ghāzī, the founder of the Māridīn line, and one of the most redoubtable of Muslim warriors against the Crusaders, gained possession of Aleppo in 1117 (*511*), and in 1121 (*515*) was also invested with the government of Mayyāfāriḳīn (in Diyār-Bakr) by the Seljūḳ Sulṭān Maḥmūd. Māridīn and Mayyāfāriḳīn continued to be held by his descendants, the latter until 1184 (*580*), the former until their submission to Tīmūr and absorption by the Ḳarā-Ḳuyunlī in 1408 (*811*); but the Māridīn Amīrs ceased to be of importance after the Ayyūbid supremacy was established in Syria and Mesopotamia. Aleppo fell 1123 (*517*) to another Ortuḳid chief, Balak b. Bahrām, who had also held Āna (*497*) and Khartapirt (*515*), and was a prominent leader in the wars with the Crusaders.

A.H.		A.D.
495—629	A. ORTUḲIDS OF KAYFÂ	1101—1231
495	Mu'īn-al-dawla Sukmân I	1101
498	Ibrāhīm	1104
c. 502	Rukn-al-dawla Dāwūd	1108
c. 543	Fakhr-al-dīn Ḳarā-Arslān	1148
570	Nūr-al-dīn Moḥammad	1174
581	Ḳuṭb-al-dīn Sukmān II	1185
597	Nāṣir-al-dīn Maḥmūd	1200
619	Rukn-al-dīn Mōdūd	1222
—629	[*Ayyūbids*]	—1231

A.H.		A.D.
502—712	B. ORTUḲIDS OF MÂRIDĪN	1108—1312
502	Najm-al-dīn Īl-Ghāzī	1108
516	Ḥusâm-al-dīn Timurtāsh	1122
547	Najm-al-dīn Alpī	1152
572	Ḳuṭb-al-dīn Īl-Ghāzī	1176
580	Ḥusām-al-dīn Yūluḳ-Arslān	1184
c. 597	Naṣir-al-dīn Ortuḳ-Arslān -Manṣūr . .	1200
637	Najm-al-dīn Ghāzī I -Sa'īd	1239
658	Ḳarā-Arslān -Muẓaffar	1260
c. 691	Shams-al-dīn Dāwūd	1292
693	Najm-al-dīn Ghāzī II -Manṣūr . . .	1294
712	'Imād-al-dīn 'Alī Alpī -'Ādil . . .	1312
712	Shams-al-dīn Ṣāliḥ	1312
765	Aḥmad -Manṣūr	1363
769	Maḥmūd -Ṣāliḥ	1367
769	Dāwūd -Muẓaffar	1367
778	Majd-al-dīn 'Isā -Ẓāhir	1376
809	Ṣāliḥ	1406
—811	[*Ḳara Ḳuyunlī*]	—1408

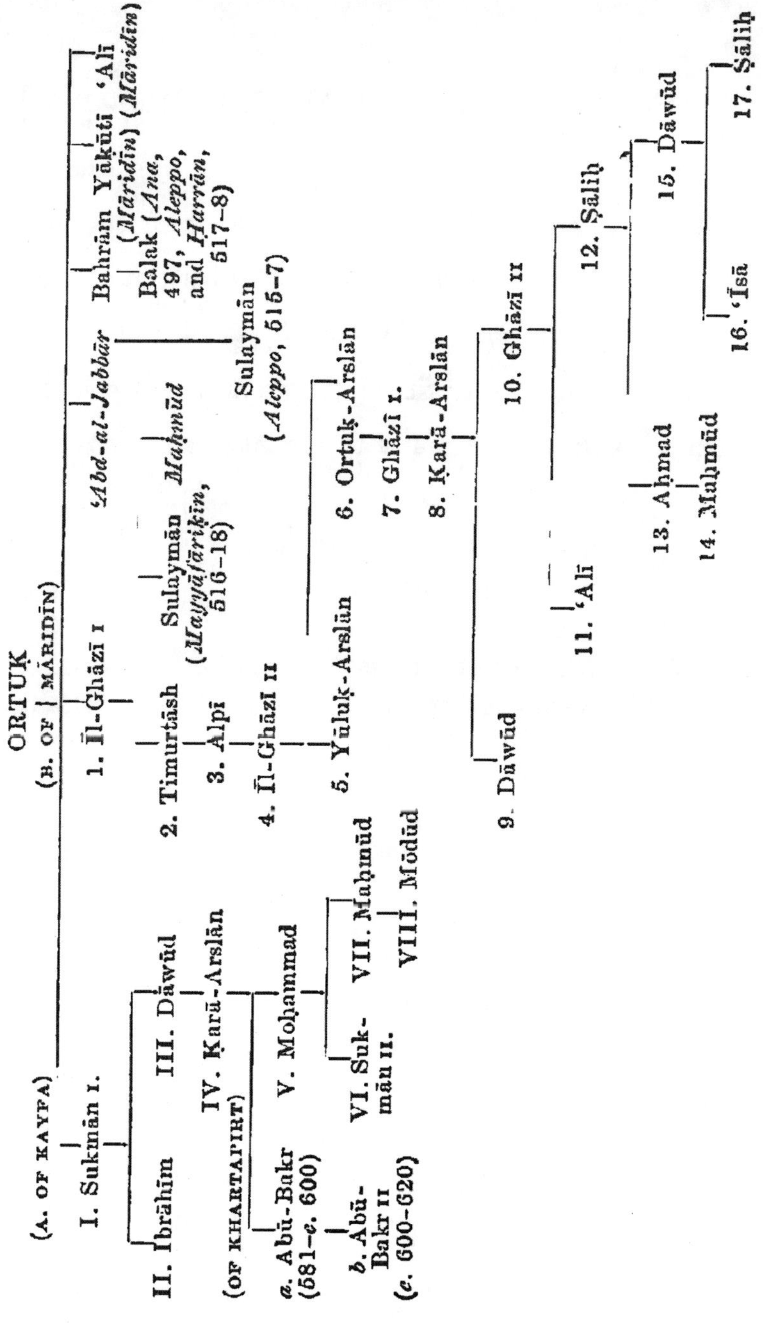
ORTUḲ
(A. OF KAYFA)
I. Suḳmān I.
II. Ibrāhīm
III. Dāwūd
IV. Ḳarā-Arslān
(OF KHARTAPIRT)
a. Abū-Bakr (581–c. 600)
b. Abū-Bakr II (c. 600–620)
V. Moḥammad
VI. Suḳmān II.
VII. Maḥmūd
VIII. Mōdūd
(B. OF MĀRIDĪN)
1. Īl-Ghāzī I
2. Timurtāsh
3. Alpī
4. Īl-Ghāzī II
5. Yuluḳ-Arslān
6. Ortuḳ-Arslān
7. Ghāzī I.
8. Ḳarā-Arslān
9. Dāwūd
10. Ghāzī II
11. ʿAlī
12. Ṣāliḥ
13. Aḥmad
14. Maḥmūd
15. Dāwūd
16. ʿĪsā
17. Ṣāliḥ
Sulaymān (*Mayyāfāriḳīn*, 516–18)
Maḥmūd
ʿAbd-al-Jabbār
Sulaymān (*Aleppo*, 515–7)
Bahrām
Balak (*Ana*, 497, *Aleppo*, and *Ḥarrān*, 517–8)
Yāḳūti (*Māridīn*)
ʿAlī (*Māridīn*)

A.H. 493—604 65. SHĀHS OF ARMENIA A.D. 1100—1207

Sukmān -Ḳuṭbī, so called because he was once the slave of Ḳuṭb-*al*-dīn Ismā'īl, the Seljūḳ governor of Marand in Adharbījān, wrested the town of -Khalāṭ in Armenia from the Marwānids in 1100 (*493*), and his descendants and their mamlūks continued to govern this region for a century until their conquest by the *Ayyūbids* in 1207.

A.H.		A.D.
493	Sukmān -Ḳuṭbī	1100
506	Ẓahīr-*al*-dīn Ibrāhīm Shāh-Arman . .	1112
521	Aḥmad	1127
522	Nāṣir-*al*-dīn Sukmān II	1128
579	Sayf-*al*-dīn Begtimur	1183
589	Badr-*al*-dīn Āḳsunḳur	1193
594	-Manṣūr Moḥammad	1198
603	'Izz-*al*-dīn Balbān	1206
—604		—1207

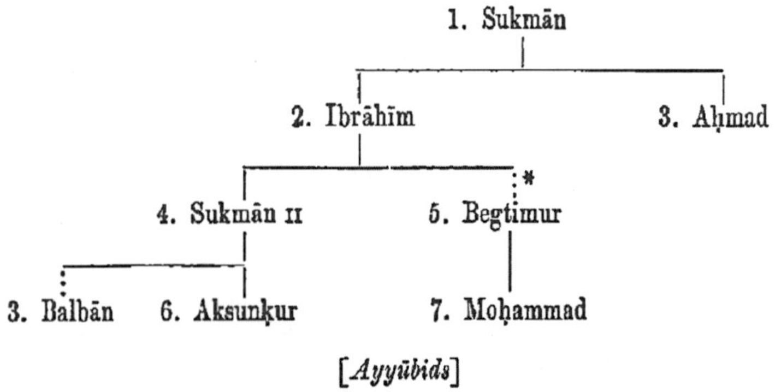

* Dotted lines indicate the relationship between master and slave.

A.H.		A.D.
531—622	**66. ATĀBEGS OF ADHARBĪJĀN**	1136—1225

Īldigiz, a Turkish slave from Kipchak, rose in favour at the court of Mas'ūd, the Seljūḳ Sulṭān of -'Irāḳ, and was finally granted the government of Adharbījān, together with the Sultan's widowed sister-in-law. His son Moḥammad was the virtual ruler of the Seljūḳ kingdom of -'Irāḳ as well as of his own province. Moḥammad's brother Ḳizil-Arslān, who had acted as his deputy in Adharbījān, succeeded to his authority, and was created *Amīr-al-Umarā*; but on his claiming sovereign rights, he was assassinated, and his two nephews, who followed him, moderated their ambition.

A.H.		A.D.
531	Shams-al-dīn Īldigiz	1136
568	Moḥammad -Pahlawān Jahān	1172
581	Ḳizil-Arslān 'Othmān	1185
587	Abū-Bakr	1191
607	Muẓaffar-al-dīn Ūzbeg	1210
—622		—1225

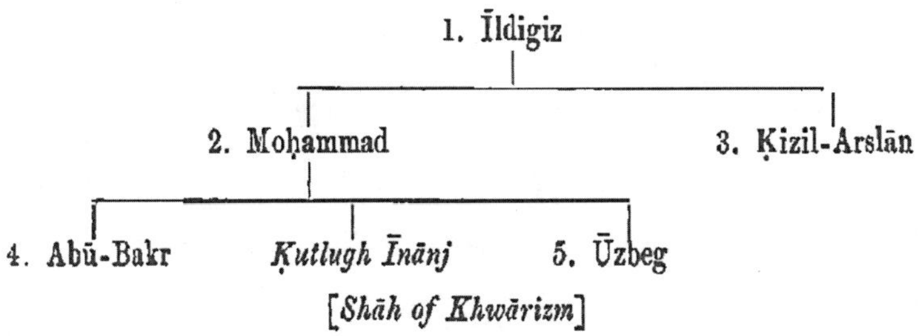

A.H.		A.D.
543—686	67. SALGHARIDS	1148—1287

(ATĀBEGS OF FĀRIS)

Salghar was the chief of a band of Turkomāns who migrated into Khurāsān, and after a career of rapine attached themselves to the Seljūḳ Ṭughril Beg, who appointed Salghar one of his chamberlains. One of his descendants, Sunḳur b. Mōdūd, made himself master of the province of Fārs in 1148 (*543*), and founded a dynasty which lasted nearly a century and a half. Atābeg Sa'd became tributary to the Shāh of Khwārizm, to whom he surrendered Iṣṭakhr and Ashkūrān; and Atābeg Abū-Bakr, in his turn, paid homage to Ogotai Khān the Mongol, and was rewarded with the title of Ḳutlugh Khān. The later Atābegs were merely vassals of the *Mongols of Persia*, and the last of them, the princess 'Abish, was the wife of Mangū-Tīmūr, a son of Hūlāgū. The poet Sa'dī lived at the court of the Atābeg Abū-Bakr.

A.H.		A.D.
543	Sunḳur*	1148
557	Zangī	1162
571	Takla	1175
591	Sa'd	1195
623	Abū-Bakr	1226
658	Moḥammad	1260
660	Moḥammad Shāh	1262
660	Seljūḳ Shāh	1262
662	'Abish	1263
—686		—1287

[*Mongols*]

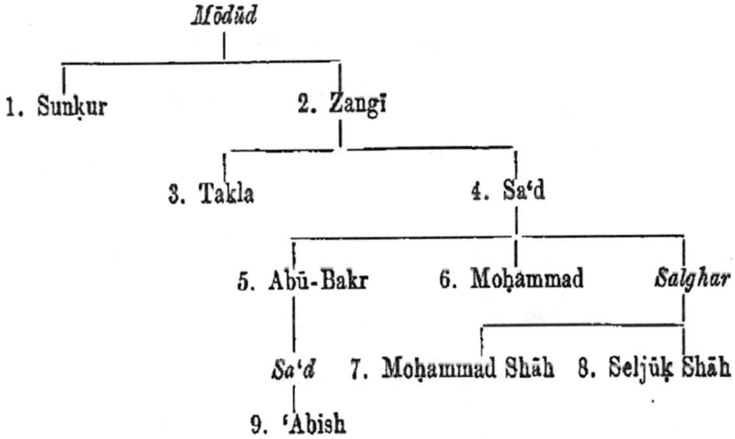

* Most of the Salgharids used the title Muẓaffar-al-dīn.

A.H.		A.D.
543–740	68. HAZĀRASPIDS	1148–1339

68. HAZĀRASPIDS

(ATĀBEGS OF LŪRISTĀN)

The founder of this line was Abū-Ṭāhir, a general who was sent by the Salgharid Atābeg to reduce the Greater Lūristān in 1148 (*543*). This original territory was augmented by a grant of the province of Khūzistān by the Mongol Abāgā. The Atābeg Afrāsiyāb I seized Iṣpahān on the death of Arghūn, but was speedily punished. This petty dynasty continued to rule till about 1339 (*740*). Many of the dates are uncertain. Their capital was Īdaj; but Yūsuf Shāh II is recorded to have annexed Shūstar, Ḥuwayza, and -Baṣra. There was also another petty dynasty of Atābegs, who governed the *Lesser* Lūristān from the end of the 12th to the 16th century.*

* For both dynasties see Sir Henry Howorth's *History of the Mongols*, Part III. pp. 140, 406, 751–6.

A.H.		A.D.
543	Abū-Ṭāhir b. Moḥammad	1148
c. 600	Naṣrat-*al*-dīn Hazārasp	*c.* 1203
c. 650	Takla	*c.* 1252
c. 657	Shams-*al*-dīn Alp-Arghū	*c.* 1259
c. 673	Yūsuf Shāh I	*c.* 1274
c. 687	Afrāsiyāb I	1288
696	Naṣrat-*al*-dīn Aḥmad	1296
733	Rukn-*al*-dīn Yūsuf Shāh II	1333
740	Muẓaffar-*al*-dīn Afrāsiyāb II	1339
756	Shams-*al*-dīn Hūshang (*or* Nūr-al-Ward) .	1355
c. 780	Aḥmad	*c.* 1378
c. 815	Abū-Sa'īd	1408
c. 820	Ḥosayn	*c.* 1417
827	Ghiyāth-*al*-dīn	1423

Expelled by Ibrāhīm b. Shāh Rukh

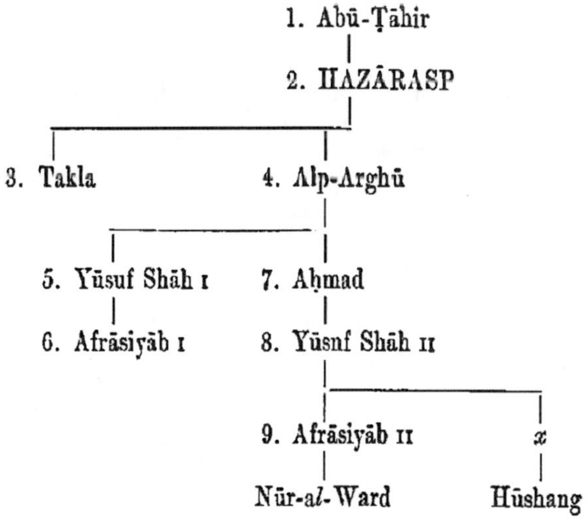

[*Tīmūrīds*]

A.H.		A.D.
c. 470–628	69. SHĀHS OF KHWĀRIZM	1077–1231

A Turkish slave of Balkātigīn of Ghazna, named Anush-tigīn, rose to be the cup-bearer of the Seljūḳ Sulṭān Malik Shāh, who made him governor of Khwārizm (Khiva), a post to which his son succeeded with the title of *Khwārizm Shāh.* Atsīz was the first of the line to show any ambition for independence, but his revolt in 1138 (*533*) was punished by his expulsion from Khwārizm by Sulṭān Sinjar. Atsīz, however, shortly returned, and henceforward the Khwārizm Shāhs enjoyed sovereign power. Atsīz extended his authority as far as Jand on the River Sīhūn (Jaxartes). Tukush added Khurāsān, -Rayy and Iṣpahān to his dominions 1193–4 (*589–590*), and his son, the celebrated 'Alā-a*l*-dīn Moḥammad, after a stubborn war with the *Ghūrids* in Khurāsān, reduced the greater part of Persia by the year 1210 (*607*), subdued Bukhārā and Samarḳand, and invading the territory of the Gūr-Khān of Ḳarā-Khitay, seized his capital Otrār. In 1214 (*611*) he entered Afghānistān and took Ghazna, and then, having adopted the 'Alid heresy (*614*) prepared to put an end to the 'Abbāsid Caliphate. His career of conquest was suddenly cut short by the appearance of the Mongol hordes of Chingiz Khān on his northern borders. Moḥammad fled incontinently before this appalling swarm, and died in despair on an island of the Caspian Sea, 1220 (*617*). His three sons wandered for some time through the provinces of Persia, and one of them, Jalāl-*al*-dīn, even visited India for two years; but after a decade of stirring adventures, during which he contrived to hold Adharbījān from *622–8*, he was finally banished by the Mongols in 1231 (*628*). At one time the rule of the Khwārizm Shāh was almost conterminous with the Seljūḳ empire, but this period of widest extent scarcely lasted a dozen years.

A.H.		A.D.
c. 470	Anushtigīn	*c.* 1077
490	Ḳutb-*al*-dīn Moḥammad	1097
521	Atsīz	1127
551	Īl-Arslān	1156
568	Sulṭān Shāh Maḥmūd († 589)	1172
568	Tukush	1172
596	'Alā-*al*-dīn Moḥammad	1199
617	Jalāl-*al*-dīn Mangbarti	1220
—628		—1231

[*Mongols*]

SHĀHS OF KHWĀRIZM

- 1. Anushtigīn
  - 2. Ḳuṭb-al-dīn Moḥammad
    - 3. Atsīz
      - 4. Īl-Arslān
        - 5. Sulṭāu Shāh
        - 6. Tukush
          - 7. 'Alā-al-dīn Moḥammad
            - Rukn-al-dīu Gūrsauchī † 619
            - Ghiyāth-al-dīn Shīr Shāh † 627
            - 8. Jalāl-al-dīn Mangbartī † 628
          - Nāṣir-al-dīu Malik Shāh (*Khurāsān* † 593)
            - Arslān Shāh
          - Yūnus Khān (-*Rayy*)
          - Tāj-al-dīn 'Alī Shāh (*Kurdistān*)

A.H.		A.H.
619–703	70. ḲUTLUGH KHĀNS	1222–1303

70. ḲUTLUGH KHĀNS
(KIRMĀN)

Burāk Ḥājib, a native of Ḳarā-Khitay, and an officer of 'Alā-*al*-dīn the Khwārizm Shāh, succeeding in establishing his power in Kirmān in 1222 (*619*), during the period of anarchy which followed the overthrow of the Khwārizm Shāh by Chingiz Khān; and his authority was confirmed by the Mongol Ogotāy, who conferred upon him the title of *Ḳutlugh Khān.* The dynasty kept within the limits of Kirmān, and were loyal vassals of the *Mongols of Persia*, two of whom married daughters of the family. The daughter of the last of the line married Moḥammad the *Muẓaffarid* of Fārs.

A.H.		A.D.
619	Burāk Ḥājib Ḳutlugh Khān	1222
632	Rukn-*al*-dīn Khōjat-al-Ḥaḳḳ . . .	1234
650	Ḳuṭb-*al*-dīn Moḥammad	1252
655	Ḳutlugh Khātūn (*widow of preceding*)* . .	1257
681	Jalāl-*al*-dīn Suyurghātmish	1282
693	Ṣafwat-*al*-dīn Pādishāh Khātūn . . .	1293
694	Jalāl-*al*-dīn Moḥammad Shāh . . .	1294
701	Ḳuṭb-*al*-dīn Shāh-Jahān	1301
–703		–1303

[*Mongol governors* till 741 ; then *Muẓaffarids.*]

* From 655 to 660 her son Ḥajjāj Sulṭān was the titular ruler.

ĶUTLUGH KHĀNS

- 1. Burāk Ḥājib
  - 2. Rukn-a*l*-dīn
  - *Taynkū*
    - 3. Ķuṭb-a*l*-dīn = 4. Ķutlugh Khātūn
      - Hajjāj Sulṭān
        - 7. Jalāl-a*l*-dīn
      - 5. Jalāl-a*l*-dīn
        - 8. Ķuṭb-a*l*-dīn
          - *daughter* = Moḥammad b. -Muẓaffar
        - *daughter* = Baydū Īl-Khān
      - 6. Ṣafwat-a*l*-dīn
      - *daughter* = Abāgā Īl-Khān

X. THE SUCCESSORS OF THE SELJŪḲS IN THE WEST

SÆC. XIV–XIX

AMĪRS OF ASIA MINOR

71. KARĀSĪ (MYSIA)
72. ḤAMĪD (PISIDIA)
73. KARMIYĀN (PHRYGIA)
74. TAKKA (LYCIA)
75. ṢĀRŪ KHĀN (LYDIA)
76. AYDĪN (LYDIA)
77. MANTASHĀ (CARIA)
78. ḲIZIL-AḤMADLĪ (PAPHLAGONIA)
79. ḲARAMĀN (LYCAONIA)

80. 'OTHMĀNLĪ SULTĀNS OF TURKEY

X. THE SUCCESSORS OF THE SELJŪḲS IN THE WEST

SÆC. XIV—XIX

We have seen how the Atābegs and other officers of the Seljūḳs succeeded to the government of the Persian, Mesopotamian, and Syrian provinces of their wide empire, but, failing to found powerful dynasties, were forced to make way for the Mongols in the thirteenth century. There was, however, one part of the Seljūḳ empire where the Mongols made no lasting impression, and where the Seljūḳs were followed by a dynasty greater than their own, the splendid line of the *'Othmānlī* or *Ottoman Turks.* Before entering upon the Mongol period of Moḥammadan history, these successors of the Seljūḳs in the West must be noticed.

In the second half of the thirteenth century the Seljūḳs of Rūm, or Hither Asia, became the vassals of the Mongols of Persia, who directed affairs in Anatolia through a governor. But the hold of the Mongols upon this distant province was slight and brief. The decayed Seljūķs might submit, but the young dynasties which sprang up among their ruins paid little heed to the remote despots of Persia, who made few efforts to restrain them. Ten States soon divided the Seljūķ kingdom of Rūm amongst themselves. The *Karāsī* dynasty occupied Mysia; the families of *Ṣārū Khān* and *Aydīn*, Lydia; the *Mantashā* princes, Caria; those of *Takka*, Lycia and Pamphylia; *Ḥamīd*, Pisidia and Isauria; *Ķaramān*, Lycaonia; *Karmiyān*, Phrygia; *Ķizil-Aḥmadlī*, Paphlagonia; whilst the house of *'Othmān* held Phrygia Epictetus.

All these dynasties were gradually absorbed by the rising power of the *'Othmānlīs*, once the least among them. Karāsī was annexed in 1336 (*737*); Ḥamīd was purchased as a marriage dower in 1382 (*783*); and in 1390 (*792*) Bāyazīd (Bajazet) I annexed Karmiyān, Takka, Ṣārū Khān, Aydīn, and Mantashā, in a single campaign, and completed his conquest by adding Ķaramān and Ķizil-Aḥmadlī in 1392–3 (*794–5*). Thus at the end of the fourteenth century, not a hundred years after the assumption of independence by 'Othmān I, the arms of his great-grandson had swept away the nine rival dynasties.

[To face p. 184.]

BITHYNIA	PHRYGIA EPICTETUS	MYSIA	PISIDIA	PHRYGIA	LYCIA	LYDIA	LYDIA	CARIA	PAPHLAGONIA	LYCAONIA
BYZANTINES	'OTHMANLIS	KARĀSĪ	ḤAMĪD	KARMIYAN	TAKKA	ṢĀRŪ KHĀN	AYDIN	MANTASHĀ	ḲIZIL-AḤMADLĪ	ḲARAMĀN
	630 Ertughril	S	E	L	J	Ū		Ḳ	S	c. 620 Ḳaramān
660 Michael Palaeologus										c. 643 Moḥammad I
682 Andronicus										678 Maḥmūd
	699 'Othmān	'Ajlān Beg	Ḥamīd	Karmiyān Beg	Takka Beg		700 Aydīn Beg	700 Mantashā Beg	690 Tīmūr	
717 *Brūsā*						713 Ṣārū Khān				719 Yakhshī
	726 Orkhān			'Alishīr			733 Moḥammad	Ya'ḳūb	Shujā'-al-dīn	750 'Alā-al-dīn 'Alī
731 *Nicaea*	761 Murād I	737	Ḥosayn	'Ālim		746 Ilyās	740 'Omar 748 'Īsā			
				'Āti						
				Ya'ḳūb		776 Isḥāḳ		Maḥmūd	'Ādil Beg	
	792 Bāyazīd		783					791 Ilyās	Bāyazīd Koturum	
	804 INVASION OF TĪMŪR			792	792	792	792	792	795	794
				ANNEXED BY BAYAZĪD; RESTORED BY TĪMŪR						
	805 Moḥammad I			805 Ya'ḳūb restored	805 'Othmān	805 Khiḍr 809? 'Omar	805 'Īsā 808 'Omar	805 Ilyās restored	805 Isfandiyār	805 Moḥammad II
	824 Murād II					*Junayd*	*Junayd* 824 Muṣṭafā	824 { Oways, Aḥmad, Layth		
				832	830	829		829	833 Ibrāhīm Ismā'īl Ḳizil-Aḥmad	829 Ibrāhīm
	855 Moḥammad II			FINAL ANNEXATION BY MURĀD II						
'O	T.	H	M	Ā	N	L	Ī	S	864	869 { Pīr Aḥmad, Isḥāḳ 877

After the battle of Angora in 1402 (*804*), when Bāyazīd was defeated and made prisoner by Tīmūr, and the 'Othmānlī power in Asia seemed to be annihilated by the Tatar hordes, seven of these dynasties (but not Karāsī or Ḥamīd) were restored by the conqueror, and enjoyed a renewed vitality for about a quarter of a century. By that time, however, the 'Othmānlīs had recovered from the blow, and in 1426–8 (*829–832*) five of the restored dynasties were re-absorbed by Murād (Amurath) II; and in 1471 (*877*), after the second conquest of Ḳaramān, the rule of the Ottoman Turks, in the strong hands of Moḥammad II, was again supreme over all the provinces which once owned the sway of the Ten Amīrs, as it is at this day.

The following table shows the division of the Seljūḳ kingdom of Rūm among the Ten States, and their absorption by the 'Othmānlīs, and gives the names and (so far as known) the dates of their princes.*

* Details may be consulted in my article on the Successors of the Seljūḳs, in *Journal* R. As. Soc., N.S. xiv. (1882).

A.H.		A.D.
699–1311	80. 'OTHMĀNLĪ OR OTTOMAN SULṬĀNS OF TURKEY	1299–1893

The 'Othmānli or Ottoman Turks were a small clan of the Oghuz tribe, who were driven westward from Khurāsān by the Mongol migration, and took refuge in Asia Minor early in the thirteenth century. In recognition of their aid in war, the Seljūḳ Sulṭān allowed them to pasture their flocks in the province anciently known as Phrygia Epictetus (henceforward called Sulṭān-öni) on the borders of the Byzantine Bithynia, with the town of Sugut (Thebasion) for their headquarters. Here 'Othmān, the eponymous founder of a dynasty which numbers thirty-five Sulṭāns in the direct male line, was born in 1258 (*656*). 'Othmān pushed the Byzantine frontier further back, and his son 'Orkhān took Brūsa and Nicaea, .absorbed the neighbouring State of Karāsī, and organized the famous corps of Janizaries (*Yani chari* 'new soldiery'), who for several centuries were the flower of the conquering armies of the 'Othmānlīs. In 1358 (*759*) the Turks crossed the Hellespont, established a garrison at Gallipoli, and began the conquest of the Byzantine Empire in Europe. Adrianople and Philippopolis fell a few years later, and the victories of the Maritza (1364), Kosovo (1389), and Nicopolis (1394) over the chivalry of all Europe gave the Turks assured possession of the whole Balkan peninsula, except the district surrounding Constantinople. The capital of the Eastern Empire was temporarily saved by the diversion caused by the invasion of Asia Minor by Tīmūr (Tamerlane) and the overwhelming defeat of the Ottoman Sulṭān Bāyazīd I (commonly called Bajazet, from an ignorant pronunciation of the German spelling) in 1402 (*804*) on the field of Angora.

For the moment an empire which had stretched from the Danube to the Orontes appeared to be almost annihilated by a single blow. Its recovery, however, under the wise rule of Moḥammad I, 'The Gentleman,' was scarcely less remarkable, and, after an interval of peace and consolidation, Murād II was able to defend the empire from the attacks of Hunyady, the 'White Knight of Wallachia,' and to avenge a violated treaty by the decisive victory of Varna (1444) over a vast army of Christian crusaders. This signal success secured the

Turks from invasion from the north, and the history of the next two centuries is a long record of triumphs. Constantinople fell to Moḥammad II in 1453, and the last remnant of the Byzantine Empire was thereby destroyed. The Crimea was annexed (1475), the Aegean islands became Ottoman soil, and the Turkish flag waved even in Italy over the castle of Otranto. In his brief reign of eight years, Selīm I, 'the Grim,' defeated the Shāh of Persia, and added Kurdistān and Diyār-Bakr to the Turkish Empire; took Syria, Egypt and Arabia from the Mamlūks (1517); and not only became the master of the Holy Cities of Mecca and Medīna, but received from the last 'Abbāsid Caliph of Cairo the relics of the Prophet Moḥammad and the right of succession to the Caliphate, in virtue of which the Ottoman Sulṭāns have ever since claimed the homage of the faithful.

Sulaymān the Great, *patris fortis filius fortior*, overshadowed Selīm's exploits by his own magnificent achievements. In 1522 he expelled the Knights of Rhodes from their corsairs' stronghold. In the north he conquered Belgrade, and in 1526 utterly crushed the Hungarians on the field of Mohács, slaying their king Louis II and 20,000 of his troops. For a century and a half Hungary became a Turkish province. Sulaymān even besieged Vienna (1529), and, though he failed to subdue it, he compelled the Archduke Ferdinand to pay him tribute. 'The Sultan's claim to be called The Great rests not merely upon his undoubted wisdom and ability, and the splendid series of his successes, but upon the fact that he maintained and improved his grand position in an age of surpassing greatness—the age of Charles I, Francis I, Elizabeth, and Leo X—of Colombus, Cortes, and Raleigh. In the great days of Charles he dared to annex Hungary and lay siege to Vienna; and in the epoch of great navies and admirals, of Doria and Drake, he swept the seas to the coasts of Spain, and his admirals Barbarossa, Pialé, and Dragut, created panic fear along all the shores of the Mediterranean, drove the Spaniards out of the Barbary States, and defeated pope, emperor, and doge together at the great sea-fight off Prevesa (1538).'* The empire of Sulaymān stretched from Buda-Pesth on the Danube to Aswān on the Cataracts of the Nile, and from the Euphrates almost to the Straits of Gibraltar.

* See my *History of Turkey*, ch. X (1888).

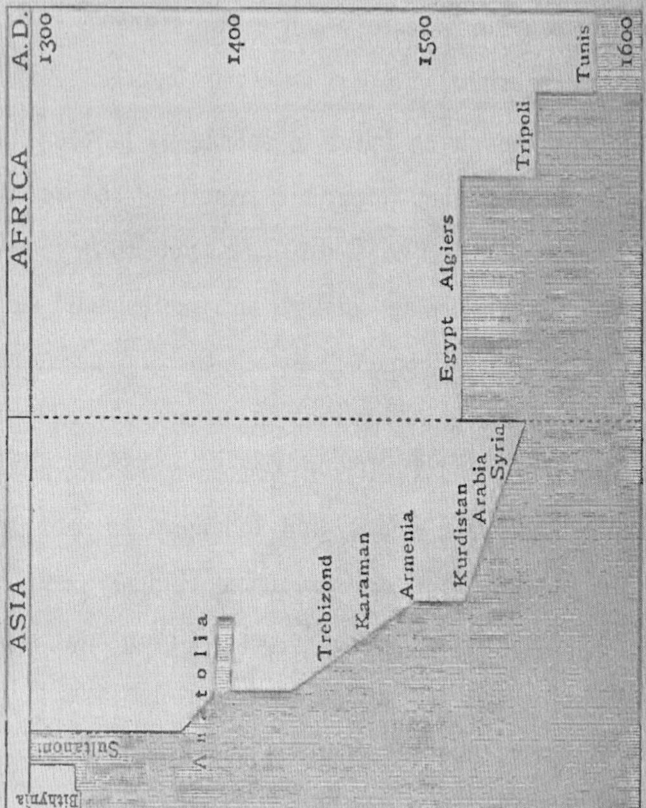

GROWTH OF THE OTTOMAN EMPIRE.

DECLINE OF THE OTTOMAN EMPIRE.

The reign of Sulaymān the Great is the apogee of Ottoman power. The downward course began with the blow inflicted upon the naval prestige of Turkey by Don John of Austria's signal victory off Lepanto (1571). In spite of the conquest of Cyprus (1571) and such successes on land as the defeat of the Austrians on the Keresztes (1596), the Turks were no longer the terror of Europe. Murād IV added Baghdād to their Asiatic dominions in 1638, and Candia and other islands were wrested from the Venetians in 1645; but on the continent of Europe the defeats at St. Gothard (1664), Choczim (1673), and Lemberg (1675) by John Sobieski, culminating in the fatal siege of Vienna (1682) and the rout at Mohácz, were followed by the total loss of Hungary (1686), and the invasion of Bosnia and Greece by the Austrians and Venetians. Prince Eugene delivered a final blow at the battle of Zenta (1697), and the treaties of Carlovitz (1699) and Passarovitz (1718) mark the end of Turkish supremacy in Hungary, Podolia, and Transylvania.

The frontiers of the empire remained almost unchanged from this epoch of humiliation up to the recent partition of 1878. Russian aggression began in 1736 with the annexation of Oczakov and Azov, and continued with the seizure of the Crimea in 1783, besides several invasions of the Danubian Principalities. Turkey itself was a prey to the exactions of a disorderly soldiery, and Maḥmūd II, the greatest of modern Sulṭāns, though he massacred the mutinous Janizaries (1826), could not arrest the process of disintegration which was going on in the Ottoman empire. In Africa, Egypt became practically independent under Moḥammad 'Alī in the first quarter of this century, and since 1883 has been still further removed from the 'sphere of Turkish influence' by the British occupation. Algiers and Tunis became semi-independent under their Deys and Beys in 1659 (*1070*) and 1705 (*1117*) respectively, and France has been the possessor of Algiers since 1830, and of Tunis, in all but name, since 1881. The regency of Tripoli is all that now remains of the Turkish empire in Africa. In Asia, however, it has lost little since the day when Murād IV took Baghdād from the Persians; though Ḳars and Batūm were awarded to Russia in 1878 by the Treaty of Berlin, when the island of Cyprus was hypothecated to Great Britain.

Turkey's most serious losses have been in Europe.

Greece parted from her in 1828; the Danubian Principalities coalesced into the State of Roumania in 1866; and Servia got rid of her Turkish garrisons in 1867. The designs of Russia, which had been checked by England and France in the Crimean War (1854–5), were again manifested in the invasion of Turkey in 1877–8; but the Great Powers did not sanction the aggrandizing ambition of Russia. The Treaty of Berlin (1878), though it gave little to Russia, carried out the partition of Turkey in Europe which had already begun. Roumania and Servia were created separate kingdoms, the independence of Montenegro was recognized, Greece was given Thessaly, Bosnia and Herzegovina were entrusted to Austria, and a new tributary principality of Bulgaria was established, to which Eastern Roumelia was added in 1885, whereby Turkey was virtually deprived of her last possession north of the Balkans. The Ottoman Empire in Europe is now reduced to a strip of territory south of the Balkans, corresponding to ancient Thrace, Macedon, Epirus, and Illyria, instead of stretching almost to the gates of Vienna as it did in the great days of Sulaymān.

A.H.		A.D.
699	'Othmān I	1299
726	Orkhān	1326
761	Murād (Amurath) I	1360
792	Bāyazīd (Bajazet) I	1389
805	Moḥammad I	1402
824	Murād II	1421
855	Moḥammad II	1451
886	Bāyazīd II	1481
918	Selīm I	1512
926	Sulaymān I	1520
974	Selīm II	1566
982	Murād III	1574
1003	Moḥammad III	1595
1012	Aḥmad I	1603
1026	Muṣṭafā I	1617
1027	'Othmān II	1618
1031	Muṣṭafā I (*restored*)	1622
1032	Murād IV	1623
1049	Ibrāhīm I	1640
1058	Moḥammad IV	1648
1099	Sulaymān II	1687
1102	Aḥmad II	1691
1106	Muṣṭafā II	1695
1115	Aḥmad III	1703
1143	Maḥmūd I	1730
1168	'Othmān III	1754
1171	Muṣṭafā III	1757
1187	'Abd-al-Ḥamīd I	1773
1203	Selīm III	1789
1222	Muṣṭafā IV	1807
1223	Maḥmūd II	1808
1255	'Abd-al-Majīd	1839
1277	'Abd-al-'Azīz	1861
1293	Murād V	1876
1293	'Abd-al-Ḥamīd II *regnant*	1876

ʻOTHMĀNLĪ OR OTTOMAN TURKS

1. ʻOthmān b. Ertughrul 1299
2. Orkhān 1326
3. Murād I 1360
4. Bāyazīd I 1389

Sulaymān *Claimant* 1403–10

5. Moḥammad I 1402

Mūsā *Claimant* 1410–16

6. Murād II 1421
7. Moḥammad II 1451
8. Bāyazīd II 1481
9. Selīm I 1512
10. Sulaymān I 1520
11. Selīm II 1566
12. Murād III 1574

13. Moḥammad III 1595

14. Aḥmad I 1603 — 15. Muṣṭafā I 1617, (2) 1622

16. 'Othmān II 1618 — 17. Murād IV 1623 — 18. Ibrāhīm 1640

19. Moḥammad IV 1648 — 20. Sulaymān II 1687 — 21. Aḥmad II 1691

22. Muṣṭafā II 1695 — 23. Aḥmad III 1703

24. Maḥmūd I 1730 — 25. 'Othmān III 1754 — 26. Muṣṭafā III 1757 — 27. 'Abd-al-Ḥamīd I 1773

28. Selīm III 1789 — 29. Muṣṭafā IV 1807 — 30. Maḥmūd II 1808

31. 'Abd-al-Majīd 1839 — 32. 'Abd-al-Azīz 1861

33. Murād V 1876 — 34. 'Abd-al-Ḥamīd II 1876 *regnant*

XI. THE MONGOLS

SÆC. XIII–XVIII

XI. THE MONGOLS*

SEC. XIII—XVIII

The history of the Mongols begins practically with the great conqueror Chingiz Khān. There are many traditions of his ancestors current among his biographers, but, as in the case of many another man of unexpected fame, his pedigree has been elaborated rather on the ground of natural propriety than of fact. All that can safely be said about the early history of the Mongols is that they were a clan among clans, a member of a great nomad confederacy that ranged the country north of the desert of Gobi in search of water and pasture; who spent their lives in hunting and the breeding of cattle, lived on flesh and sour milk (kumis), and made their profit by bartering hides and beasts with their kinsmen the Khitans, or with the Turks and Chinese, to whom they owed allegiance. The name Mongol was not known abroad until the tenth century, and probably came to be applied to the whole group of clans only when the chief of a particular clan bearing that name acquired an ascendancy over the rest

* The following introduction, and those to the succeeding sections of the Mongol dynasties, are reprinted from my *Catalogue of Oriental Coins in the British Museum*, vol vi. They are of course based upon Sir Henry Howorth's great History.

of the confederacy, and gave to the greater the name of the less. If not the founder of the supremacy of his clan, Yissugāy was a notable maintainer of it, and it was probably he who first asserted the independence of the Mongols from Chinese rule. In spite, however, of conquest and annexation, the people who owned the sovereignty of Yissugāy numbered only forty thousand tents. Yet it was upon this foundation that Yissugāy's son, Chingiz Khān, built up in twenty years the widest empire the world has ever seen. The father died in 1175 A.D., and Temujin his son, a child of thirteen years, and not yet called by the high title of Chingiz Khān, ruled in his stead over the tribes that wandered by the banks of the Onon.

A detailed chronicle of the career of conquest inaugurated by this Asiatic Alexander is no part of the present purpose.* It is sufficient to say that after thirty years of struggle against home-foes, in which he succeeded in firmly establishing his authority over his own and the neighbouring clans, in face of powerful and treacherous conspiracies, Temujin found himself free to devote the twenty years that remained of his life to wider and more ambitious designs. Having reduced all the tribes north of the desert

* See Sir H. H. Howorth's *History of the Mongols*, i. 49—115.

of Gobi, from the Irtish to the Khinggan Mountains, and having incorporated among his subjects the Karaits, who had forfeited their independence by the treachery of their king, Wang Khān (the Prester John of European fable, and an old but perfidious ally of Yissugāy and his son), Temujin summoned, in 1206, a Kuriltāy or Diet of the chiefs of all the tribes; and a *shaman*, or priest, announced to the assembled nobles that a higher title than belonged to others had been decreed by Heaven to Temujin, and henceforward his name should be Chingiz Ḳaān, 'the Very Mighty King.' Thus at the age of forty-four did Chingiz begin his undisputed reign. Three years later, after receiving the submission of the Uighurs, he began his invasion of China, and though it was reserved for his grandson to complete the subjugation of the Celestial Empire, a great part of the northern provinces, the ancient kingdom of Liau-tung, and the Tangut Kingdom of Hia, were added, as subject provinces or feudatory states, to the Mongol dominions during the great Khān's own lifetime. The next obstacle in the path to universal sovereignty was the old Turkish kingdom of Ḳarā-Khitay, which corresponded nearly to the modern limits of Eastern Turkistān, and was ruled by a line of kings called Gūr-

Khāns, who exacted homage from the border states of Persia and Transoxiana. Chingiz and his horsemen, however, instead of paying homage, speedily rode down all resistance, and soon found themselves masters of Kāshghar, Khoten, and Yārkhand, with the rest of the territory of Gūr-Khāns. The Mongol dominions now marched with the wide kingdom which had recently been conquered by the Khwārizm Shāh; and this, therefore, became the next object of attack and the next example of the futility of resistance. The Mongol armies, divided into several immense brigades, swept over Khwārizm, Khurāsān, and Afghānistān, on the one hand, and on the other over Adharbījān, Georgia, and southern Russia, whilst a third division continued the reduction of China. In the midst of these diverging streams of conquest, Chingiz Khān died, in 1227 (*624*), at the age of sixty-four. The territory he and his sons had conquered stretched from the Yellow Sea to the Euxine, and included lands or tribes wrung from the rule of Chinese, Tanguts, Afghāns, Persians, and Turks.

It was the habit of a Mongol chief to distribute the clans over which he had ruled as appanages among his sons; and this tribal rather than territorial distribution obtained in the division of the empire among the sons of Chingiz. The founder appointed a special appanage of tribes in certain loosely defined camping-grounds to each son, and also nominated a successor to himself in the supreme Khānate. Beginning therefore with the *Khāḳaāns*, or supreme suzerains over all the other Mongol chiefs, the following seems the natural order:

1. *The line of Ogotāy*, ruling the tribes of Zungaria; *Khāḳaāns*, till their extinction by the family of Tulūy.
2. *The line of Tulūy*, ruling the home clans of Mongolistān; *Khāḳaāns* after Ogotāy's line, down to the Manchu supremacy.
3. *The Persian branch of the line of Tulūy*; Hūlāgū and his successors, the Īl-khāns of Persia.
4. *The line of Jūjī*, ruling the Turkish Tribes of the Khānate of Kipchak; the Khāns of the Golden and White Hordes, with the sequel, the Khānate of Astrakhān, and the offshoots, the Khānates of Kazan, Kazimof, and Ḳrim; and finally the Khāns of Khiva and Bukhārā.
5. *The line of Chagatāy*, ruling Mā-warā-*l*-nahr, or Transoxiana.

SKETCH-TREE OF THE DYNASTIES SPRUNG FROM CHINGIZ KHĀN

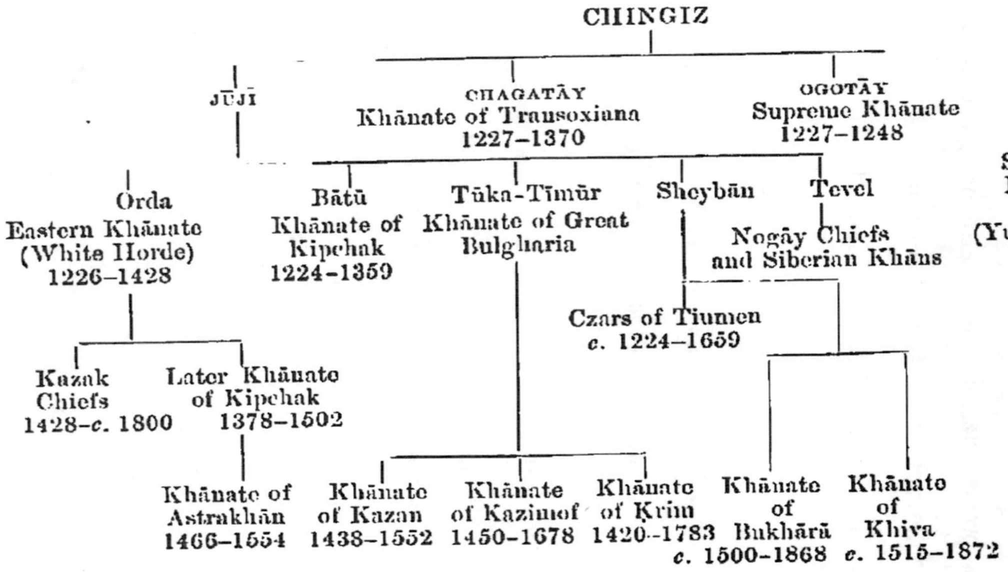

A.H.		A.D.
603–1043	81. GREAT KHĀNS	1026–1634

1. *Line of Ogotāy*:—Appanage, Zungaria*; Supreme Khākaāns (1227—1248).

By the will of Chingiz, Ogotāy besides receiving his appanage in Zungaria was appointed to succeed to the supreme authority; and it is a singular testimony to the reverence in which the intentions of the great founder of Mongol power were held that Ogotāy, although neither the eldest nor the most capable of the sons of Chingiz, was suffered quietly to assume the sovereignty over all the chiefs of the family and tributaries, and received their loyal homage at the general Diet held in 1229. His reign was marked by a considerable extension of the Mongol dominions. The Kin empire, or northern half of China, which had only been partially reduced in the lifetime of Chingiz, was now (1234) entirely subdued; (the southern

* It will be simpler thus to indicate roughly the position of the camping-grounds of Ogotāy's subjects, than to say "the clans camping in or about Zungaria," etc. In this instance the tribes in question were the Naymans and the ancestors of the modern Kalmuks.

half, or Sung empire, resisted the invaders till the time of Khubilāy.) Korea was annexed (1241). The gallant and unfortunate Jalāl-*al*-dīn, son of the late Khwārizm Shāh Moḥammad, was hunted through the wide territory which had once owned his father's rule. A great expedition into Europe was conducted by Bātū, son of Jūjī; the Mongols entered Moscow and Novgorod, penetrated to Hungary, burned Cracow, and laid siege to Pesth. The opportune death of Ogotāy called for a general assembly of the family, and a reverse sustained at Liegnitz, at the hand of the Grand Duke of Austria, saved Europe. Meanwhile the internal affairs of the empire had been organized and ably administered under the wise and just rule of the prime minister Yeliu Chutsāy, a Khitan, who did much to restore order and security to the provinces, in spite of the incapacity of his imperial master, who was given over to the prevailing Mongol vice of habitual drunkenness.

Ogotāy's death in A.D. 1241 (*637*) was followed by an interregnum of several years, during which his widow Turakina governed the empire as regent for her eldest son Kuyuk, until he should return from Europe, where he had been distinguishing himself in the invasion of

Hungary under his cousin Bātū. He received the summons in Hungary, and on his return to Karakorum in 1246, was elected Khāḳaān by a general Kuriltāy attended by most of the chiefs of the family, except the sons of Jūjī, who were dissatisfied with the succession and excused themselves. Kuyuk restored the tranquility which had been disturbed during the rule of his mother, and armies were now despatched to continue the work of extension in China and Persia.

Kuyuk was the only member of the family of Ogotāy who succeeded to the supreme throne, and on his death in 1248 the empire passed to the line of Tulūy, and neither Kuyuk's sons nor any of his brothers succeeded him. Under the first Khāḳaān of the new line, the family of Ogotāy offered no opposition to their dethronement; but when Mangū died and Khubilāy was elected to the sovereignty by an informal Diet held in China, the discontent of Ogotāy's descendants manifested itself in immediate and general revolt, and a series of disastrous campaigns ensued.* Kaydū, the grandson of Ogotāy, fought no less than forty-one battles with the supporters of Tulūy on the east, and fifteen with their Kipchak allies on

* See Howorth, i. 173—186.

the west: but the struggle was unequal, and soon after Kaydū's death (about 1301, *701*) the family of Ogotāy did homage to the line of Tulūy; their clans were dispersed among the tribes of Transoxiana and Kipchak, and their chiefs lived in obscurity under the rule of the Chagatāy Khāns. Once and again, in a period of confusion, some representative of Ogotāy's house was raised to the throne of Transoxiana; and it was the fancy of the great Tīmūr to bring again to light the heirs of the heir of Chingiz by setting up Suyurghātmish and his son Maḥmūd in the stead of the deposed house of Chagatāy; but this was only a fictitious revival, and these two *rois fainéants* cannot be said to represent the original Khaḳaāns.

2. *Line of Tulūy*:—Appanage, Mongolistān; Khāḳaāns (1248–1634) in three stages, (1) Yuen dynasty in China (1248–1370), (2) Diminished empire at Karakorum (1370–1543), (3) Divided tribes and gradual submission to Manchus (1543–1634).

Mangū, the son of Tulūy, owed his accession partly to his personal reputation as a warrior and general, and partly to the adherence of the numerous tribes of Mongolia proper, the nucleus of the Mongol armies under Chingiz, which formed the appanage of Tulūy. In 1251 his inauguration took place, and in 1257 he died. Yet in this short reign there was room for the beginning of two important changes. Mangū kept his court at the usual capital Karakorum, north of the desert of Gobi, and appointed his brother Khubilāy governor of the southern provinces: this was the beginning of the transfer of the seat of government from Karakorum to Peking. The other change was the despatch of another brother, Hūlāgū, to Persia, where in place of the shifting rule of provincial governors he established his own dynasty, and thus Persia now possessed a line of kings of the royal house of Chingiz, like the other great divisions of the Mongol empire.

The death of Mangū in 1257 was the signal for a general struggle. The house of Ogotāy laid claim to the supreme sovereignty, as has been said; and Arikbuka, a brother of Mangū and Khubilāy, was the candidate in the Mongol homeland. Khubilāy was saluted Khāḳaān by the chiefs of the army in China; Arikbuka was elected by another Diet at Karakorum; and Kaydū received the like title and homage from the tribes of Ogotāy and Chagatāy further west. Jūjī's line in Kipchak did not attempt to gain the Khāḳaānship, but supported the house of Tulūy. The fine generalship, large resources, and wide personal popularity of Khubilāy—Marco Polo's Great Khān and Coleridge's Kubla Khan—carried him safely through these early complications. Arikbuka was speedily routed, and Kaydu was kept at a distance, though he did not cease from troubling till after Khubilāy's death.

The Khāḳaāns of the blood of Chingiz now became a Chinese dynasty. By 1280 Khubilāy had conquered the southern or Sung empire of China, and, having thus united the whole country under his sole rule, fixed his court at Khān Baligh (Cambaluk) or the 'City of the Khān,' now called Peking; whilst the old capital Karakorum became a provincial centre during the first of the three periods into which the history of his descendants may be divided. This *first period* includes the century which elapsed between his founding of the Mongol empire in China and the expulsion of the invaders under his tenth successor, Tughān-Tīmūr (1370).* The Mongol Khāḳaāns of this period are known in Chinese annals as the *Yuen Dynasty.* With what sumptuous glory this dynasty began we know from Marco Polo: the causes of its decay—the extravagance of the court, the favouritism of the Lamas, the poverty and sickness of the people, the plagues and famines, earthquakes and other 'signs'—may be read in Sir Henry Howorth's History. The attempts of various pretenders were crowned by the successful attack of Chu Yuen Chang, prince of U, the founder of the Ming Dynasty, who assumed the royal title and seized Peking in 1368. In two years China was rid of the Mongols; and the most prosperous period of the history of the Khāḳaāns was over.

The *second period* extends from the expulsion from China to the temporary revival under Dayan Khān (1370–1543). This is the time of the *Diminished Empire,* when the Mongols were confined to the steppes from which they

* Howorth, i. 284-340

first went forth to conquer, the camping-grounds by the rivers Kerulon and Onon, north of the desert of Gobi. Even here they were not absolutely independent. The Ming armies surprised the Mongols by Lake Buyur and totally routed them, capturing 80,000 prisoners, lifting 150,000 head of cattle, and carrying off an immense booty. This defeat effectually tamed the spirit of the Khāḳaāns, supreme now in name alone; and they became actual vassals of the Ming emperors, who appointed the rulers of the tribes by patents drawn up in Peking. In the 15th century a worse thing happened to them; many of the clans became for a while subject to the Uirats. But at the end of the same century Dayan Khān, the fourteenth Khāḳaān in succession from Tughān-Tīmūr, effected a temporary union among the scattered tribes, and organized them in certain groups.

The *third period* is the history of the disastrous results of Dayan's decentralizing policy—civil war among the *Divided Tribes*, and the consequent absorption of them one by one by the Manchu power which had newly risen on the ruins of the Ming in China. Internal wars, separate dynasties, and universal disunion, soon brought even the nominal sovereignty of the Khāḳaāns to an end; and after 1634 the descendants of Khubilāy were mere vassals of China.

GREAT KHĀNS

A.H.		A.D.
603	Chingiz Khān	1206
624	Ogotāy	1227
639	*Interregnum*: Turakina	1241
644	Kuyuk	1246
646	Mangū	1248

YUEN DYNASTY

A.H.		A.D.
655	Khubilāy	1257
693	Ūljā·itū	1294
706	Kuluk	1307
711	Buyantu	1311
720	Gegen	1320
723	Yisun-Tīmūr	1323
728	Rajipeka	1328
729	Kushala	1329
729	Jiyaghatu	1329
732	Rintshenpal	1332
732	Tughān-Tīmūr	1332

DIMINISHED EMPIRE

A.H.		A.D.
771	Biliktu	1370
780	Ussukhal	1378
790	Engke Soriktu	1388
794	Elbek	1392
802	Gun-Tīmūr	1400
805	Uljai-Tīmūr	1403
814	Delbek	1411
837	Adsai	1434
843	Taisong	1439
856	Akbarji	1452

857	Ukektu	1453
857	Molon	1453
867	Mandaghol	1463
875	Dayan	1470

DIVIDED TRIBES

951	Bodi	1544
955	Kudang	1548
964	Sasaktu	1557
1001	Setzen	1593
1013	Lingdan	1604
—1043		—1634

[*Manchu Tatars*]

THE HOUSES OF OGOTÁY AND TULÚY (To face p. 216)

SUPREME KHĀNS

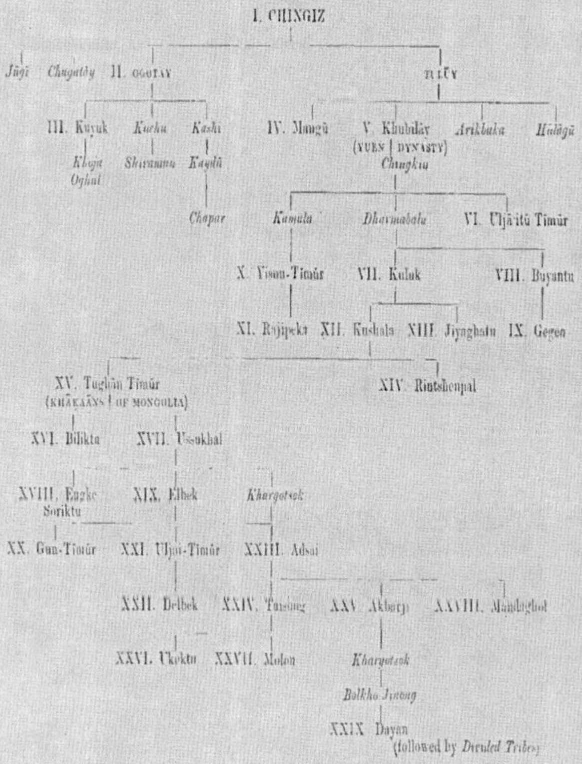

A.H. A.D.

654–750 82. MONGOLS OF PERSIA * 1256–1349

It was in the reign of Mangū that Persia was given a royal dynasty in the House of Hūlāgū (of the line of Tulūy), called Īl-khāns, or provincial Khāns, to indicate the homage they owed and invariably acknowledged (very cheaply) to the supreme Khāḳaāns. Hūlāgū had little difficulty in establishing his authority over the country allotted to him. The ambitious Shāh of Khwārizm whom Chingiz haḍ routed had already cleared the way by conquering the better part of Persia, and there were no formidable opponents to meet. Hūlāgū speedily drove before him the small princes who were trying to build their little dynastics on the ruins of the great empire of Khwārizm; came to Baghdād and cruelly murdered -Musta'ṣim, the feeble representative of the 'Abbāsid Caliphs; and discovered no serious obstacle in his path till he was checked in Syria by the valiant Mamlūks of Egypt, who kept him successfully at arm's length. Hūlāgū was now master of

* Howorth, iii.

all the provinces of Persia and Asia Minor from India to the Mediterranean. His dominions marched with those of Chagatāy and Jūjī on the north, and with the territory of the Egyptian Sulṭāns on the south; and within these limits for nearly a century his dynasty reigned in practical independence, whilst rendering a certain feudal homage to the remote Khāḳaān in China. Save for an occasional contest over the succession, the country was quietly and peaceably governed, and the Īl-khāns showed a praiseworthy desire to emulate the examples of earlier rulers of Persia in the encouragement of science and letters.

In the reign of Abū-Sa'īd, however, the dynasty was undermined by the same causes which had previously destroyed the power of the Caliphs and the Seljūḳs, and were destined at last to bring about the downfall of the Mamlūks in Egypt: rival amīrs, generals, ministers, fanatics, began to take a large share in the government of the country, and in their jealousies and animosities lay the prime danger of the Īl-khāns. After Abū-Sa'īds death the throne of Persia became the toadstool on which the puppet sovereigns set up by rival amīrs seated themselves only to find it crumbling beneath them. Two great houses tore Persia in sunder: that of Amīr Chūpān, a favourite general of Ghāzān and of his successors; and that of Amīr Ḥosayn the Jalayr, also called the Ilkānian. Each of these had a son named Ḥasan, distinguished by the epithets Great and Little; the son of Chūpān was Amīr Ḥasan Kūchuk or the Little; and the son of the Jalayr was Amīr Shaykh Ḥasan Buzurg or the Great. Their power was immediately felt. Arpā Khān, a descendant not of Hūlāgū but of Arikbuka his brother, was placed on the throne after Abū-Sa'īd's death, but was deposed the same year (1336) by Mūsā, who drew his pedigree from Baydū the sixth Īl-khān. Mūsā was quickly displaced by the nominees of the Greater Ḥasan, whose rival of the line of Chūpān presently set up an opposition in the sovereignty in the person of Sātī-Beg, a sister of Abū-Sa'īd, who had been the wife of Chūpān, then of Arpā, and was finally married to Sulaymān, who nominally supplanted her in the supremacy. After the troubled reign of Nūshīrwān, the Jalayrs were the chief power in Persia, and the dynasty of Hūlāgū became extinct. The Jalayrs, Muẓaffarids, Sarbadārids etc., made havoc of the country till the great Tīmūr came and swept them away.

A.H.		A.D.
654	Hūlāgū	1256
663	Abāgā	1265
680	Aḥmad	1281
683	Arghūn	1284
690	Gaykhātū	1291
694	Baydū	1295
694	Ghāzān Maḥmūd	1295
703	Uljāi·tū	1304
716	Abū-Sa'īd	1316
736	Arpā	1335
736	Mūsā	1336

RIVAL KHĀNS*

736–8	Moḥammad	1336–8
739–52	Tughā-Tīmūr	1338–51
739–41	Jahān-Tīmūr	1339–40
739–40	Sātī-Beg (princess)	1339
740–4	Sulaymān (m. Sātī Beg)	1339–43
745	Nūshīrwān	1344

---

* Moḥammad, Tughā-Tīmūr, and Jahān-Tīmūr were set up as puppet-khāns by the Jalayr Amīr, Shaykh Ḥasan Buzurg; Sātī-Beg and her husband Sulaymān were nominees of the rival Amīr Ḥasan Kūchuk Chūpānī; and Nūshīrwān of -Ashraf Chūpānī. All were of the posterity of Hūlāgū, except Tughā-Tīmūr who was descended from a brother of Chingiz Khān, and Nūshīrwān whose pedigree is doubtful.

ĪL-KHĀNS OF PERSIA

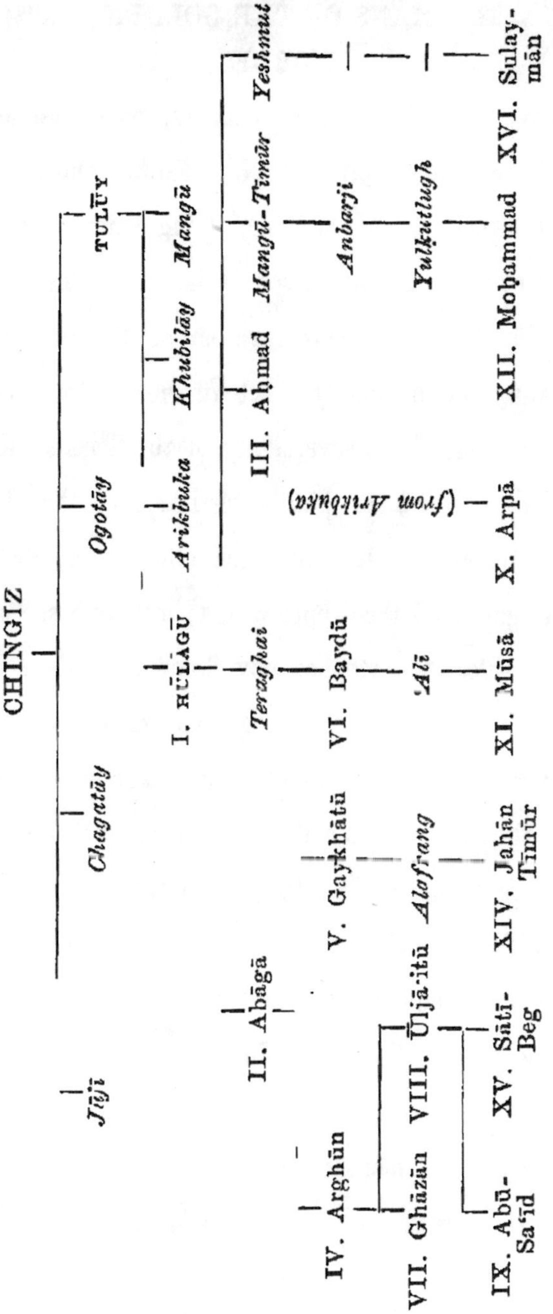

A.H. 621—907 83. KHĀNS OF THE GOLDEN HORDE A.D. 1224—1502

To Jūjī, the eldest son of Chingiz, were assigned the tribes of the old empire of Ḳarā-Khitay, north of the Sīhūn or Jaxartes, and here he, dying before his father, was succeeded by his eldest son Orda. A younger son of Jūjī, Bātū, by his famous invasion of Europe, extended the appanage of his family much further to the west, and secured for himself the sovereignty of the Turkish Khānate of Kipchak. North of Bātū's territory, another brother, Tūka-Tīmūr, appears to have been allotted the district of Great Bulgaria, on the Upper Volga; a fourth son of Jūjī, Shaybān, ruled the steppes now known as those of the Kirghiz Kazaks, north of Orda's appanage, and a fifth, Teval, led the Pechenegs, afterwards known as Nogāys, between the Ural and Yemba. All these tribes and their chiefs were more or less subject to the family of Bātū, which, although a younger branch, had acquired the greatest power and had made their capital Sarāy on the Volga the metropolis of the Jūjid empire; and all these tribes are included in the general name *Golden Horde*, so-called from the Khān's royal camp, *Sir Orda* or Golden Camp. It must be added that only the ruling family and the cream of the army were of Mongol race: the vast majority of the tribes allotted to the sons of Jūjī were conquered Turks or Turkomans.

The family of Jūjī has, therefore, to be considered in the following distinct lines:—

A. *The line of Bātū*, chief Khāns of the Golden Horde, ruling the Blue Horde in Western Kipchak (1224–1359).

B. *The line of Orda*, titular heads of the family, ruling the White Horde in Eastern Kipchak (1226–1428), Khāns of the Golden Horde in Western Kipchak after Bātū's line (1378–1502); and finally decaying as Khāns of Astrakhān (1466–1554).

C. *The line of Tūka-Tīmūr*, Khāns of Great Bulgaria, north of Kipchak; occasional Khāns of the Golden Horde in Western Kipchak; finally Khāns of Kazan (1438–1552), Kazimof (1450–1678), and Ḳrim (1420–1783).

D. *The line of Shaybān*, in the Uzbeg or Kirghiz Kazak steppes (1224–1659); afterwards migrating and becoming Khāns of Khiva and Bukhārā (1500–1872).

A. *The line of Bātū*:—Chief Khāns of the Golden Horde; appanage, the Blue Horde in Western Kipchak* (1224–1359).

Bātū's line had the privilege of ruling what was emphatically the Great Khānate of the West. Its history is important in its relations with the growth of Russia. At first the liege-lords of the Russian princes, receivers of their tribute, and owners of their daughters, it was the fate of the Great Khāns of Kipchak eventually to become the vassals of those whom they had once held in bondage. But before this stage in the decay of the Golden Horde, Bātū's line had become extinct, and the Khāns had been supplied from his brothers' families. So long as the descendants of Bātū held the reins of government, the great domain of the Khānate of Kipchak was maintained in all its power. The history of this line, through ten Khāns, to Jānī-Beg, the last great ruler of this branch of Jūjī's family, is comparatively plain. But on his death in 1357 anarchy ensued. His son Birdī-Beg reigned for

* The country watered by the Don and the Volga, extending east and west from the Ural or Yaik to the Dnieper, and north and south from the Black Sea and Caspian to Ukek. Howorth, ii. 36–194.

two years; two Khāns asserting themselves to be sons of Jānī-Beg succeeded in a single year; and then follows an intricate period of twenty years of rival candidates.

There were five branches of Jūjī's house from which claimants for the Golden Khānate might spring, on the extinction of Bātū's line. North and south, in Great Bulgaria and the Ḳrim, ruled the numerous progeny of Tūka-Tīmūr. South also, by the Caucasus, camping along the Terek and Kuma, were the descendants of Baraka, the younger brother and second successor to Bātū, to whom the Golden Horde owed much of its terrible prestige. East of the Great Khānate was the White Horde with its chiefs of the family of Orda; and also east, but further north, were the Uzbeg tribes of Shaybān's leading; whilst along the northern shore of the Caspian the clans of Nogāy pastured their herds. The attribution of the fifteen khāns of this period of rival families to their several ancestors in the table on page 230 is partly conjectural, but their dates are established by coins. In 1378, the sovereignty of the Golden Horde passed into the family of Orda in the person of Tōḳtāmish.

B. *The line of Orda*:—Appanage, the White Horde in Eastern Kipchak,* 1226–1428; Khāns of the Golden Horde in Western Kipchak, 1378–1502; Khāns of Astrakhān, 1466–1554.

Although Bātū was the most powerful of the sons of Jūjī, Orda the eldest inherited his father's appanage by the Jaxartes, and received a special homage as hereditary head of the family. He ruled the left division of the Golden Horde, known as the White Horde (Āḳ Orda), (a colour which ranked higher than the Blue), in distinction from the right wing, or Bātū's tribes, which were designated the Blue Horde (Kōk Orda) in token of imaginary dependence. Living in the far-away steppes beyond the Caspian, the White Horde soon yielded the palm to its Blue brethren on the Don and Volga; but in its rough wintry life it retained a vigour and hardihood which eventually placed its rulers on the throne of the more civilized and decayed descendants of Bātū.

Of the earlier rulers of the White Horde little is

* The country of the Lower Jaxartes and the Ulugh and Kūchuk Tāg Mountains: bounded on the west by Bātū's Blue Horde, on the north by Shaybān's Uzbegs, on the east by Chagatāy's Khānate, on the south by the desert of Ḳizil Ḳumm and the Alexandrovski range. Howorth, ii. 216–362.

known; the Khānate passed regularly from father to son; and the only noticeable fact is the possession by Kūchī of a territory at Ghazna and Bāmiyān under the suzerainty of either the Chagatāy Khāns or the Īl-khāns of Persia. Ūrūs Khān is the first chief of Orda's line who possesses any individuality in the history of the White Horde. He had the distinction of defeating the troops of Tīmūr more than once. Tīmūr in his overbearing fashion had appointed to the sovereignty of the tribes of Jūjī's appanage a member of Orda's family, Tōḳtāmish, whose father had been killed and he himself exiled by Ūrūs Khān. Assisted by the troops supplied by Tīmūr to carry his nomination into effect, Tōḳtāmish sustained several repulses at the hands of Ūrūs, and it was not till after the death of this Khān and the short reign of Tōḳtakya his son that Tōḳtāmish was able to wrest the command of the White Horde from another son of Ūrūs, Tīmūr Malik.

Tōḳtāmish is 'the last really great figure in the history of the Golden Horde.' After seizing the throne of the White Horde he marched upon Western Kipchak, defeated Mamāy, the king-maker of Sarāy, and by this victory in 1378 (*780*) put an end to the division between the White and the Blue Hordes, and united Eastern and Western

Kipchak under his sole rule. Henceforward Orda's family ruled the Blue Horde, bringing no doubt the cream of the White Horde with them; and their original camping-grounds gradually passed into the hands of the descendants of Shaybān. Under Tōḳtāmish the Golden Horde recovered much of its prestige. A great campaign was carried into Russia, Moscow was sacked and burnt (1382), and the Grand Principality was ravaged with the ancient fury of the Mongols. This revival of the glory of Kipchak, however, was only the flicker of a dying torch. Tōḳtāmish had the misfortune or the ingratitude to quarrel with the prince who had helped him to his success; and no one offended Tīmūr with impunity. The great conqueror in two campaigns, one marked by the battle of Urtupa on the 18th June, 1391, and the second by a crushing defeat near the Terek in 1395, when Tōḳtāmish had returned from exile, destroyed for ever the power of the Khāns of Kipchak. Tōḳtāmish indeed re-entered Sarāy in 1398, after Tīmūr's departure, but he was speedily driven out again by Tīmūr Ḳutlugh, son of his old enemy, Ūrūs, and forced to take refuge with the Lithuanian prince Vitut, whom he involved in war with the Tatars; he died in 1406.

The period succeeding the overthrow of Tōḳtāmish is one of the most obscure in the labyrinth of dark passages which the history of the Golden Horde affords. It is filled with the incessant struggles of *Rival Families* for the throne. There were at least three distinct sets of candidates for the decayed Khānship: the family of Ūrūs Khān, supported by the Nogāy chief Idiku, the second king-maker of Kipchak; the sons of Tōḳtāmish; and some younger members of the family of Shaybān. The table on page 232 will give an idea of this confused period. The rival Khāns not only ruled simultaneously in Kipchak, but held the same cities in the same years; and the history of Sarāy and other large towns must have been the record of continual sieges and recaptures.

This is the end of the Golden Horde. It was absorbed by Russia in 1502 (*907*), and its history degenerates into the petty annals of its scattered fragments. Of these one alone belonged to the family of Orda—the insignificant Khānate of Astrakhān,* founded by Ḳāsim, a grandson of Kūchuk Moḥammad, about 1466, and held by his descendants until its abolition in 1554 by the Grand Prince of Moscow.

* Howorth, ii. 349-362.

KHĀNS OF THE GOLDEN HORDE

i. THE BLUE HORDE OF WESTERN KIPCHAK

a. FAMILY OF BĀTŪ

A.H.		A.D.
621	Bātū	1224
654	Sartak	1256
654	Baraka	1256
664	Mangū-Tīmūr	1266
679	Tūda-Mangū	1280
686	[Tūla Bughā]	1287
689	Tōḳtū	1290
712	Ūzbeg	1312
741	Tīnī-Beg	1340
741	Jānī-Beg Maḥmūd	1340
758	Birdī-Beg Moḥammad	1357
760	Ḳūlnā	1359
760	Nūrūz-Beg	1359

b. RIVAL FAMILIES

A.H.	OF SHAYBĀN		OF ORDA		OF TŪKA-TĪMŪR
760	Khiḍr				
762	Mardūd	762	Tīmūr Khōja	762	Kildī Beg
		762	Murīd Khōja		
764–8	Pūlād Khōja	764	Ḳutlugh Khōja	764	'Azīz Shaykh
		764	'Abd-Allāh		
				768	Ḥasan
772	Tūlūn-Beg	771	Moḥammad Būlāk	—772	
775	Ilbān	—780			
777	Khāghān				
779	'Arab Shāh				
—780					

[780 *United to White Horde* 1378]

ii. THE WHITE HORDE OF EASTERN KIPCHAK

FAMILY OF ORDA

A.H.		A.D.
623	Orda	1226
679	Kūchī	1280
701	Bāyān	1301
709	Sāsibūkā	1309
c. 715	Ibisan	1315
720	Mubārak Khōja	1320
745	Chimtāy	1344
762	Ūrūs	1361
777	Tōḳtakya	1375
777	Tīmūr Malik	1375
778	Tōḳtāmish Ghiyāth-*al*-din	1376
—793	(who unites Blue and White Hordes 1378)	—1391

[*Rival Families*]

iii. RIVAL FAMILIES

	OF ORDA					OF SHAYBĀN	
A.H.	Eastern Kipchak Brauch		House of Ūrūs		House of Tōḳtāmish		
797	Koirijak	797	Tīmūr Ḳutlugh	793	Beg Pūlād		
		802	Shādī Beg				
		{ 810–15	Pūlād			805-22	Darwīsh
		{ 809–18	Tīmūr	814	Jalāl-al-dīn		
				815	Karīm Birdī		
				817	Kibak		
		818	Chakra	c. 818	Jabar Birdī		
823	Burāḳ (seizes part of West Kipchak 827–831)					822	Sayyid Aḥmad
		827	Kūchuk Moḥammad				
		—c. 864					
	FAMILY OF TŪKA-TĪMŪR						
830	Dawlat Birdī (in absence of Burāḳ)						
		c. 864	Maḥmūd				
		864	Aḥmad				
		886 {	Sayyid Aḥmad				
			Murtaḍā				
			Shaykh Aḥmad				

[907 *Final submission to Russia.* 1502]

A.H.		A.D.
c. 823—1197	84. KHĀNS OF THE ḲRIM (CRIMEA)	*c.* 1420—1783

C. *The Line of Tūka-Tīmūr*:—Appanage, Great Bulgaria, and subsequently Ḳrim and Kaffa; occasional Khāns of the Golden Horde; finally, Khāns of Kazan, Kazimof, and Ḳrim.*

Tūka-Tīmūr was the youngest son of Jūjī, and was attached to the left (or Orda's) wing of the Golden Horde, but probably had his own camping-grounds on the Upper Volga, including part at least of Great Bulgaria. Almost nothing is known of this branch in its original seats. Mangū-Tīmūr (of Bātū's line) gave Urang-Tīmūr, son of Tūka-Tīmūr, Ḳrim and Kaffa, and the family being thus established north and south of Bātū's Khānate soon began to interfere in its dynastic succession. We have seen how three Khāns of the first period of rival families belonged probably to Tūka-Tīmūr's line, and one of the second period. But the chief importance of this branch is after the downfall of the Golden Khānate which followed upon Tīmūr's invasions.

* Howorth, ii. 198–216, 274, 363–626, 1074–5

One of the line, Ulugh Moḥammad, after attempting to seize the Great Khānate on Burāḳ's death, betook himself in 1438 to his old possession of Great Bulgaria, and there revived his forefathers' Khānate, under the title of *Khānate of Kazan*, which, no longer overshadowed by the Great Khānate on its south, became an independent thorn in the side of the growing Muscovite giant. With the death, however, of Moḥammad Amīn, in 1519, the Moḥammadan posterity of the founder of Kazan came to an end, and Khāns of the true faith had to be transplanted from the Kazimof, Ḳrim, Astrakhān and other stocks, under the auspices of Russia, who finally suppressed the Khānate and appointed a Russian governor of Kazan in 1552.

When Ulugh Moḥammad was murdered by his son Maḥmūdak, in 1446, two of his other sons fled to Russia, and after some service in the Muscovite army one of these, Ḳāsim, was granted the town and district of Gorodetz on the Oka, in the division of Riazan. He gave the town his own name, and the line of Khāns ruling here, and known as the *Khāns of Kazimof*, were used by Russia to play off against their more powerful neighbour at Kazan, and were allowed to supply a couple of Khāns to the greater Khānate on the extinction of Ulugh Moḥammad's direct Muslim line. This Khānate, which never had a really independent existence, was absorbed by Russia in 1678.

The most important of the three Khānates sprung from the house of Tūka-Tīmūr was that of the Ḳrim. Ulugh Moḥammad had a brother, Tāsh-Tīmūr, who was once a general under Tōḳtāmish, and was the actual founder of the powerful dynasty of the *Khāns of the Ḳrim* or Crimea, though his son, Hājji Girāy, is generally regarded as the first Khān. The Ḳrim dynasty was always an element in the Eastern Question, and as an outpost of Turkey or an ally of Russia was an object of consideration on both sides. Eventually the inconvenience of these violent neighbours was agreed between Russia and Turkey, and the Khānate of the Ḳrim was extinguished by treaty in 1783. A lineal descendant of these powerful Khāns, one Sulṭān Ḳrim Girāy Kattī Girāy, settled in Edinburgh and married a Scottish lady.*

* *Athenæum*, No. 2762

KHĀNS OF THE ḲRIM (CRIMEA)

A.H.		A.D.
c. 823	Ḥājjī Girāy	c. 1420
871	Nūr-Dawlat	1466
873	Manglī Girāy I	1469
878	Nūr-Dawlat (*restored*)	1474
882	Jānī-Beg Girāy I	1477
883	Manglī Girāy (*restored*)	1478
921	Moḥammad Girāy I	1515
929	Ghāzī Girāy I	1523
929	Sa'ādat Girāy I	1523
938	Islām Girāy I	1532
938	Ṣāḥib Girāy I	1532
958	Dawlat Girāy I	1551
985	Moḥammad Girāy II	1577
992	Islām Girāy II	1584
996	Ghāzī Girāy II	1588
1002	Fatḥ Girāy I	1594
1002	Ghāzī Girāy II (*restored*)	1594
1017	Salāmat Girāy I	1608
1019	Jānī-Beg Girāy II	1610
1031	Moḥammad Girāy III	1627
1036	Jānī-Beg II (*restored*)	1635
1045	Ināyat Girāy	1638
1048	Bahādur Girāy	1642
1052	Moḥammad Girāy IV	1644
1054	Islām Girāy III	
1064	Moḥammad IV (*restored*)	1654
1075	'Ādil Girāy	1665
1081	Selīm Girāy I	1670
1088	Murād Girāy	1677
1094	Ḥājjī Girāy II	1683

1095	Selīm I (*restored*)	1684
1102	Sa'ādat Girāy II	1691
1102	Ṣafā Girāy	1691
1103	Selīm I (*again restored*)	1692
1109	Dawlat Girāy II	1698
1114	Selīm I (*again restored*)	1702
1117	Ghāzī Girāy III	1705
1119	Kaplan Girāy I	1707
1119	Dawlat Girāy (*restored*)	1707
1125	Kaplan I (*restored*)	1713
1127	Ḳarā Dawlat Girāy	1715
1127	Sa'ādat Girāy III	1715
1136	Manglī Girāy II	1724
1142	Kaplan I (*again restored*)	1730
1149	Fatḥ Girāy II	1736
1150	Manglī II (restored)	1737
1152	Salāmat Girāy II	1739
1156	Selīm Girāy II	1743
1161	Arslān Girāy	1748
1168	Ḥākim Girāy	1755
1171	Ḳrīm Girāy	1758
1177	Selīm Girāy III	1764
1180	Arslān Girāy (*restored*)	1767
1181	Makhṣūd Girāy I	1767
1182	Ḳrim Girāy (*restored*)	1768
1184	Dawlat Girāy III	1770
1184	Kaplan Girāy II	1771
1184	Selīm III (*restored*)	1771
1185	Makhṣūd Girāy II	1771
1185	Ṣāḥib Girāy II	1772
1189	Dawlat III (*restored*)	1775
1191	Shāhīn Girāy	1777
—1197	[*Crimea ceded to Russia*]	—1783

D. *The Line of Shaybān*:—Appanage, the Uzbeg country (between the Ural and Chu rivers); occasional Khāns of the Golden Horde; Khāns or Czars of Tiumen, *circ.* 1226—1659; Khāns of Bukhārā, 1500—1868, and of Khiva, 1515—1872.*

When Bātū invaded Hungary in 1240, his brother Shaybān accompanied him, and acquitted himself so well that Bātū not only made him King of Hungary, a title of a somewhat nominal value, but gave him an appanage of certain tribes north of Orda's Khānate. Shaybān was to camp in summer from the Ural mountains to the rivers Ilek and Irghiz, and in winter about the lands watered by the Sir, Chu, and Sarisu. His descendant in the sixth generation, Mangū-Tīmūr, was a contemporary of the great Khān Uzbeg of the Golden Horde, and from him the tribes of Shaybān's appanage took the name of Uzbegs, which has since become famous. On the extinction of Bātū's line, the family of Shaybān supplied several Khāns to the Golden Horde; and in the second period of rival families, after the overthrow of

* Howorth, ii. 686–1010

Tōḳtāmish, the house of Shaybān is represented, in all probability, by Darwīsh Khān and Sayyid Aḥmad.

The home-line of Shaybān remained in the original camping-grounds and assumed the title of *Czars of the Tiumen,* under which they were obeyed over a great part of Siberia. They survived till 1659, when their country was occupied by the Kalmuks: but for some time before this their authority had been purely nominal.

Much more important were the branches descended from Pūlād, son of Mangū-Tīmūr, and once ruler of the Golden Horde. Pūlād's two sons, Ibrāhīm and 'Arab-Shāh, were respectively ancestors of the *Khāns of Bukhārā* and *Khwārizm* or *Khiva.* The former Khānate was founded by Moḥammad Shaybānī, grandson of Abū-l-Khayr, who was grandson of Ibrāhīm, in 1500, and survives to the present day, although General Kaufmann made it a Russian dependency in 1868. 'Arab-Shāh, the founder of the Khānate of Khiva, is also known as, if not a Khān of the Golden Horde, at least a striker of coins in Kipchak just before the invasion of Tōḳtāmish. His descendant in the fifth generation, Ilbars Khān, took forcible possession of Transoxiana and adjacent provinces after Shaybānī's death, probably about 1515, and his posterity are still called Khāns of Khiva, but they have been tributary to Russia since 1872. The history of these Khānates, which sprang up on the ruins of the empire of Tīmūr, belong to a later section (XIII).

It should be added that another son of Jūjī, Teval, was the chief of the Pechenegs, camping about the river Bug in Southern Russia, and was the grandfather of Nogāy, who took a large part in the affairs of the Golden Horde, but afterwards fell out with Tōḳtū and was driven, along with his tribes, who adopted the name of Nogāys, beyond the Volga, and found settlements between the Ural and the Yemba. The history of this horde is very fragmentary, and their state was peculiarly migratory.*

* Howorth, ii. 1011–1068

A.H. A.D.

624—760 85. CHAGATĀY KHĀNS 1227—1358
(TRANSOXIANA)

The Khānātes founded by three sons of Chingiz—Ogotāy, Tulūy, and Jūjī—have in turn been noticed. There remains Chagatāy, who was allotted the appanage of Mā-warā-*l*-nahr, or Transoxiana (Bukharia), with part of Kāshghar, Badakhshān, Balkh, and Ghazna, and who founded the Khānate of those regions. The history of his descendants is very scantily recorded, and, beyond occasional raids over the Persian border and internal disputes, nothing of note has been set down. Two members of Ogotāy's family ('Alī and Dānishmandja) intrude themselves into the series, proving the presence of Ogotāy chiefs of rank and importance in the Chagatāy dominions (pp. 210, 265). The genealogy and chronology of this branch are alike doubtful; and the following list is merely tentative.

A.H.		A.D.
624	Chagatāy	1227
639	Ḳarā-Hūlāgū	1242
645	Yīsū Mangū	1247
650	Ḳarā-Hūlāgū (*restored*)	1252
650	Orgána Khātūn	1252
659	Algū	1261
664	Mubārak Shāh	1266
664	Burāḳ Khān	1266
668	Nikpāy	1270
670	Tūka-Tīmūr	1272
c. 672	Duwā Khān	c. 1274
706	Kunjuk Khān	1306
708	Tālikū	1308
709	Kibak Khān	1309
709	Yisunbughā	1309
c. 718	Kibak Khān (*restored*)	1318
721	Ilchīkadāy	1321
721	Duwā Tīmūr	1321
722	Tirmashirīn	1322
730–4 ?	Sinjar ?	1330–4 ?
734	Jingishay	1334
c. 735	Būzūn	c. 1335
c. 739	Yisun Tīmūr	c. 1339
c. 741	'Alī (of Ogotāy stock)	c. 1340
c. 743	Moḥammad	c. 1342
744	Kazan	1343
747	Dānishmandja (of Ogotāy stock)	1346
749	Būyān Kulī	1348
—760		—1358

[*Anarchy and rival chiefs, until*

771 *Supremacy of Tīmūr* 1370.]

To face p. 242

THE HOUSE OF CHAGATÁY*

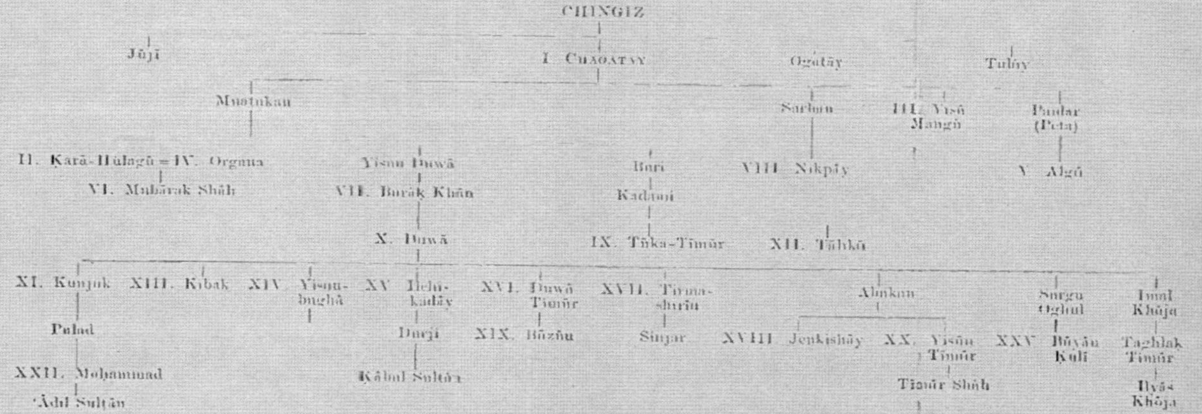

* This table has been kindly arranged for me by Sir Henry Howorth

XII. PERSIA

SÆC. XIV—XIX

86. JALAYRS (-'IRĀḲ)

87. MUẒAFFARIDS (FĀRS)

88. SARBADĀRIDS (KHURĀSĀN)

89. KARTS (HERĀT)

TĪMŪRIDS (*See* XIII)

90. ḲARĀ-ḲUYUNLĪ (ADHARBĪJĀN)

91. AḲ-ḲUYUNLĪ (ADHARBĪJĀN)

92. ṢAFAVIDS
93. AFGHĀNS
94. AFSHĀRIDS
95. ZANDS
96. ḲĀJĀRS

} SHĀHS OF PERSIA

XII. PERSIA

SEC. XIV–XIX

On the decay of the power of the Persian Mongols a number of prominent chiefs and provincial governors asserted their independence. Of these the Jalayrs were the most powerful, and held the provinces of -'Irāḳ and Adharbījān, in which they were succeeded by the Turkomāns of the Black and White Sheep. The more eastern provinces were ruled by the Muẓaffarids, but not without a severe struggle with Abū-Isḥāḳ and other members of the family of Maḥmūd Shāh Injū, whose seat was Iṣpahān. In the north-east, Khurāsān was for a time divided between the Sarbadārids and the Kart Maliks of Herāt. Tīmūr swept across Persia in 1384–93, and his descendants held part of the country for a century. At the beginning of the 16th century, however, Shāh Ismā'īl the Ṣafavid established his authority over all the provinces governed by the Tīmūrids, Turkomāns, and minor dynasties, and presently added Khurāsān, since which time the modern kingdom of the Shāhs of Persia has remained practically unchanged in its boundaries, save for some losses on the west to Turkey.

A.H.		A.D.
736—814	86. JALAYRS	1336–1411

86. JALAYRS
(-'IRĀḲ, ETC.)

The chiefs of the tribe of Jalayrs, also called Ilkānians, became the leading family in Persia after the death of the Mongol Abū-Sa'īd. Their head, Shaykh Ḥasan Buzurg ('the Great'), as has been seen (pp. 219, 220), set up three puppets on the Mongol throne; after which he assumed sovereign functions himself, and taking possession of -'Irāḳ made Baghdād his capital. His son Oways, who succeeded him in *757* (1356), took Adharbījān and Tabrīz from the Golden Horde (*759*), and added -Mōṣil and Diyār-Bakr to his dominions (*766*). Ḥusayn, his successor, was engaged in wars with his neighbours the Muẓaffarids of eastern Persia, and with the Turkomāns of the Black Sheep, who had made themselves dominant in Armenia and the country south of Lake Van; until the latter agreed to become his allies (*779*). On his death in 1382 (*784*), the kingdom was divided between his two sons; Adharbījān and -'Irāḳ falling to Sulṭān Aḥmad, and part of Kurdistān (for a year) to Bāyazīd. On the invasion of Tīmūr, who overran northern Persia and Armenia in 1384–7, and reduced Baghdād, Mesopotamia, Diyār-Bakr, and Vān in 1393 (*796*), Sulṭān Aḥmad fled to Egypt, where he took refuge with the Mamlūk Sulṭān Barḳūḳ, who assisted him to recover Baghdād after Tīmūr's return to Samarḳand. From this time until Tīmūr's death in 1405 (*807*) Sulṭān Ahmad's life was spent in losing and recapturing his dominions, and when in *808* he was once more actual ruler of Baghdād, his breach with Ḳarā-Yūsuf the Turkomān and his ensuing invasion of Adharbījān ended in his defeat and death, 1410 (*813*). His nephew Shāh Walad continued to govern Baghdād until the arrival of the Black Sheep in 1411; and Shāh Walad's widow, Tandū (who had previously been married to the Mamlūk Barḳūḳ) reigned at Wāsiṭ, Baṣra, and Shūstar (doing homage, however, to the Tīmūrid Shāh Rukh) till *819*, when her stepson succeeded to the government, and was followed by his brothers Oways (*822–829*) and Moḥammad, and by their cousin Ḥusayn, who was killed by the Black Sheep Turkomāns.*

* See Sir H. H. Howorth, *History of the Mongols*, iii, 654-679.

A.H.		A.D.
736	Shaykh Ḥasan Buzurg	1336
757	Shaykh Oways	1356
777	Ḥosayn	1374
784–5	Bāyazīd (in Kurdistān) . . .	
784	Sulṭān Aḥmad	1382
	(*Repeatedly expelled by Tīmūr* 796–807)	
813	Shāh Walad	1410
—814		—1411

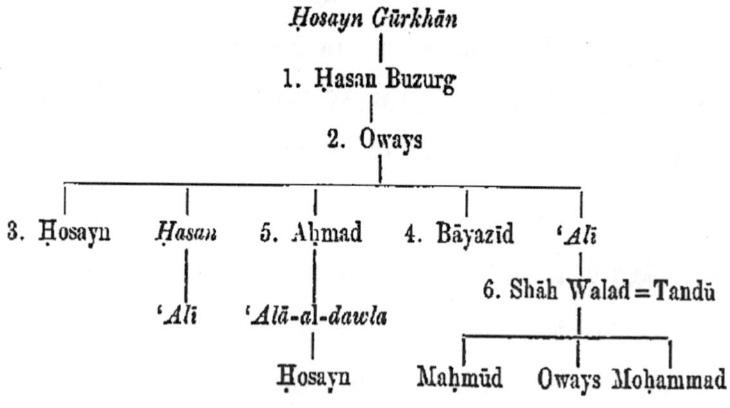

[*Ḳarā-Ḳuyunlī*]

A.H.		A.D.
713—795	87. MUẒAFFARIDS	1313—1393

(FĀRS, KIRMĀN, AND KURDISTĀN)

The Amīr Muẓaffar, founder of this dynasty, a grandson of Ghiyāth-al-dīn Ḥājjī of Khurāsān, after holding various posts at the court of the Mongols of Persia, was appointed governor of Maybudh near Iṣpahān. His son Mubāriz-al-dīn Moḥammad succeeded him in his government in 1313 (*713*), and received the much more important command of Yazd in Fārs in 1319 (*719*) from the Mongol Abū-Sa'īd. Kirmān was added in 1340 (*741*), and after a prolonged struggle with Abū-Isḥāḳ Injū, Moḥammad captured Shīrāz and all Fārs in 1353 (*754*), and added Iṣpahān in 1356 (*758*), when Abū-Isḥāḳ was executed. After carrying his arms successfully as far north as Tabrīz, Moḥammad was deposed and blinded in 1357 (*759*), and, although restored for a brief space, died in a second exile in 1364 (*765*). His successors retained the government of Fārs, Kirmān, and Kurdistān until the irruption of Tīmūr in 1387.* The poet Ḥāfiẓ lived at the court of Shāh Shujā'.

* Howorth, iii, 693-716.

A.H.		A.D.
713	Mubāriz-*al*-dīn Moḥammad b. -Muẓaffar .	1313
759	Jalāl-*al*-dīn Shāh Shujā'	1357
786–9	Mujāhid-*al*-dīn 'Alī Zayn-al-'Abidīn . .	1384–
	(*Expelled by Tīmūr*)	—1387
789	Shāh Yaḥyā (*at Yazd*) Sulṭán Aḥmad (*at Kirmān*) Shāh Manṣūr (*at Iṣpahān*) } *contemporary* .	1387
—795		—1393

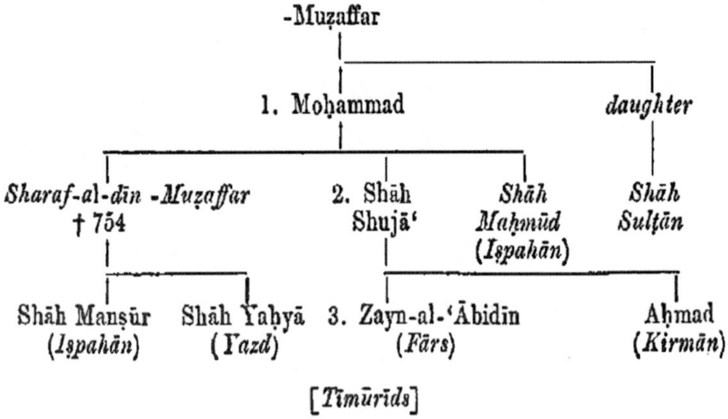

A.H.		A.D.
737–783	88. SARBADĀRIDS	1337–1381

(KHURĀSĀN)

'Abd-*al*-Razzāķ, a native of the village of Bashtīn in Khurāsān, and at one time in the service of the Ilkhān Abū-Sa'īd, in 1337 (*737*) headed a rebellion of his countrymen against the oppression of the local governor. The rebels took the name of *Sar-ba-dār* or "Head to the gibbet" in token of the neck-or-nothing-ness of their cause. Nevertheless they obtained possession of Sabzawār and the neighbouring district, and held it for nearly half a century, during which period twelve successive chiefs assumed the command, nine of whom suffered violent deaths.

A.H.		A.D.
737	'Abd-*al*-Razzāķ b. Faḍl-Allāh	1337
738	Wajīh-*al*-dīn Mas'ūd b. Faḍl-Allāh . .	1338
744	Ay-Tīmūr Moḥammad	1344
746	Isfandiyār	1346
747	Faḍl-Allāh	1346
748	Shams-*al*-dīn 'Alī	1347
753	Yaḥyā	1352
756	Ẓahīr-*al*-dīn	1355
760	Haydar -Ķaṣṣāb	1359
760	Luṭf-Allāh	1359
761	-Ḥasan -Dāmighānī	1360
766	'Alī -Mu'ayyad	1364
—783	[*Abolished by Tīmūr*]	—1381

A.H. 643–791 — A.D. 1245–1389

89. KARTS
(HERĀT)

The Maliks of Herāt of the Kart race of Ghōr had held their government from the early days of the Mongol rule in Persia. As the Mongols grew weak, the Karts became an important power in Khurāsān, until Herāt was conquered by Tīmūr in 1381 (*783*), and, after a period of vassalage, the dynasty was extinguished in 1389 (*791*).

A.H.		A.D.
643	Shams-al-dīn I	1245
	677–82 Rukn-al-dīn, *contemp.* 1278-83	
684	Fakhr-al-dīn	1285
708	Ghiyāth-al-dīn	1308
729	Shams-al-dīn II	1328
730	Ḥāfiẓ	1329
732	Mu'izz-al-dīn	1331
772	Ghiyāth-al-dīn Pīr 'Alī	1370
—791		—1389

Rukn-al-dīn Abū-Bakr b. 'Othmān

1. Shams-al-dīn I

2. Rukn-al-dīn

3. Fakhr-al-dīn — 4. Ghiyāth-al-dīn

5. Shams-al-dīn II — 6. Ḥāfiẓ — 7. Mu'izz-al-dīn

Mohammad (*Sarakhs*) — 8. Ghiyāth-al-dīn Pīr 'Alī

[*Tīmūrids*]

A.H.		A.D.
780—874	90. ḲARĀ-ḲUYUNLĪ	1378—1469

90. ḲARĀ-ḲUYUNLĪ

TURKOMANS OF THE BLACK SHEEP

(ADHARBĪJĀN, ETC.)

In the last quarter of the fourteenth century a clan of Turkomāns, known as the Black Sheep, from the device on their standard, dominated the country south of the lake of Van, and, having allied themselves with the Jalayr Sulṭān Ḥosayn, established a dynasty in Armenia and Adharbījān. Ḳarā-Yūsuf, the second chief of the line, was several times driven into exile by Tīmūr, but as often returned, and after the conqueror's death in 1405 (*807*) resumed his former dominions, and in 1411 added those of the Jalayrs. The Black Sheep were superseded in 1469 (*874*) by Uzun Ḥasan of the rival clan of the White Sheep.

A.H.		A.H.
780	Ḳarā-Moḥammad	1378
c. 790	Ḳarā-Yūsuf	c. 1388
802	*Invasion of Tīmūr*	1400
808	Ḳarā Yūsuf (*restored*)	1405
823	Iskandar	1420
841	Jahān Shāh	1437
872	Ḥasan 'Alī	1467
—874		—1469

[*Āḳ-Ḳuyunlī*]

A.H.		A.D.
780—908	91. ĀḲ-ḲUYUNLĪ	1378—1502

TURKOMANS OF THE WHITE SHEEP.

(ADHĀRBĪJAN, ETC.)

The White Sheep or Aḳ-Ḳuyunlī succeeded their rivals the Black Sheep in Adharbījān and Diyār-Bakr, but after some thirty years of sole authority they were defeated by Shāh Ismā'īl the Ṣafavid at the great battle of Shurūr in 1502 (*907*), and the dynasty soon afterwards expired.

A.H.		A.D.
780	Ḳarā-Yūluḳ 'Othmān	1378
809	Ḥamza	1406
848	Jahāngīr	1444
871	Uzun Ḥasan	1466
883	Khalīl	1478
884	Ya'ḳūb	1479
896	Baysunḳur*	1490
897	Rustam	1491
902	Aḥmad	1496
903	Murād	1497
905	Alwand	1499
906	Moḥammad	1500
907	Murād (*restored*)	1501
—908		—1502

[*Ṣafavids*]

* 'Alī and Masīḥ were rival claimants in 896.

A.H. A.D.

907—1311 92—6. SHĀHS OF PERSIA 1052—1893

The series of the Shāhs of Persia is composed of five distinct dynasties of different races: the Ṣafavids, Afghāns, Afshārids, Zands, and Ḳājārs. Of these the first claimed Arab lineage, for the Ṣafavids traced their descent from the seventh Imām Mūsā -Ḳazam († *183*), of the family of Ḥosayn the grandson of the prophet Moḥammad (p. 72). Many shaykhs of the family acquired a reputation for sanctity, and among these the most celebrated saint was Shaykh Ṣafī-*al*-dīn of Ardabīl, from whom his descendants took their name of Ṣafawī or *Ṣafavid.* It was not till four generations after Shaykh Ṣafī that one of his descendants, Haydar, added the rôle of warrior to the profession of saint. He engaged in a contest with Uzun Ḥasan of the White Sheep Turkomāns, and his third son Ismā'īl, preserving a continuity of policy, seized Shīrwān, utterly defeated the Turkomāns at the battle of Shurūr in the spring of 1502 (*907*), and making Tabrīz his capital proceeded to conquer all Persia. The Tīmūrid governors and other petty dynasts were rapidly subdued, and in a few years Shāh Ismā'īl's arms had advanced through Khurāsān as far as Herāt, besides annexing the southern provinces, till his dominions stretched from the Oxus to the Persian Gulf, from Afghānistān to the Euphrates. His territories now marched with those of the 'Othmānlīs, and the religious antagonism between the Shī'ite Ṣafavids and the Sunnite 'Othmānlīs, embittered by the wide-spread Shī'ite propaganda in Asia Minor, brought about a war. Selīm the Grim, after massacring or imprisoning 40,000 Shī'ites in his Asiatic dominions, led a campaign against Shāh Ismā'īl. At the head of 80,000 horsemen and 40,000 foot, Selīm marched upon Persia and forced the Shāh to give battle at Chāldirān (1514), when the fine generalship of Sinān Pasha and the valour of the Janizaries won the day. Selīm entered Tabrīz in triumph, and after annexing Diyār-Bakr and some surrounding districts abandoned the idea of further conquests in the East in favour of an invasion of Egypt. From this time onwards there have been frequent contests over the Turko-Persian frontier, and provinces in Georgia and Armenia have been taken and re-taken, but the general boundary has not greatly varied, except when Murād IV conquered Baghdād and annexed Mesopotamia to the Turkish Empire in 1638. In the like manner the northern frontier was long contested by the Uzbegs; and Afghānistān has been alternately part of India and part of Persia, until the establishment of an independent dynasty by Aḥmad Durrānī in 1747. Bābar, the founder of the Mogul empire in India, was an ally of Shāh Ismāʻīl, and his son Humāyūn was aided in his recovery of Hindūstān by Shāh Tahmāsp. The greatest of the Ṣafavid kings was Shāh ʻAbbās (1587–1629), who, seconded by Sir Anthony Shirley, the organizer of the Persian army, recovered several of the western provinces from the ʻOthmānlīs, and whose reign was celebrated for the cultivation of the arts and literature, the increase of public works, and the observance of an enlightened foreign policy. He belonged to the great epoch which produced such rulers as Sulaymān the Great, Akbar, and Elizabeth.

The Ṣafavid dynasty practically ended when the *Afghāns* under Maḥmūd rose in revolt, seized Herāt and Mashhad, defeated Shāh Ḥosayn, and after a seven months' siege took the capital Iṣpahān in 1722 (*1135*). Members of the Ṣafavid family, however, still retained a vestige of authority, chiefly in Mazandarān, and after ten years of anarchy, revolts, and Russian and Turkish invasions, Nādir Ḳulī the *Afshārid* Turk, made use of the pretext of restoring the enfeebled Ṣafavids, to seize the supreme power, to which he soon added the avowed as well as the real sovereignty in 1736 (*1148*). Nādir Shāh not only maintained the Persian kingdom in its fullest extent, but subdued Afghānistān, seized Kābul and Ḳandahār (1737), pushed on to Lahore, defeated the Mogul army after an obstinate battle near Karnāl, and sacked Dehlī in March 1738 (*1151*). Peace was made, and for a time the Persian empire extended from the Indus to the Caucasus.

The Afshārid dynasty, numbering four Shāhs, ended in a period of anarchy, during which the Afghān Āzād held Adharbījān; 'Alī Mardān the Bakhtiyārī, Iṣpahān; Moḥammad Ḥosayn, the chief of the Ḳājārs, ruled Astarabād; and Ḳarīm Khān the Zand fought with Shāh Rukh the Afshārid for the supreme throne. The *Zand* eventually got the upper hand, and from 1750 (*1163*) to 1779 (*1193*) governed all Persia except Khurāsān, where Shāh Rukh the Afshārid, though old and blind, still maintained some show of authority. On the death of Ḳarīm Khān a contest was waged for a dozen years between his Zand successors and Āḳā Moḥammad the *Ḳājār*, which ended in the triumph of the latter, whose nephew in the fourth generation now reigns over the relics of a great people from his throne at Ṭihrān.

A.H.		A.D.
907—1148	92. ṢAFAVIDS	1502—1736
907	Ismā'īl I	1502
930	Ṭahmāsp I	1524
984	Ismā'īl II	1576
985	Moḥammad Khudabanda . . .	1578
985	'Abbās I	1587
1038	Ṣafī I	1629
1052	'Abbās II	1642
1077	Sulaymān I	1667
1105	Ḥosayn I	1694
1135	Ṭahmāsp II	1722
1144	'Abbās III	1731
—1148		—1736

93. AFGHĀNS

1135	Maḥmūd	1722
1137	Ashraf	1725
—1142		—1729

94. AFSHĀRIDS

1148	Nādir	1736
1160	'Ādil	1747
1161	Shāh Rukh	1748
—1210		—1796

95. ZANDS

A.H.		A.D.
1163	Ḳarīm Khān	1750
1193	Abū-l-Fatḥ	1779
1193	ʻAlī Murād	1779
1193	Moḥammad ʻAlī	1779
1193	Ṣādiḳ	1779
1196	ʻAlī Murād (again)	1782
1199	Jaʻfar	1785
1203	Luṭf ʻAlī	1789
—1209		—1794

96. ḲĀJARS

A.H.		A.D.
1193	Aḳā Moḥammad	1779
1211	Fatḥ ʻAlī	1797
1250	Moḥammad	1834
1264	Nāṣir-*al*-dīn, *regnant*	1848

ṢAFAVIDS*

- 1. Ismā'īl I
  - 2. Ṭahmāsp I
    - 3. Ismā'īl II
      - *Shāh Shujā'*
    - 4. Moḥammad Khudabanda
      - 5. 'Abbās I
        - *Ṣafī Mirza*
          - 6. Ṣafī I
            - 7. 'Abbās II
              - 8. Sulaymān
                - 9. Ḥosayn
                  - 10. Ṭahmāsp II
                    - 11. 'Abbās III
                    - Ḥosayn
                      - *Moḥammad Mirza*
                  - *Sāni*
                  - *daughter*
                    - Ismā'īl
                  - *daughter* = *Riẓā Ḳulī Afshārid*
                    - Shāh Rukh
      - *Ḥamza*
    - *Haydar*

* The pedigrees of the Shāhs of Persia are abridged from the *Catalogue of Persian Coins in the British Museum*, by R. S. Poole, LL.D.

AFSHĀRIDS

- *Imām Ḳulī*
  - *Ibrāhīm*
    - 2. 'Adil Shāh
    - 3. Ibrāhīm
  - 1. Nādir
    - Riẓā Ḳulī
      - 4. Shāh Rukh

ZANDS

- 1. Ḳarīm Khān
  - 2. Abū-l-Fatḥ
  - 4. Moḥammad 'Alī
- 5. Ṣādiḳ = *wife*
  - 6. Ja'far
    - 7. Luṭf 'Alī
  - 3. 'Alī Murād (son of the *wife*)
- *Zakī*

ḲĀJĀRS

- Moḥammad Ḥasan
  - 1. Āḳā Moḥammad
    - 2. Fatḥ 'Alī
      - *'Abbās*
        - 3. Moḥammad
          - 4. Nāṣir-*al*-dīn
      - *Ḥosayn*
      - *'Alī Ẓill-i Sulṭān*

XIII. TRANSOXIANA

SÆC. XIV–XIX

97. TĪMŪRIDS

98. SHAYBĀNIDS

99. JĀNIDS OF ASTRAKHĀN

100. MANGITS

101. KHĀNS OF KHOḲAND

102. KHĀNS OF KHIVA

XIII.—TRANSOXIANA

SÆC. XIV—XIX

A.H.		A.D.
771—906	97. TĪMŪRIDS	1369—1500

Tīmūr, or Tīmūr Lang (Tīmūr the Lame), commonly corrupted into Tamerlane, was related to the family of Chingiz Ḳaān, and one of his ancestors had been Vizīr to Chagatāy the son of Chingiz and ruler of Transoxiana. Tīmūr, who was born in 1335 (*736*), was appointed to the government of Kash by Tughā-Tīmūr, (p. 220), and became Vizīr to the Chagatāy Khān Suyurghātmish, whose authority he completely usurped before 1369 (*771*), though he allowed the Khān and his successor Maḥmūd to retain the nominal sovereignty until 1397 (*800*). In 1380 (*782*) Tīmūr began a long series of campaigns in Persia; and in seven years overran Khurāsān, Jurjān, Mazandarān, Sijistān, Afghānistān, Fārs, Adharbījān, and Kurdistan. An invasion by Tōḳtāmish, the Khān of the Golden Horde, called his attention nearer home in 1388, but in 1391 (*793*) he inflicted a total defeat on the Khān, which, however, had to be repeated in 1395

(*797*). Meanwhile in 1393 he had taken Baghdād from the Jalayrs, and had reduced Mesopotamia. In 1397 he entered northern India, and in the following year (*801*) raided Kashmīr and Dehlī. His next great movement was to the west. In 1401 he invaded Anatolia, and took Sīwās and Malatia; and in 1402 (*804*) totally routed the 'Othmānlī Turks at Angora and took Sulṭān Bāyazīd prisoner (p. 185). He reinstated the minor princes of Asia Minor, and, having subdued Syria and taken Aleppo and Damascus (*803*), he received the homage of their former possessor, the Mamlūk Sulṭān of Egypt. Whilst on the march for a still more ambitious campaign against China, Tīmūr died at Otrār, 1405 (*807*), aged 70.

The conquests of Tīmūr raised the kingdom of *Mā-warā*-l-*nahr* ('Beyond the River' Oxus) or Transoxiana to an importance it had never before attained. Samarḳand became the capital of an empire which stretched, in name at least, from Dehlī to Damascus, and from the Sea of Aral to the Persian Gulf; and although much of Tīmūr's conquest was rather a raid than an annexation, yet Transoxiana remained for some time the centre of a kingdom which embraced most of Persia and Afghānistān besides the provinces beyond the Oxus. But Tīmūr's empire was too unwieldy to be maintained in all its original vastness. When the petty dynasties of Persia, Karts and Sarbadārids, Muẓaffarids and Jalayrs, had been swept away, and the Turks had been driven out of Anatolia, and all Western Asia from the Hindū Kūsh to the Mediterranean trembled before one man, a reign of terror and not an organized empire had been established. As soon as the great conqueror was dead, Ottomans, Jalayrs and Turkomāns began to recover their lost provinces in the west. Although Tīmūr's descendants retained their hold of the north of Persia for a century, they were able to offer but a feeble resistance to the rising power of the Ṣafavids; and when in the sixteenth century the line of Shaybān (of the house of Chingiz) succeeded to the capital of Tamerlane, the dominions of his descendants had shrunk to the limits which the Khānate of Bukhārā long afterwards preserved. The table (facing p. 268) of Tīmūr's descendants, who struggled with one another for the disjointed fragments of his empire, shows one cause of their weakness; there were too many rivals. Shāh Rukh, indeed, for a while succeeded in subduing the jealousies of his kinsmen and maintaining the power and dignity of the empire; but after his death in 1447 (*850*) his dominions were split up into various petty principalities, which made way for the *Ṣafavids* in Persia and the *Shaybānids* in Transoxiana. Yet the line did not become extinct with the loss of Tīmūr's dominions. His descendant Bābar founded a new empire in Hindūstān which, known to us as that of the '*Great Moguls*,' lasted down to the present century (see XIV.).

A.H.		A.D.
771	Tīmūr	1369
	[771 Suyūrghātmish, nominal Khān	
	790-800 Maḥmūd ,, ,,]	
807–12	Khalīl	1404–9
807	Shāh Rukh	1404
850	Ulugh Beg	1447
853	'Abd-al-Laṭīf	1449
854	'Abd-Allāh	1450
855	Abū-Sa'īd	1452
872	Aḥmad	1467
899	Maḥmūd	1493
900	*Anarchy*	1494
—906		—1500

[*Shaybānids*]

THE DESCENDANTS OF TĪMŪR AND THEIR GOVERNMENTS

[To face p. 260]

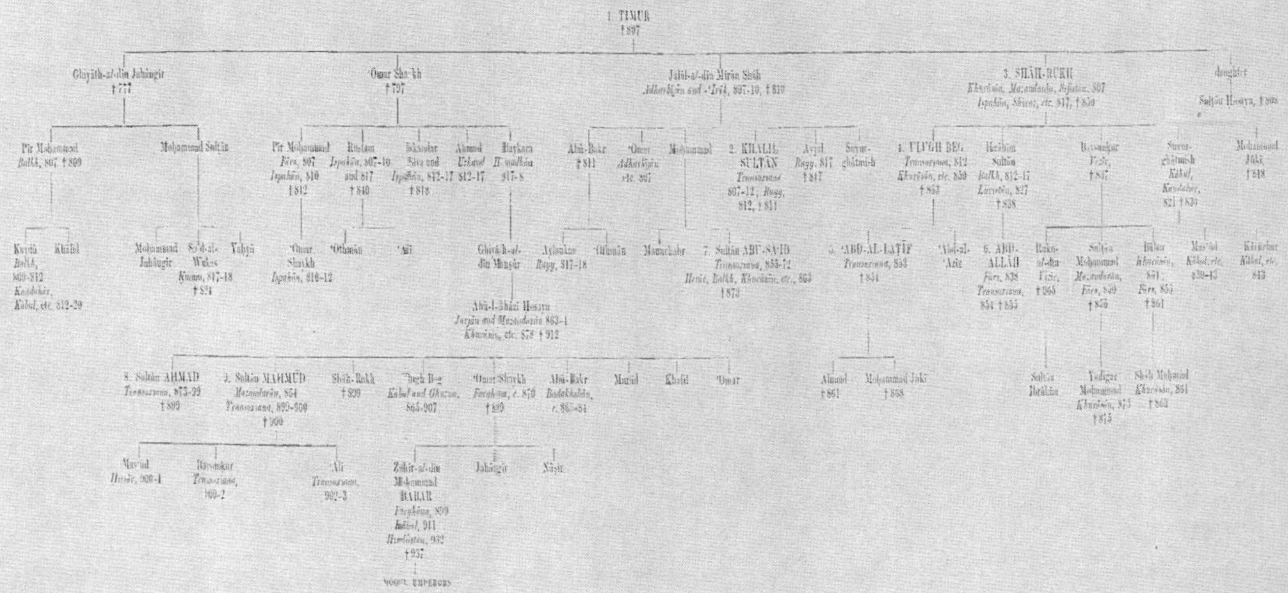

CONNEXION OF THE TRANSOXINE KHĀNATES

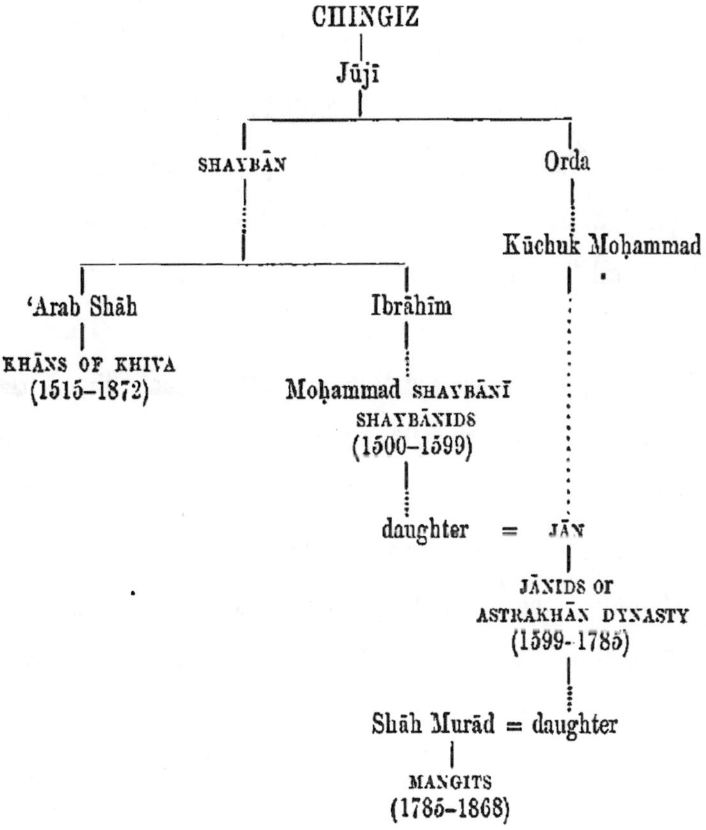

A.H.		A.D.
906—1007	98. SHAYBĀNIDS	1500—1599

Whilst the three sons of Maḥmūd, the last Tīmūrid Sulṭān of Transoxiana, were fighting over the ruins of an empire, a new power was approaching, which made an end of all the princes of Mā-warā-*l*-nahr and re-established a strong government in the place of anarchy. This was the Uzbeg horde led by Moḥammad Shaybānī, almost the last of the great warriors of the lineage of Chingiz. The early history of the family of Shaybān has been mentioned (pp. 238–40). Their home-line remained in Siberia as Czars of Tiumen; but a large proportion of the clan migrated to Transoxiana under Shaybānī, overthrew the rival princes of Tīmūr's line, and founded the Uzbeg kingdom, which survived in the Khānates of Bukhārā and Khiva until their submission to Russia within the last quarter of a century. This Uzbeg kingdom was ruled by several successive dynasties. First, the Shaybānids governed Transoxiana for the whole of the sixteenth century, leaving Khwārizm

(Khiva) to be ruled by its own line of Khāns (p. 278), who were also descended from Shaybān, and abandoning Khurāsān to the Ṣafavids. Next, the Jānids or Astrakhān dynasty, connected in the female line with the Shaybānids, governed the same gradually diminishing territory during the seventeenth and eighteenth centuries. Thirdly, their connexions by marriage, the Mangits, usurped the Khānate of Bukhārā, which was now greatly restricted by the growth of the neighbouring Khānate of Khoḳand, by the rise of various independent principalities at Tashkand, Uratippa, and elsewhere, and by the aggrandizement of the Durrānids of Afghānistan. Finally Bukhārā, Khiva, and Khoḳand, all fell before the aggression of Russia in 1868–1872.

A.H.		A.D.
906	Moḥammad Shaybānī	1500
916	Köchkünjī	1510
937	Abū-Sa'īd	1530
940	'Obayd-Allāh	1533
946	'Abd-Allāh I	1539
947	'Abd-al-Laṭīf	1540
959	Nūrūz Aḥmad	1551
963	Pīr Moḥammad I	1555
968	Iskandar	1560
991	'Abd-Allāh II	1583
1006	'Abd-al-Mu'min	1598
1007	Pīr Moḥammad II	1599

[*Astrakhān*]

Samarḳand was the capital of the Shaybānids, but there was generally a powerful, and sometimes independent, government at Bukhārā. More than once the governor of Bukhārā was practically the ruler of Transoxiana, and this province became almost as much the Dauphiné of Samarḳand under the Shaybānids as Balkh was under the succeeding dynasty of Astrakhān.

SUB-DYNASTY OF BUKHĀRĀ

A.H.		A.D.
947	'Abd-al-'Azīz	1540
957	Yār Moḥammad	1549
961	Burhān Sulṭān	1553
964	'Abd-Allāh (*who united Sāmarḳand in* 986, *and became from* 991 *'Abd-Allāh* II *of the Chief Khānate, q. v.*)	1556

SUB-DYNASTY OF SAMARḲAND

968	Khusrū Sulṭīn	1560
975	Sulṭān Sa'īd	1567
980	Juvanmard 'Alī	1572
986	*'Abd-Allāh of Bukhārā*	1578

SHAYBÂNIDS

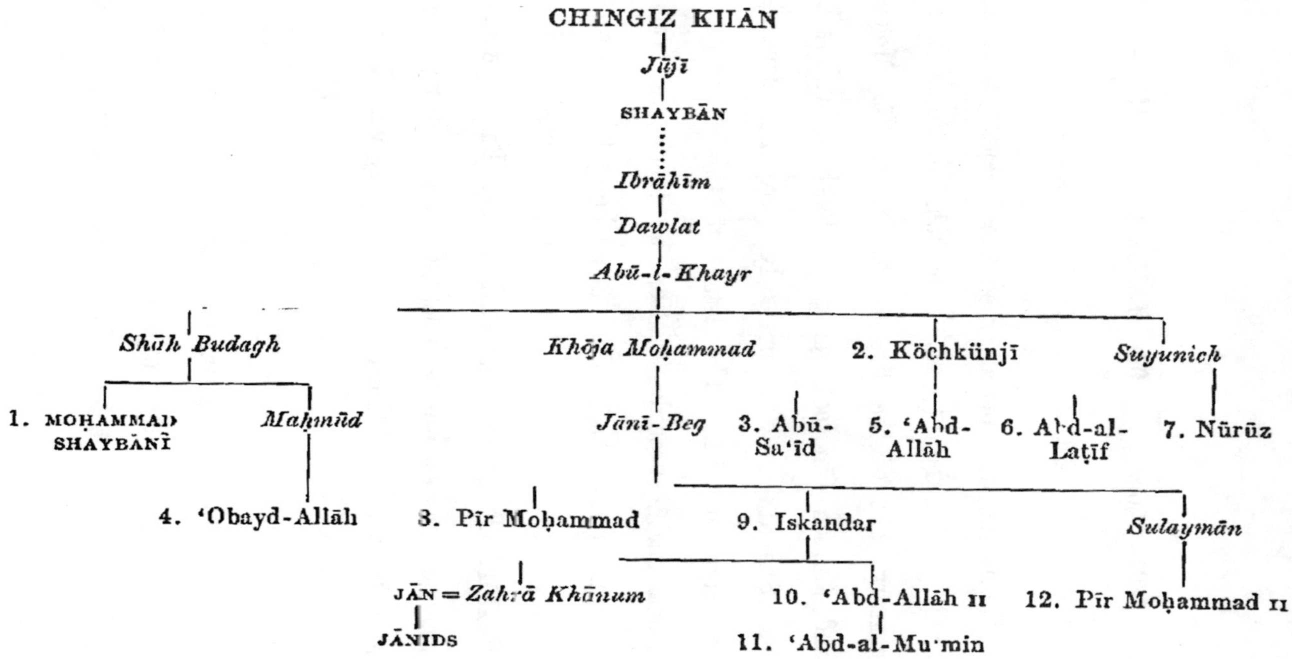
CHINGIZ KHĀN
Jūjī
SHAYBĀN
Ibrāhīm
Dawlat
Abū-l-Khayr
Shāh Budagh
Khōja Moḥammad
2. Köchkünjī
Suyunich
1. MOḤAMMAD SHAYBĀNĪ
Maḥmūd
Jānī-Beg
3. Abū-Sa'īd
5. 'Abd-Allāh
6. Abd-al-Laṭīf
7. Nūrūz
4. 'Obayd-Allāh
8. Pīr Moḥammad
9. Iskandar
Sulaymān
JĀN = Zahrā Khānum
JĀNIDS
10. 'Abd-Allāh II
11. 'Abd-al-Mu'min
12. Pīr Moḥammad II

A.H.		A.D.
1007—1200	99. JĀNIDS	1599—1785

OR ASTRAKHĀN DYNASTY

When the Russians absorbed the Khānate of Astrakhān or Ḥājjī Tarkhān (p. 229) in the middle of the 16th century, two of the dispossessed chiefs, Yār Moḥammad and his son Jān took refuge at Bukhārā with Iskandar the Shaybānid, who presently gave his daughter in marriage to Jān. The issue of this marriage, Bāḳī Moḥammad, succeeded (after a year's interval) his maternal uncle 'Abd-Allāh II, and he and his descendants, during most of the 17th century, ruled Samarḳand, Bukhārā, Farghāna, Badakhshān, and Balkh, which last province was sometimes independent. Their power gradually decayed; the Durrānids eventually gained possession of all their Cisoxine territories (1752 ff.); a rival Khānate sprang up at Khoḳand (Farghāna) about 1700; and the Jānids were finally ousted in 1785 by the chiefs of the Mangit tribe, who had possessed the real power for some years before the actual dethronement of the last Jānid, Abū-l-Ghāzī.

A.H.		A.D.
1007	Bāḳī Moḥammad	1599
1014	Vālī Moḥammad*	1605
1017	Imām Ḳulī († 1060)	1608
1050	Nādir Moḥammad († 1061) . . .	1640
1057	'Abd-al-'Azīz	1647
1091	Subḥān Ḳulī †	1680
1114	'Obayd-Allāh ‡	1702
1117	Abū-l-Fayḍ §	1705
1160	'Abd-al-Mu'min	1747
1164	'Obayd-Allāh II	1751
1167	*Moḥammad Raḥīm* (*Mangit*) . .	1753
1171	Abū-l-Ghāzī	1758
—1200		—1785

[*Mangits*]

* Governed Balkh from 1007.

† Previously ruled Balkh for 23 years.

‡ Makīm Khān held Balkh 1111 1119.

§ Ruled only beyond the Oxus.

JĀNIDS AND MANGITS

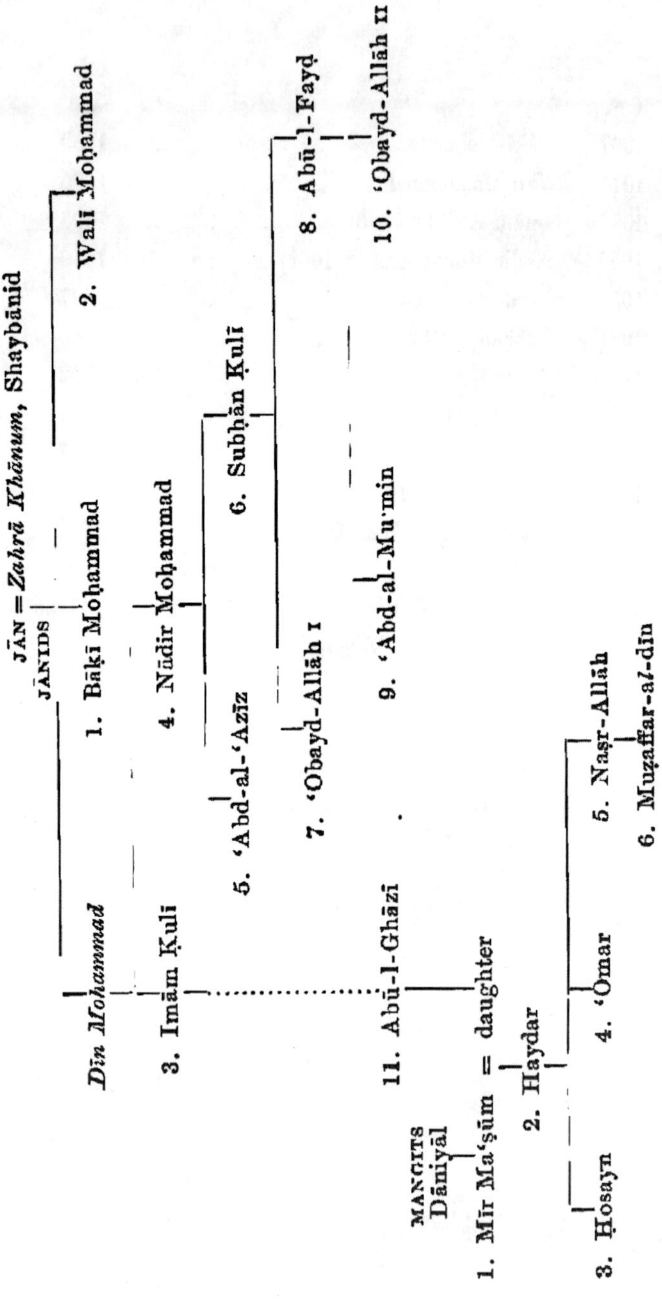

A.H.		A.D.
1200—1284	100. MANGITS	1785—1868

The Mangits, or "Flat-noses," a tribe akin to the Nogāys, left their Kipchak camping-grounds to follow the fortunes of Moḥammad Shaybānī at the beginning of the 16th century. Under the Astrakhān dynasty they gradually increased in influence, and in the second half of the eighteenth century their chiefs became the vizīrs of the rulers of Bukhārā and eventually supplanted their masters. Their dominions had shrunk considerably from the wide extent of the Shaybānids' kingdom, and Ma'ṣūm Shāh's wars with the Durrānids for the recovery of the Cisoxine territory were rewarded with but temporary success. The present Khān has been tributary to Russia since the campaign of 1868.

A.H.		A.D.
1200	Mīr Ma'ṣūm Shāh Murād	1785
1215	Ḥaydar Tora	1800
1242	Ḥosayn	1826
1242	'Omar	1826
1242	Naṣr-Allāh	1827
1277	Muẓaffar-al-dīn	1860
—1284	*Tributary to Russia*	—1868

A.H. c. 921—1289 — 101. KHĀNS OF KHIVA — A.D. c. 1515—1872

Khwārizm or Khiva, which had once furnished an ambitious line of Shāhs of its own (p. 176), was an appanage of the house of Jūjī, and never properly belonged to the Khānate of Transoxiana; up to the time of Tīmūr it was held by the Golden Horde. After the confusion of the Tīmūrīd period, the Uzbegs of Moḥammad Shaybānī occupied Khiva as well as Transoxiana, and about 1515 an independent Uzbeg Khānate was established there, the early history of which is exceedingly obscure. Wars were constantly waged with Bukhārā with varying success. Nādir Shāh of Persia conquered Khiva in 1740 and a Persian governor ruled there for a year. Finally General Kaufmann annexed it on the part of Russia in 1872.

A.H.		A.D.
c. 921	Ilbars I	c. 1515
c. 931	Sulṭān Ḥājjī	c. 1525
	Ḥasan Ḳulī	
	Ṣufyān	
	Bujugha	
	Avanak	
	Kal	
c. 946	Akatāy	c. 1540
953	Dost	1546

A.H.		A.D.
965	Ḥājjī Moḥammad I	1558
1011	ʻArab Moḥammad I	1602
1032	Isfandiyār	1623
1053	Abū-l-Ghāzī I	1643
1074	Anusha	1663
c. 1085	Moḥammad Arank	c. 1674
1099	Isḥāḳ Aḳā Shāh Niyāz	1687
1114	ʻArab Moḥammad II	1702
	Ḥājjī Moḥammad II	
1126	Yadighār	1714
1126	Arank	1714
1127	Shīr Ghāzī	1715
114*x*	Ilbars II	173*x*
1153	*Annexation by Nādir Shāh*	1740
1154	*Tagir (for Nādir Shāh)*	1741
1154	Abū-Moḥammad	1741
115*x*	Abū-l-Ghāzī II	174*x*
1158	Kaip	1745
c. 1184	Abū-l-Ghāzī III	c. 1770
1219	Iltazar	1804
1221	Moḥammad Raḥīm	1806
1241	Allāh Ḳulī	1825
1258	Raḥīm Ḳulī	1842
1261	Moḥammad Amīn	1845
1271	ʻAbd-Allāh	1855
1272	Ḳutlugh Moḥammad	1855
1272?	Sayyid Moḥammad	1856?
1282	Sayyid Moḥammad Raḥīm	1865
—1289	[*Annexation by Russia*]	—1872

A.H. c. 1112—1293 102. KHĀNS OF KHOḲAND A.D. c. 1700—1876

Shāh Rukh, who claimed to be a descendant of Chingiz Khān, made himself independent in Farghāna and founded the Khānate of Khoḳand about 1700. The chronology of the earlier Khāns is uncertain. In 1800 Tāshkand was annexed by Khoḳand. The Khānate passed into the possession of Russia in 1876.

A.H.		A.D.
c. 1112	Shāh Rukh Beg	c. 1700
	Raḥīm	
	'Abd-al-Ḳarīm	
	Erdeni	
1184	Sulaymān	1770
1184	Shāh Rukh II	1770
1184?	Narbuta	1770?
1215	'Ālim	1800
1224	Moḥammad 'Omar	1809
1237	Moḥammad 'Alī	1822
c. 1256	Shīr 'Alī	1840
1261	Murād	1841
c. 1261	Khudāyār	1845
1273	Malla	1857
1275	Shāh Murād	1859
c. 1277	Khudāyār (*2nd reign*)	1861
c. 1280	Sayyid Sulṭān	1864
1288	Khudāyār (*3rd reign*)	1871
1292	Nāṣir-al-dīn	1875
—1293	[*Annexed by Russia*]	—1876

XIV. INDIA

AND AFGHĀNISTĀN

SÆC. X—XIX

103. GHAZNAWIDS
104. GHŌRIDS
105. SULṬĀNS OF DEHLĪ
106. KINGS OF BENGAL
107. KINGS OF JAUNPŪR
108. KINGS OF MĀLWA
109. KINGS OF GUJARĀT
110. KINGS OF KHĀNDĒSH
111. BAHMANIDS OF THE DECCAN
112. 'IMĀD SHĀHS OF BERĀR
113. NIẒAM SHĀHS OF AḤMADNAGAR
114. BARĪD SHĀHS OF BĪDAR
115. 'ĀDIL SHĀHS OF BĪJĀPŪR
116. ḲUṬB SHĀHS OF GOLKONDA
117. MOGUL EMPERORS OF HINDŪSTĀN
118. AMĪRS OF AFGHĀNISTĀN

XIV. INDIA

AND AFGHĀNISTĀN

SÆC. X–XIX

No considerable part of India ever belonged to the Caliphate. Soon after their conquest of Herāt, indeed, the Arabs pushed on to Kābul in 664 (*44*) and thence descended to Multān; but this reconnaissance did not lead to continuous occupation. An advance from the south produced more permanent results. Piratical expeditions by sea to the mouths of the Indus were frequent in the early days of Islām, and in 711 (*92*) Moḥammad Ḳāsim, a nephew of -Ḥajjāj, the celebrated governor of -Baṣra, conquered Sind from the coast as far as Multān, and although no attempt was made to enlarge this dominion, the province continued to be ruled by Arab governors for nearly two centuries.

The conquest of Hindūstān by the Moḥammadans, however, sprang not from Sind but from Afghānistān. The early annexation by the Arabs of the mountainous country south of the Hindū Kūsh had been nominal and temporary, and Ya'ḳūb b. Layth the Ṣaffārid of Sijistān (p. 129) was the first to establish a settled Moḥammadan government at Kābul. Here his dynasty was succeeded by governors appointed by the Sāmānids (p. 131), and it was Alptigīn, one of the local governors of the Sāmānids, who laid the foundations at Ghazna of the first independent Moḥammadan dynasty in Afghānistān.

Henceforward for two centuries Ghazna was the capital of a powerful dynasty to which it gave the name of *Ghaznawids.* The incursions of the Ghaznawids into India and their settlement at Lahore formed the true beginning of Muslim rule in Hindūstān. The Ghaznawid kingdom at Lahore prepared the way for Moḥammad b. Sām the Ghōrid and his successors the Sulṭāns of Dehlī, who brought the whole of northern India under Moḥammadan sway. The invasion of the Mongols under Bābar put an end to the divisions which had weakened the Dehlī kingdom in its later years, and Bābar's grandson Akbar organized the splendid Empire of the Great Moguls which lasted down to the present century.

A.H.		A.D.
351—582	103. GHAZNAWIDS	962—1186

(AFGHĀNISTĀN AND PANJĀB)

Among the Turkish slaves whom the Sāmānid princes delighted to honour with the chief posts in the government of their dominions, Alptigīn rose by favour of 'Abd-al-Malik to be commander of the forces in Khurāsān, but, being deprived of this office on the death of his patron, he retired in dudgeon in 962 (*351*) to the city of Ghazna, in the heart of the Sulaymān mountains, where his father had been governor under the Sāmānids, and where the son had succeeded to his authority. In the mountain fastnesses he could safely defy the ill-will of his masters in the plains; but he died in a year's time without enlarging the dominion he had assumed; nor did his son Isḥāḳ or his slave Balkātigīn enhance the power of the Ghaznawids. The true founder of the dynasty was Sabaktigīn, another slave of Alptigīn, and the husband of his daughter. Sabaktigīn widened his territories on both sides; in India by the defeat of the Rājputs and the establishment of a government at Peshāwar: in Persia by the acquisition of Khurāsān, of which he was appointed governor by the Sāmānid Nūḥ in 994 (*384*) in reward for his assistance in quelling a rebellion in Transoxiana. Sabaktigīn out of loyalty or prudence accepted the position of a vassal of the Sāmānids, but the vassalage was nominal; he had become more powerful than his liege-lord before his death in 997 (*387*).

Maḥmūd of Ghazna, the son of Sabaktigīn, is one of the greatest figures in Moḥammadan history. After overcoming his younger brother Ismā'īl, who had forced a contest, he repudiated the supremacy of the feeble representative of the Sāmānids, and received an investiture for the governments of Khurāsān and Ghazna direct from the Caliph of Baghdād, 'the dispenser of powers which he himself no longer enjoyed.'* Having made peace with his powerful neighbours the Īlak Khāns, who were then giving the *coup de grâce* to the expiring Sāmānids, Maḥmūd began a series of campaigns in India. Twelve several

* It is commonly asserted that Maḥmūd then adopted the title of Sulṭān, which had never before been assumed by a Moḥammadan ruler: but the statement is not warranted by his coins, whereon he styles himself occasionally Amīr and Sayyid, and very rarely Malik, but never Sulṭān. The first of the dynasty to use the new title was Ibrāhīm, who doubtless imitated the Seljūḳs, who were the earliest to adopt the style of Sulṭān, according to the evidence of the coins. It is singular that this first of Indian Sulṭāns should be described as a 'professed devotee,' who copied Ḳorāns and left seventy-six children.

times, between 1001 and 1024, he descended from his highlands into the plains of Hindūstān, and, gradually enlarging the scope of his expeditions, beyond Kashmīr and the Panjāb, at length he occupied Kanauj and Muttra (1017) and seized Sōmnāth and Anhalwāra, the capital of Gujarāt, 1024 (*415*). These expeditions were more or less raids undertaken with a view to plunder and to satisfy the righteous iconoclasm of a true Muslim, and the 'Idol-Breaker' returned to Ghazna laden with costly spoils from the Hindū temples of Sōmnāth and Muttra; but they led to far-reaching results. The way into India had been opened; the Panjāb had been permanently annexed; and the kingdom of Gujarāt had accepted a rāja from the hands of its conqueror.

Besides his Indian wars, Maḥmūd beat off the attack of the Īlak Khān, reduced Ghōr (1010) and the country of the Upper Marghāb (1012), and even annexed Transoxiana with its two great cities of Samarḳand and Bukhārā in 1016 (*407*). Towards the close of his reign he discovered a serious danger in the growing power of the Seljūḳ chiefs Ṭughril and Chagar Beg, whom he had at first unwisely encouraged; but, after reducing them to apparent submission in 1027 (*418*), he did not live to witness their final triumph. On his return from an expedition into the heart of the old Caliphate, in which he took Iṣpahān from the Buwayhids (p. 142), Maḥmūd died at Ghazna in the spring of 1030 (*421*). His magnificent encouragement of science, art, and literature, was no less remarkable than his genius as a general and statesman. He founded and endowed a university at Ghazna, and his munificence drew together perhaps the most splendid 'assemblage of literary genius,' including the poet Firdausī, that any Asiatic capital has ever contained.* Ghazna was enriched with palaces and mosques, aqueducts and public works, beyond any city of its age: for Maḥmūd had known how to learn from India, as well as how to plunder it.

The empire which had thus been founded stretched from Lahore to Samarḳand and Iṣpahān; but it was soon lopped of its western limbs. In a few years the Seljūḳs (p. 151), after defeating Mas'ūd the son of Maḥmūd near Merv, had taken possession of all the Persian and Transoxine provinces of the Ghaznawids, from Balkh and Khwārizm to Iṣpahān and Rayy (1037–1045); and the rulers of Ghazna learned to turn their eyes to the east, now that the west was closed to them. Lahore

* Elphinstone, *History of India*, 341–5 (5th ed. 1866).

became their capital when Ghazna fell to the Ghōrids in 1161. Thus the losses in the west confirmed the settlement in Hindūstān, and when in 1186 (*582*) the successors of of Maḥmūd, who had not emulated his ambition, gave place to the hardy Afghāns of Ghōr, the Indian provinces soon separated from the highlands; and thus began the series of independent Moḥammadan dynasties of India.

A.H.		A.D.
351	Alptigīn	962
352	Isḥāḳ	963
355	Balkātigīn*	966
362	Pīrī	972
366	Sabaktagīn	976
387	Ismā'īl	997
388	Maḥmūd, Yamīn-al-dawla	998
421	Moḥammad, Jalāl-al-dawla	1030
421	Mas'ūd I, Nāṣir-dīn-Allāh	1030
432	Mōdūd, Shihāb-al-dawla	1040
440	Mas'ūd II	1048
440	'Alī Abu-l-Ḥasan, Baha-al-dawla	1048
440	'Abd-al-Rashīd, 'Izz-al-dawla	1049
444	*Ṭughril* (usurper)	1052
444	Farrukhzād, Jamāl-al-dawla	1052
451	Ibrāhīm, Ẓahīr-al-dawla	1059
492	Mas'ūd III, 'Alā-al-dawla	1099
508	Shīrzād, Kamāl-al-dawla	1114
509	Arslān, Sulṭān-al-dawla	1115
512	Bahrām Shāh, Yamīn-al-dawla	1118
547	Khusrū Shāh, Mu'izz-al-dawla	1152
555	Khusrū Malik, Tāj-al-dawla	1160
—582	[*Ghōrids*]	—1186

* On the chronology of the early Ghaznawids see E. E. Oliver, *The Decline of the Sāmānīs*, in *Journ. As. Soc. Bengal*, lv. pt. i. 1886.

GHAZNAWIDS

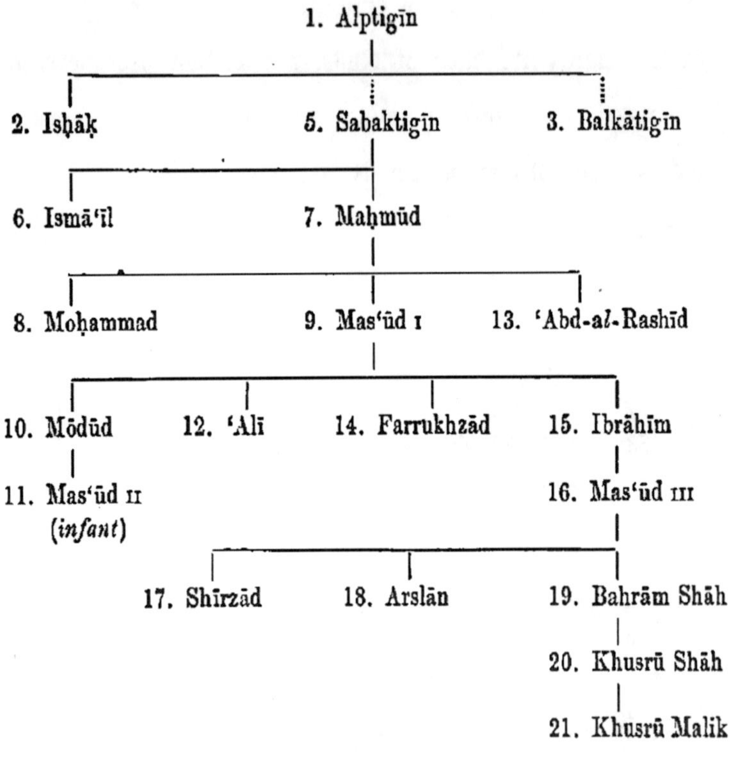

(..... Dotted lines indicate the relation of master to slave.)

A.H. 543—612 — 104. GHŌRIDS — A.D. 1148—1215

104. GHŌRIDS

(AFGHĀNISTĀN, HINDŪSTĀN)

From early times the mountainous district of Ghōr (or Ghūr), between Herāt and Ghazna, had been the seat of a small but practically independent dynasty, who usually made the fortress of Fīrūz-kōh their headquarters. Maḥmūd of Ghazna had reduced this principality in 1010 (*401*), when the Afghāns of Ghōr were ruled by Moḥammad b. Sūrī; and the descendants of this chief continued to govern at Fīrūz-kōh and Bāmiyān under the orders of the Ghaznawids, with whom they allied themselves by marriage. The execution of one of the family (Ḳuṭb-al-dīn Moḥammad) by his father-in-law Bahrām Shāh the Ghaznawid was avenged by the capture of Ghazna in 1148 (*543*) by the murdered man's brother, Sayf-al-dīn Sūrī, the ruler of Ghōr; but in the following year Bahrām Shāh succeeded in re-entering his capital, and tortured the invader to death. This second act of barbarity brought down a signal punishment upon Ghazna at the hands of a third brother, 'Alā-al-dīn Ḥosayn, surnamed Jahān-sōz, or 'world-incendiary,' from the ferocity with which he gave up the splendid city of Maḥmūd the idol-breaker to fire and sword. Contemptuously leaving the ashes of Ghazna, 'Alā-al-dīn returned to Ghōr; and after a brief captivity in the hands of Sulṭān Sinjar the Seljūḳ of Khurāsān, he died in 1161 (*556*) in a time of anarchy, when the Ghuzz Turkomāns swept over Afghānistān and for a while abolished both Ghōrid and Ghaznawid governments.

The Ghuzz soon wended their migratory way into Persia, and on their departure two brothers, nephews of the 'World-Incendiary,' became the leaders of the Ghōrid family. The elder, Ghiyāth-al-dīn b. Sām, had taken Ghazna from the Ghuzz in 1173 (*569*), and annexed Herāt two years later. He remained titular sovereign of all the wide possessions of his family until his death in 1202 (*599*). The younger brother, however, Shihāb-al-dīn, afterwards styled Mu'izz-al-dīn, and commonly known as Moḥammad Ghōrī, was the real ruler and extender of the kingdom. He conquered part of Khurāsān from the Seljūḳs, and then began a series of campaigns in India, in which he reduced Sind and Multan (*571*), where Arab governors had made Muslim rule familiar; subdued the Ghaznawids in their last retreat at Lahore in 1186 (*582*); and then proceeded to attack the leader of the Chohān Rājputs, Prithwī Rāja of Ajmīr. His first onslaught was repulsed with terrible loss (*587*), but in the following year, 1192, a hard-fought battle on the same field of Thaneswar ended in the total defeat of the Rājputs, and the death of Prithwī Rāja and many others of the 150 princes who had assembled for the defence of Hindūstān. The victory meant nothing less than the submission of nearly the whole of northern India; for Kanauj fell in 1194, and Gwāliōr, Bandalkhand, Bihār, and Bengal were successively reduced by the generals of Moḥammad Ghōrī. For the first time the whole of Hindūstān admitted, in a greater or less degree, Moḥammadan sway.

So long as his brother lived, Moḥammad Ghōrī always remained a loyal viceroy, but on Ghiyāth-a*l*-dīn's death in 1202 (*599*) he succeeded to the supreme authority, when his first duty was to defend his realm against the Khwārizm Shāh, who had overrun Persia and was forcing his way into Afghānistān. In the midst of the confusion of this invasion, Moḥammad Ghōrī was assassinated by a party of Ghakkars in 1206 (*602*). His dynasty did not long survive him. His nephew Maḥmūd was indeed proclaimed Sulṭān throughout the wide dominions conquered by the uncle; but the unity of the kingdom vanished with its founder. The Turkish slaves who had served as generals under Moḥammad Ghōrī assumed independent power. Ḳuṭb-al-dīn Aybak became the first of the Slave Kings of Dehlī; Nāṣir-al-dīn Kubācha ruled in Sind; and Yildiz governed Ghazna. The titular successor of the great Ghōrid, from his capital of Fīrūz-kōh, reigned over little more than western Afghānistān (Ghōr and Herāt) with part of Khurāsān; and from all these the Ghōrids were expelled by the armies of the *Khwārizm Shāh* in 1215 (*612*). Long afterwards, however, their descendants recovered some relics of their ancient dominions, and the *Kart* princes of Herāt traced their origin to the family of Moḥammad Ghōrī.

The opposite table shows the relationship and places of government of the chief members of the Ghōrid family.*

* For further details see E. Thomas, *Supplementary Contributions to the Series of the Coins of the Kings of Ghaznī* (1859).

To face p. 294)

GHORIDS

1. Izz-al-dīn Ḥasan (*Ghōr*)
   - Kuṭb-al-dīn Moḥammad (*Fīrūz-kōh*; killed by Bahrām Shāh)
   - 2. Sayf-al-dīn Sūrī (*Ghōr*; *Ghazna*, 543–4; killed by Bahrām Shāh, 544)
     - 9. ʿAlā-al-dīn Atsuz (*Ghōr*, 607–610)
   - 3. ʿAlā-al-dīn Ḥesayn Jahānsōz (*Ghōr*, 544–556; *Ghazna*, 550)
     - 4. Sayf-al-dīn Moḥammad (*Ghōr*, 556–8)
   - Bahā-al-dīn Sām (*Fīrūz-kōh*, 544)
     - 5. Ghiyāth-al-dīn Moḥammad (*Ghōr*, 558; *Herāt*, 571; † 599)
       - 7. Maḥmūd (*Bost*, 599; *Ghōr and Fīrūz-kōh*, 603; † 607)
         - 8. Bahā-al-dīn Sām (*Ghōr*, etc., 607)
     - 6. Shihāb-al-dīn Muʿizz-al-dīn Moḥammad Ghōrī (*Ghazna*, 569; *Sind*, 571; *Lahore*, 582; *Hindūstān*, 588 ff.; *Ghōr and Ghazna*, 599; † 602)
   - *Shihāb-al-dīn Moḥammad (*Mādīn*)
   - Shujāʿ-al-dīn ʿAlī (*Khirmās*)
     - 10. ʿAlā-al-dīn Moḥammad (*Ghōr and Fīrūz-kōh*, [under 6]; 599–603; *restored* 610; surrenders to *Khwārizm Shāh* 612)
   - BAMIYAN LINE
     - i. Fakhr-al-dīn Masʿūd (550–?)
       - ii. Shams-al-dīn Moḥammad
         - iii. Bahā-al-dīn Sām † 602
           - ʿAlā-al-dīn (*Ghazna*, 602–3)
           - iv. Jalāl-al-dīn 602–9 (killed by *Khwārizm Shāh*)

A.H.		A.H.
602—962	105. SULṬĀNS OF DEHLĪ	1206—1554

(HINDŪSTĀN)

Moḥammad Ghōrī, after conquering northern India to the mouth of the Ganges, either by his own campaigns or by those of his generals, appointed his slave Ḳuṭb-*al*-dīn Aybak to act as his viceroy at Dehlī; and on the death of the master in 1206 (*602*) the slave proclaimed himself sovereign of Hindūstān, and founded the first Moḥammadan dynasty which ruled exclusively in India; for hitherto Moḥammadan India had been but an outlying province of the kingdom of Ghazna. This dynasty, the first of five which preceded the Mogul conquest, is commonly known as the *Slave Kings*. The greatest of the line was Altamish (more correctly Īltutmish), who subdued the governor of Sind, Nāṣir-*al*-dīn Kubācha; compelled the viceroy of Bengal to acknowledge the supremacy of Dehlī; repelled the attempt of Yildiz to revive in India the kingdom of which the Khwārizm Shāh had robbed him at Ghazna; and in turn withstood the attempts of Jalāl-al-dīn, the son of that Shāh, to set up his rule in Hindūstān when driven over the Hindū-Kūsh by the Mongols of Chingiz Khān. Fortunately for India these Mongols stopped short at the Indus, though their raids were a frequent source of alarm for many years. Altamish vigorously maintained his authority over the whole country north of the Vindhya mountains; and the Caliph of Baghdād, for the first time recognizing a distinct Moḥammadan kingdom of India, gave its sovereign the sanction of a formal diploma of investiture from the spiritual head of Islām. Riḍīya, the daughter of Altamish, was the only woman who ever sat on the throne of Dehlī, until Queen Victoria figuratively took her seat there in 1858. Under the later Slave Kings the Hindūs began to pluck up the courage which had oozed away before the arms of Moḥammad Ghōrī and Altamish; and Balban had to sternly suppress many serious native outbreaks, which were in some degree the fruit of his policy of getting rid of the Slave governors—a policy which led to the subversion of his own dynasty.

The *Khaljī* Turks, the second Muslim dynasty of India, began to extend Moḥammadan rule beyond the Vindhyas into the Deccan. 'Alā-*al*-dīn Moḥammad re-conquered Gujarāt, 1297; took Chitōr and temporarily subdued the Rājputs, 1303; and his eunuch general Malik Kāfūr seized Deogīri and Warangal, and founded a Deccan province of the Dehlī kingdom. The extent of the dominion, however, tended towards disruption. After power had again changed hands, and a Turkish slave had established the *Taghlaḳid* dynasty, Moḥammad b. Taghlaḳ, a man of remarkable but bizarre genius, perceived the impossibility of ruling the Deccan from Dehlī, and accordingly sought to transplant by force both court and population from the northern capital to Deogīri, which he re-named Dawlatābād, the 'seat of government.' But he could not check the disintegrating process which had begun; whole provinces revolted, and he was ever on the wing from end to end of his empire to suppress rebellion; and his successors were forced to witness the separation of province after province from the central stock, until the Sulṭān of Dehlī sometimes commanded but a small district round his capital. The invasion of Tīmūr, who turned northern India into a shambles in 1398–9, hastened the catastrophe. The *Sayyids* and *Lōdīs*, who followed the house of Taghlaḳ, held but one government out of the many that now prevailed in Hindūstān. Bengal, Jaunpūr, Mālwa, and Gujarāt were the seats of independent Moḥammadan dynasties, and the Rājputs and the Hindūs of the Deccan had recovered much of their former possessions.

The irruption of the Moguls under Bābar, who established his authority over most of northern India, save Bengal, in 1526–30, was too brief to accomplish the work of re-uniting the scattered fragments of the empire of 'Alā-*al*-dīn the Khaljī. After Bābar's death the Moguls were driven out of India by Shīr Shāh and the Afghāns of Bengal 1539–40 (*946–7*), and the courage and genius of the Afghān conqueror almost availed to restore the waning prestige of the Moḥammadan power. But the provinces refused to obey an Afghān sovereign, and their disunion opened the way for the return of Bābar's son Humāyūn in 1554 (*962*) and the establishment under Akbar of the famous Mogul Empire, which lasted to the present century.

A. SLAVE KINGS

A.H.		A.D.
602	Aybak, Ḳuṭb-a*l*-dīn	1206
607	Ārām Shāh	1210
607	Altamish (Iltutmish), Shams-a*l*-dīn	1210
633	Fīrūz Shāh I, Rukn-a*l*-dīn	1235
634	Riḍīya	1236
637	Bahrām Shāh, Mu'izz-a*l*-dīn	1239
639	Mas'ūd Shāh, 'Alā-a*l*-dīn	1241
644	Maḥmūd Shāh I, Nāṣir-a*l*-dīn	1246
664	Balban, Ghiyāth-a*l*-dīn	1265
686	Kay-Ḳubād, Mu'izz-a*l*-dīn	1287

B. KHALJĪS

A.H.		A.D.
689	Fīrūz Shāh II, Jalāl-a*l*-dīn	1290
695	Ibrāhīm Shāh I, Rukn-a*l*-dīn	1295
695	Moḥammad Shāh I, 'Alā-a*l*-dīn	1295
715	'Omar Shāh, Shihāb-a*l*-dīn	1315
716	Mubārak Shāh I, Ḳuṭb-a*l*-dīn	1316
720	Khusrū Shāh, Nāṣir-a*l*-dīn	1320

C. TAGHLAḲIDS

A.H.		A.D.
720	Taghlaḳ Shāh I, Ghiyāth-al-dīn	1320
725	Moḥammad II b. Taghlaḳ	1324
752	Fīrūz Shāh III	1351
790	Taghlaḳ Shāh II	1388
791	Abū-Bakr Shāh	1388
792	Moḥammad Shāh III	1389
795	Sikandar Shāh I	1392
795	Maḥmūd Shāh II	1392
797	Naṣrat Shāh (*interregnum*)	1394
802	Maḥmūd II *restored*	1399
815	Dawlat Khān Lōdī	1412

D. SAYYIDS

817	Khiḍr Khān	1414
824	Mubārak Shāh II, Mu'izz-al-dīn	1421
837	Moḥammad Shāh IV	1433
847	'Ālim Shāh	1443

E. LŌDĪS

855	Bahlōl Lōdī	1451
894	Sikandar II b. Bahlōl	1488
923	Ibrāhīm II b. Sikandar	1517
—930	*Invasion of Bābar*	—1526

F. AFGHĀNS

946	Shīr Shāh	1539
952	Islām Shāh	1545
960	Moḥammad v. 'Adil Shāh	1552
961	Ibrāhīm III Sūr	1553
962	Sikandar Shāh III	1554

[*Mogul Emperors*]

A. SLAVE KINGS

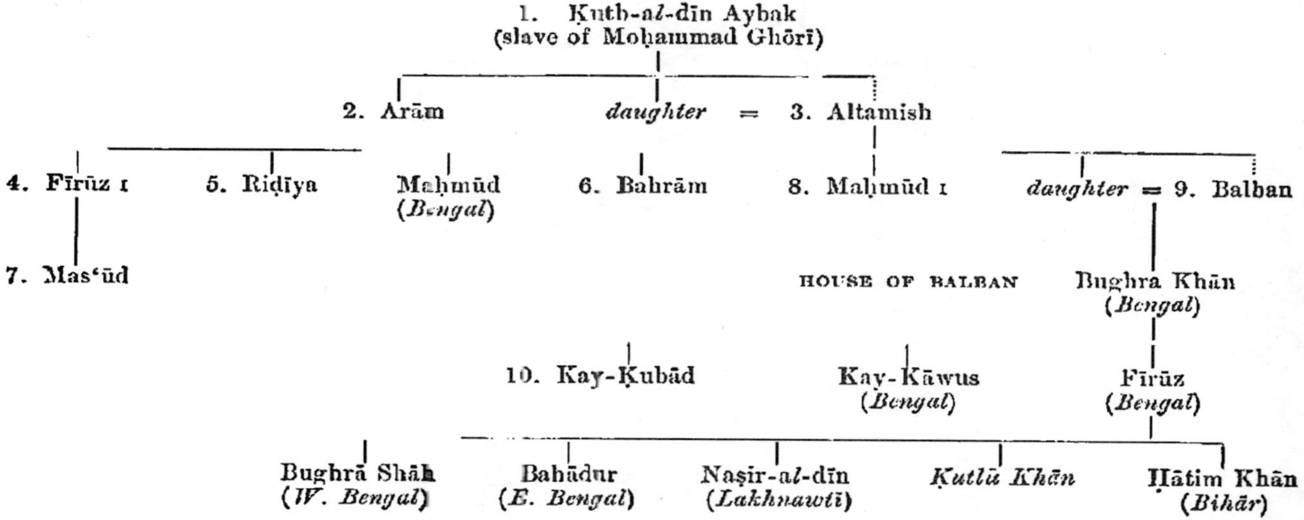

B. KHALJĪS

- 11. Fīrūz II
  - 12. Ibrāhīm I
- *x*
  - 13. Moḥammad I
    - 14. 'Omar
    - 15. Mubārak I
      - 16. Khusrū

C. TAGHLĀḲIDS

- 17. Taghlaḳ I
  - 18. Moḥammad Jūnā
    - *Maḥmūd*
- *Sipāh-Salār Rajab*
  - 19. Fīrūz III
    - Fatḥ
      - 20. Taghlaḳ II
      - 25. Naṣrat
    - Ẓafar
      - 21. Abū-Bakr
    - 22. Moḥammad III
      - 23. Sikandar I
      - 24. Maḥmūd II

D. SAYYIDS

- 27. Khiḍr
  - 28. Mubārak II
  - *Farīd*
    - 29. Moḥammad IV
      - 30. ʻĀlim

F. AFGHĀNS

- 34. Shīr Shāh
  - 35. Islām Shāh
    - *Fīrūz*
- *x*
  - 36. Moḥammad ʻĀdil
    - *Shīr Khān*
- *Ghāzī Khān Sūr*
  - 37. Ibrāhīm III Sūr
- 38. Sikandar III

PROVINCIAL DYNASTIES OF INDIA

The Empire of Moḥammad b. Taghlaḳ included the whole of Hindūstān, together with Telingana and other districts in the Deccan. Before his death the more distant provinces began to grow into independence, and soon after the beginning of the fifteenth century the greater part of his dominions was in the hands of seven provincial Moḥammadan dynasties, besides the Hindū Rājas.

A.H.		A.D.
599—984	1. Governors and Kings of Bengal .	1202—1576
796—905	2. Sharḳī Kings of Jaunpūr . .	1394—1500
804—937	3. Kings of Mālwa. . . .	1401—1530
799—980	4. Kings of Gujarāt . . .	1396—1572
735—995	5. Kings of Kashmīr . . .	1334—1587
801—1008	6. Fārūkids, Kings of Khāndēsh .	1399—1599
748—933	7. Bahmanids, Kings of Kulbarga .	1347—1526

On the decay of the Baḥmanids, the following five dynasties divided their dominions between them:—

890—980	8. 'Imād Shāhs of Berār . .	1484—1572
896—1004	9. Niẓām Shāhs of Aḥmadnagar .	1490—1595
897—1018	10. Barīd Shāhs of Bīdar . .	1492—1609
895—1097	11. 'Ādil Shāhs of Bījāpūr . .	1489—1686
918—1098	12. Ḳuṭb Shāhs of Golkonda . .	1512—1687

The Hindūstān dynasties were absorbed into the Mogul Empire by Akbar, and those of the Deccan succumbed to the attacks of Aurangzīb.

A.H. 599–984 | 106. GOVERNORS AND KINGS OF BENGAL | A.D. 1202–1576

106. GOVERNORS AND KINGS OF BENGAL

Moḥammad Bakhtiyār, the conqueror and first governor of Bengal, subdued but a small part of the present province, chiefly in the neighbourhood of his capital Lakhnawtī. In the early part of the thirteenth century Sonārgāon and Sātgāon became seats of Moḥammadan governors, and the name Bangāla included these as well as Lakhnawtī. Fīrūzābād (Pandūah) was the capital of the triple province, until in 1446 (*850*) the seat of government was again moved to Lakhnawtī, which was now first called Gaur, and remained the capital until 1564 (*972*), when it was succeeded by Tāndah. The governors of Bengal sometimes also held Bihār, and occasionally Chittagong and Orīsa. When the Dehlī kings grew weak, the Bengal governors waxed independent, and several dynasties assumed kingly powers. Humāyūn occupied Bengal in *944-6*, but after the successful defeat of the Moguls by Shīr Shāh in 1539 (*946*) governors were again appointed, and again (*960*) founded independent dynasties. In *982*, however, Bihār fell before the arms of Akbar, and by 1576 (*984*) the Mogul was supreme in Bengal.

A. GOVERNORS

A.H.			A.D.
599	Moḥammad Bakhtiyār Khaljī		1202
602	'Izz-a*l*-dīn Moḥammad Shirān		1205
605	'Alā-a*l*-dīn Mardān		1208
608	Ghiyāth-a*l*-dīn 'Iwaz		1211
624	Nāṣir-a*l*-dīn Maḥmūd		1226
627	'Alā-a*l*-dīn Jānī		1229
627	Sayf-a*l*-dīn Aybak		1229
631	'Izz-a*l*-dīn Ṭughril Ṭughān Khān		1233
642	Ḳamar-a*l*-dīn Tamar Khān-Ḳirān		1244
644	Ikhtiyār-a*l*-dīn (Mughīth-a*l*-dīn) Yūsbak		1246
656	Jalāl-a*l*-dīn Mas'ūd Malik Jānī		1258
657	'Izz-a*l*-dīn Balban		1258
659?	Moḥammad Arslān Tatar Khān		1260?
	Shīr Khān		
	Amīn Khān		
677	Mughīth-a*l*-dīn Ṭughril		1278
681	*Nāṣir-a*l*-dīn Bughrā Khān		1282
691	Rukn-a*l*-dīn Kay-Kāwus		1291
702	Shams-a*l*-dīn Fīrūz Shāh		1302
718	Shihāb-a*l*-dīn Bughrā Shāh	(West Bengal)	1318
710	Ghiyāth-a*l*-dīn Bahādur Shāh	(East Bengal)	1310
719	,, ,,	(All Bengal)	1319
723–6	Nāṣir-a*l*-dīn	(Lakhnawtī)	1323–5
725–31	Bahādur Shāh *restored, with Bahrām*	(East Bengal)	1324–30
731–9	Bahrām Shāh (alone)		1330–8
726–40	Ḳadr Khān	(Lakhnawtī)	1325–39
724–40	'Izz-a*l*-dīn A'zam-al-mulk	(Satgāon)	1323–39

* The following six governors belonged to the family of Balban, the Sulṭān of Dehlī, see the genealogy p. 301.

B. KINGS

A.H.			A.D.
739—984			1338—1576
739–50	Fakhr-*al*-dīn Mubārak Shāh	(East Bengal)	1338–49
750–3	Ikhtiyār-*al*-dīn Ghāzī Shāh	(East Bengal)	1349–52
740–6	‘Alā-*al*-dīn ‘Alī Shāh	(West Bengal)	1339–45

HOUSE OF ILYĀS

740–6	Shams-*al*-dīn Ilyās Shāh	(contending in West Bengal)	1339–45
746	,,	(West Bengal)	1345
753-9	,,	(all Bengal)	1352–8
759-92	Sikandar Shāh I b. Ilyās		1358–89
792	Ghiyāth-*al*-dīn A‘zam Shāh b. Sikandar (*rebels* 1370) *reigns*		1389
799	Sayf-*al*-dīn Ḥamza Shāh b. A‘zam . .		1396
809	Shams-*al*-dīn b. Ḥamza		1406

HOUSE OF RĀJA KĀNS

812	Shihāb-*al*-dīn Bāyazīd Shāh (with Rāja Kāns)	1409
817	Jalāl-*al*-dīn Moḥammad Shāh b. Rāja Kāns .	1414
835	Shāms-*al*-dīn Aḥmad Shāh b. Moḥammad .	1431

HOUSE OF ILYĀS (*restored*)

846	Nāṣir-*al*-dīn Maḥmūd Shāh I	1442
864	Rukn-*al*-dīn Bārbak Shāh b. Maḥmūd I .	1459
879	Shams-*al*-dīn Yūsuf Shāh b. Bārbak . .	1474
886	Sikandar Shāh II b. Yūsuf	1481
886	Jalāl-*al*-dīn Fatḥ Shāh b. Maḥmūd I . .	1481

HABSHI KINGS

A.H.		A.D.
892	Sulṭān Shāhzāda Bārbak	1486
892	Sayf-al-dīn Fīrūz Shāh I	1486
895	Nāṣir-al-dīn Maḥmūd Shāh II b. Fatḥ Shāh (*of Ilyās stock*)	1489
896	Shams-al-dīn Abū-l-Naṣr Muẓaffar Shāh .	1490

HOUSE OF ḤOSAYN SHĀH

A.H.		A.D.
899	'Alā-al-dīn Hosayn Shāh	1493
925	Nāṣir-al-dīn Naṣrat Shāh b. Ḥosayn . .	1518
939	'Alā-al-dīn Fīrūz Shāh II b. Naṣrat . .	1532
939	Ghiyāth-al-dīn Maḥmūd Shāh III b. Ḥosayn (partial rule 1526)	1532
—944	(*Conquest by Humāyūn*)	—1537

HOUSE OF MOḤAMMAD SŪR

A.H.		A.D.
960	Shams-al-dīn Moḥammad Sūr Ghāzī Shāh .	1552
962	Bahādur Shāh (Khiḍr) b. Moḥammad Sūr .	1554
968	Ghiyāth-al-dīn Jalāl Shāh b. Moḥammad Sūr	1560
971	(Son of preceding)	1563

HOUSE OF SULAYMĀN ḲARĀRĀNĪ

A.H.		A.D.
971	Sulaymān Khān Ḳarārānī (Bihār and Bengal)	1563
980	Bāyazīd Shāh b. Sulaymān	1572
980	Dāwūd Shāh b. Sulaymān	1572
—984	[*Mogul Emperors*]	—1576

A.H.		A.D.
796—905	107. SHARKĪ KINGS OF JAUNPŪR	1394—1500

('KINGS OF THE EAST')

Khwāja-Jahān, the vezīr of Maḥmūd of the house of Taghlaḳ, deserted his youthful sovereign and founded an independent government at Jaunpūr, whence he and his successors held sway for a time over Bihār, Oudh, Kanauj, and Barāich, with considerable state, as their noble monuments testify; and made war upon their former masters at Dehlī (which they twice besieged), and their neighbours the kings of Mālwa. In 1476 (*881*, or according to some historians *879*) Jaunpūr was conquered by Sikandar b. Bahlōl and reunited to Dehlī; but the adherents of the banished Ḥosayn Shāh endeavoured for some years to restore the fallen dynasty.

A.H.		A.D.
796	Khwāja-Jahān	1394
802	Mubārak Shāh	1399
803	Shams-al-dīn Ibrāhīm Shāh Sharḳī b. Mubārak	1400
844	Maḥmūd Shāh b. Ibrāhīm	1440
861	Moḥammad Shāh (jointly with his father Maḥmūd)	1456
863 —905	Ḥosayn Shāh b. Maḥmūd . . . . . . fled to Bengal 881, died 905	1458 —1500

[*Sulṭāns of Dehlī*]

A.H. 804–937 — 108. KINGS OF MĀLWA — A.D. 1401–1530

Mālwa was among the old Rājput kingdoms which longest withstood the Moḥammadan invasion. It had boasted one of the most illustrious of the ancient Hindū dynasties, who made their capital, Ujjayn, a seat of learning and science. Three centuries of contest elapsed before it was subdued, in the time of Sulṭān Balban of Dehlī. Its natural boundaries were the Narbadā on the south, the Chambal on the north, and Gujarāt and Bandalkhand on the west and east. Under the Khaljī kings, however, it included Hūshangābād, Ajmīr, Rantambhor, and Elichpūr, and even Chitōr was sometimes forced to pay tribute. Its Moḥammadan capital, Mandū, founded by Hūshang Ghōrī, stood on a spacious plateau surrounded by precipices, and was famous for its palaces and mosques.

Two successive Moḥammadan dynasties reigned in Mālwa. The first was founded by Dilāwar Khān Ghōrī, a governor of the king of Dehlī, and consisted of himself, his son, and his grandson. The second dynasty was established by Maḥmūd Khaljī, the vezīr of the grandson of Dilāwar, and fell when Mālwa was annexed in 1530 (*937*) by the neighbouring king of Gujarāt, with whom the rulers of Mālwa had waged perpetual war. The Khaljīs were a fighting race, and had carried the arms of Mālwa to the gates of Dehlī in the north and Bīdar in the south, whilst with the Rājputs of Chitōr and Chanderī their hostilities were unceasing.*

I. GHŌRĪS

A.H.		A.D.
804	Dilāwar Khān Ghōrī	1401
808	Hūshang (Alp Khān) b. Dilāwar	1405
838	Moḥammad Ghaznī Khān b. Hūshang	1434

II. KHALJĪS

A.H.		A.D.
839	Maḥmūd Shāh I Khaljī	1435
880	Ghiyāth Shāh b. Maḥmūd	1475
906	Nāṣir Shāh b. Ghiyāth	1500
916	Maḥmūd II b. Nāṣir	1510
—937	[*Kings of Gujarāt*]	—1530

* The list of the Kings of Kashmīr should follow here; but their chronology is so uncertain that an accurate table can hardly be constructed. See my *Catalogue of the Coins of the Muhammadan States of India*, xlvii, 68.

A.H. 799—980 109. KINGS OF GUJARĀT A.D. 1396—1572

Gujarāt owed its long immunity from Moḥammadan subjection to its inaccessible position, beyond the great desert and the hills connecting the Vindhya with the Aravali range, which rendered it difficult to invade except by sea. It was not until the time of 'Alā-al-dīn of Dehlī, at the close of the 13th century, that Gujarāt became a Moḥammadan province. At the end of the 14th century it became independent again, but its rulers were now Muslims instead of Hindūs. Ẓafar Khān, the son of a Rājput convert, was appointed to the government of Gujarāt in *794*, and assumed independence in 1396 (*799*). He found himself surrounded by enemies, Rājput rājas and wild tribes of Bhīls, and possessed of but a narrow territory between the hills and the sea, including, however, a considerable stretch of the coast, as far as Sūrat at least. He soon enlarged his dominions by the conquest of Īdar and Diu; plundered Jhalor; and even took possession of Mālwa for a space in 1407. Aḥmad Shāh I, his successor, founded Aḥmadābād, which became the capital of the dynasty and afterwards of the Mogul province, and is still an important city. Maḥmūd Shāh I not only carried on the traditional wars of his family with Mālwa and Khāndēsh, but added the stronghold of Jūnagarh in Kattiāwār, and Champanīr, to his dominions, and kept a large fleet to subdue the pirates of the islands and to attack the Portuguese; to whom Bahādur Shāh, the conqueror of Mālwa, conceded the right to build a factory at Diu, and at whose hands he met his death. The last years of the dynasty were clouded by the intrigues of factious nobles, and the kings became mere puppets; until Akbar's conquest in 1572 (*980*) restored prosperity to the harassed province.

A.H.		A.D.
799	Muẓaffar Shāh I Ẓafar Khān	1396
814	Aḥmad Shāh I	1411
816	Moḥammad Ḳarīm Shāh	1443
855	Ḳuṭb-al-dīn	1451
863	Dāwūd Shah	1458
863	Maḥmūd Shāh I Baykara	1458
917	Muẓaffar Shāh II	1511
932	Sikandar Shāh	1525
932	Nāṣir Khān Maḥmūd II	1525
932	Bahādur Shāh	1526
943	Mīrān Moḥammad Shāh Fārūkī (of Khāndēsh)	1536
944	Maḥmūd Shāh III	1537
961	Aḥmad Shāh II	1553
969	Muẓaffar Shāh III Ḥabīb	1561
—980	[*Mogul Emperors*]	—1572

KINGS OF GUJARĀT

- 1. Muẓaffar I
  - *Tatar Khān*
    - 2. Aḥmad I
      - 3. Moḥammad I
        - 4. Ḳuṭb-*al*-dīn
        - 6. Maḥmūd I
          - 7. Muẓaffar II
            - 8. Sikandar
            - 9. Maḥmūd II
            - 10. Bahādur
            - *Laṭīf Khān*
              - 12. Maḥmūd III
                - 14. Muẓaffar III
            - *daughter* = *ʿAdil of Khāndēsh*
              - 11. Mīrān Moḥammad
      - 5. Dāwūd

A.H. A.D.

801—1008 110. KINGS OF KHĀNDĒSH 1399—1599

Nāṣir Khān, the first Moḥammad ruler of Khāndēsh who asserted his independence of the kingdom of Dehlī, claimed to be descended from the caliph 'Omar. He was related by marriage to the kings of Gujarāt, from whose dominions Khāndēsh (comprising the lower valley of the Taptī) was separated only by a belt of forest. The capital Burhānpūr was founded near the fortress of Asīrgarh. Akbar took Burhānpūr and received the homage of its king in 1562; but Khāndēsh was not fully incorporated in the Mogul Empire until 1599 (*1008*), when Asīrgarh fell after a six months' siege.

A.D.		A.H.
772	*Malik Rāja*	1370
801	Nāṣir Khān	1399
841	Mīran 'Ādil Khān I	1437
844	Mīrān Mubārak I	1441
861	'Ādil Khān II	1457
909	Dāwūd Khān	1503
916	'Ādil Khān III	1510
926	Mīrān Moḥammad Shāh I	1520
942	Mīrān Mubārak II	1535
974	Mīrān Moḥammad II	1566
984	'Alī Khān	1576
1005	Bahādur Shāh	1596
—1008	[*Mogul Emperors*]	—1599

THE DECCAN

A.H.		A.D.
748—933	111. BAHMANIDS	1347—1526

(KINGS OF KULBARGA, ETC.)

The Deccan was partly conquered by Moḥammadans for the first time by 'Ala-al-dīn Moḥammad of Dehlī, who in 1294 seized Deogīri and Elichpūr and thus formed a new province south of the Sātpura mountains. Moḥammad b. Taghlaḳ enlarged the Deccan province by an invasion of Telingana in 1322, and for a time made Deogīri (re-named Dawlatābād) the capital of his empire. Among the numerous revolts which disturbed his reign that of the recently organized province of the Deccan was the earliest to achieve independence. From 1347 for nearly two centuries the Bahmanid kings of Kulbarga, Warangal and Bīdar, held sway over the northern half of the Deccan above the Kistna. Their founder was Ḥasan Gāngū, an Afghān in the employment of a Brahman at Dehlī. He rose to high office under the Taghlaḳ Sulṭāns and received the title of Ẓafar Khān. When the revolt against Moḥammad b. Taghlaḳ broke out in the Deccan, Ḥasan placed himself at the head of the insurgents, drove the royal troops from the country, and ascended the throne at Kulbarga under the style of 'Alā-al-dīn Ḥasan Gāngū Bahmanī.* His dominions marched on the north with Berār, on the east with Telingana, whilst the river Kistna and the sea formed the southern and western boundaries. They included the greater part of the modern Bombay Presidency south of Sūrat and most of the Nizām's territory. In addition, the Rājas of Telingana and Vijāyanagar were from time to time compelled at the point of the sword to pay homage and tribute. Under 'Alā-al-dīn Aḥmad II the Konkan was reduced and the neighbouring kings of Khāndēsh and Gujarāt were defeated. In 1471 Moḥammad Shāh II carried his arms into Orīsa, seized Conjeveram, and made war in the south upon the Rāja of Belgāon; so that the Bahmanids' sway extended from sea to sea and included nearly the whole of the Deccan north of Mysore. The extension of territory was followed by a new division into provinces, and the division led to disintegration. Yūsuf 'Ādil Shāh, a successful general of Moḥammad Shāh II, declared the independence of the

* See an article by James Gibb in *Numismatic Chronicle*, III. i. 91–115; and my *Catalogue of the Coins of the Muhammadan States of India in the British Museum*, lxii–lxvi.

new province of Bījāpūr; Nizām-al-mulk prepared the way for the separation of Junayr; ‘Imād-al-mulk was proclaimed king in Berār, and the loss of these provinces was speedily followed by the independence of the rest and the extinction of the parent dynasty. The *‘Imād Shāhs* of Berār, *Niẓām Shāhs* of Aḥmadnagar, *Barīd Shāhs* of Bīdar, *‘Ādil Shāhs* of Bījāpūr, and *Ḳuṭb Shāhs* of Golkonda divided the kingdom of the Bahmanids amongst them.

A.H.		A.D.
748	Ḥasan Gāngū ‘Alā-*al*-dīn Ẓafar Khān . . .	1347
759	Moḥammad Shāh I	1358
776	Mujāhid Shāh	1375
780	Dāwūd Shāh	1378
780	Maḥmūd Shāh I	1378
799	Ghiyāth-*al*-dīn	1397
799	Shams-*al*-dīn	1397
800	Tāj-*al*-dīn Fīrūz Shāh	1397
825	Aḥmad Shāh I	1421
838	‘Alā-*al*-dīn Aḥmad Shāh II	1435
862	‘Alā-*al*-dīn Humāyūn Shāh	1457
865	Niẓām Shāh	1461
867	Moḥammad Shāh II	1463
887	Maḥmūd Shāh II	1482
924	Aḥmad Shāh III	1518
927	‘Alā-*al*-dīn Shah	1520
929	Walī-Allāh Shāh	1522
932	Kalīm-Allāh Shāh	1525
—933	[*Five Deccan Dynasties*]	—1526

BAHMANIDS

1. Ḥasan Gāngū

2. Moḥammad I — 4. Dāwūd — 5. Maḥmūd I

3. Mujāhid — 8. Fīrūz — 9. Aḥmad I — 6. Ghiyāth-al-dīn — 7. Shams-al-dīn

10. Aḥmad II — *Moḥammad*

11. Humāyūn

12. Niẓām — 13. Moḥammad II

14. Maḥmūd II

15. Aḥmad III — 16. 'Alā-al-dīn — 17. Walī-Allāh

18. Kalīm-Allāh

A.H.		A.D.
890—980	**112. 'IMĀD SHĀHS**	1484—1572

(BERĀR)

890	Fatḥ-Allāh	1484
910	'Alā-al-dīn	1504
c. 936	Daryā	c. 1529
c. 968	Burhān	c. 1560
976	Tufāl (usurper)	1568
—980		—1572

[*Nizām Shāhs*]

A.H.		A.D.
896—1004	**113. NIZĀM SHĀHS**	1490—1595

(AḤMADNAGAR)

896	Aḥmad I b. Nizām Shāh	1490
914	Burhān I	1508
961	Ḥosayn	1553
972	Murtaḍā	1565
996	Mīrān Ḥosayn	1588
997	Ismā'īl	1589
999	Burhān II	1590
1003	Ibrāhīm	1594
1004	Aḥmad II	1594
1004	Bahādur*	1595

[*Mogul Emperors*]

* Murtaḍa II reigned nominally from 1598–1607; and the province then came under the domination of Malik Amber.

A.H.		A.D.
897—*c*. 1018	114. BARĪD SHĀHS (BĪDAR)	1492—*c*. 1609
897	Ḳāsim I.	1492
910	Amīr I	1504
945	'Alī	1549
990	Ibrāhīm	1562
997	Ḳāsim II	1569
1000	Mirza 'Alī	1572
c. 1018	Amīr II	*c*. 1609

A.H.		A.D.
895—1097	115. 'ĀDIL SHAHS (BĪJĀPŪR)	1489—1686
895	Yūsuf 'Ādil Shāh.	1489
916	Ismā'īl	1511
941	Mallū	1534
941	Ibrāhīm I	1535
965	'Alī I	1557
987	Ibrāhīm II	1579
1035	Moḥammad	1626
1070	'Alı II	1660
—1097	[*Mogul Emperors*]	—1686

A.H.		A.D.
918—1098	116. ḲUṬB SHĀHS (GOLKONDA)	1512—1687
918	Sulṭān Ḳulī	1512
940	Jamshīd	1543
957	Subḥān Ḳulī	1550
957	Ibrāhīm	1550
989	Moḥammad Ḳulī	1581
1020	Abd-Allāh	1611
1083	Abū-l-Ḥasan	1672
—1098	[*Mogul Emperors*]	—1687

A.H. A.D.

932--1275 117. MOGUL EMPERORS OF HINDŪSTĀN 1525—1857

Bābar, the Mongol conqueror of Hindūstān, was descended in the fifth generation from Tīmūr (see the genealogical table p. 268) and was born in 1482, in Farghāna, where his father was governor. Driven from his native province by the Uzbegs of Shaybānī about 1504, Bābar sought his recompense in the subjection of Afghānistān. He took possession of Badakhshān in 1503 (*909*), occupied Kābul in the following year, and annexed Ḳandahār in 1507. For many years he meditated the invasion of India, but it was not until 1525 (*932*) that he felt himself strong enough to descend at the head of his Turks (he abhorred the name of Mongol*) upon the Panjāb and occupy Lahore. On the 20th April 1526 he signally defeated the army of Sulṭān Ibrāhīm Lōdī of Dehlī on the historic plain of Pānīpat, and the victory was followed by the rapid

* In Arabic Mughal, whence the English Mogul or Moghul.

occupation of Dehlī and Agra, and the submission of the northern parts of Hindūstān, from the Indus to the borders of Bengal. Bābar died in 1530 (*937*) before he could subdue the kingdoms of Bengal, Gujarāt and Mālwa; still less had he approached the Deccan.

His son Humāyūn, though but nineteen years of age, endeavoured to complete his father's work. His attempt to reduce the united kingdom of Gujarāt and Mālwa was, however, abortive; and the Afghāns of Bengal, led by the genius of Shīr Shāh, the usurping king of Bihār, succeeded after an obstinate struggle in driving Humāyūn step by step to the west. A treacherous attack on the Mogul camp at Chonsa in 1539 (*946*) banished them from Bengal; and a total defeat at Kanauj in the following year gave Shīr Shāh the command of all Hindūstān (but not Gujarāt), and compelled Humāyūn to seek refuge, first in Sind, and then in Persia. Fifteen years passed before the Mogul Emperor returned to re-conquer his empire. Meanwhile Shīr Shāh, after laying the foundations of the administrative organization which Akbar afterwards perfected, died, and the disunion among his successors paved the way for the invader. In 1555 Humāyūn recovered Dehlī, and there died in January 1556 (*963*).

Humāyūn had only begun the work of reconquest; it was left to his son Akbar, a youth of fourteen, to finish it. The boy's guardian Bayrām Khān, a Turkomān, utterly defeated the Indian forces under Hīmū on the 5th November 1556 on the same plain of Pānīpat where Bābar had won his great victory. By this single blow Akbar found himself master of the better part of Hindūstān, and, young as he was, he soon took the reins of power into his own hands. Dehlī and Agra were his by the victory of Pānīpat; Gwāliōr fell in 1558 (*966*), Jaunpūr in 1559, and Mālwa and Khāndēsh were temporarily overrun in 1561–2. Rājputāna submitted after the storming of Chitōr in 1567 (*975*), and Gujarāt was reduced in 1572 (*980*). Bengal, which had nominally admitted the Mogul sovereignty, rose in rebellion, but was subdued in 1575–7 (*983–4*). Kashmīr was annexed in 1587 and Ḳandahār six years later.*

'Akbar was too wise to meddle seriously in Deccan politics. All he wanted was to secure himself against invasion from the south; and with this view he annexed the rugged borderland of Khāndēsh, and used its capital,

* See my *History of the Mogul Emperors of Hindustan illustrated by their Coins*, xii. ff.

Burhānpūr, with the rocky fastness of Asīrgarh, [which had withstood his siege and his English gunners for six months before it succumbed in 1601 (*1008*),] as outposts to defend his southern frontier. He also subdued Berār and took the fortress of Aḥmadnagar (1600).'* The kings of Bījāpūr and Golkonda paid him homage and offered him tribute: but he never attempted annexation in the Deccan, beyond securing his frontier; nor had the Deccan *sūbah* or province, even in this limited sense, been organized as thoroughly as the rest of the empire at the time of his death in 1605 (*1014*).

The true successor of Moḥammad b. Taghlaḳ in his dreams of Deccan conquest was Aurangzīb, the sixth Mogul Emperor. As governor during Shāh-Jahān's reign in 1636–43 he had organized the four divisions of the Deccan province—Dawlatābād (including Aḥmadnagar), Khāndēsh, Telingana, and Berār; and he made the king of Golkonda a vassal in 1656. The fratricidal struggle which preceded his accession to the throne at Dehlī in 1659 (*1069*), and the work of ordering his administration, diverted his attention from the Deccan for some years; and it was not till 1681 that he began that long series

* See my *Aurangzib* (Rulers of India) pp. 144—204.

of campaigns in the south which did not end till his own death twenty-six years later. He besieged and took Bījāpūr in 1686 and Golkonda in 1687, and put an end to the dynasties of the 'Ādil and Kuṭb Shāhs. But against the new power of the Marāthas which had arisen in the Deccan in the middle of the 17th century he could make no head; and though his armies traversed the Deccan in all directions and took many forts, the country and its hardy mountaineers were never subdued. Yet when Aurangzīb died in 1707 his dominions stretched from Kābul to the mouths of the Hūglī, and from Sūrat across Haydarābād to Masulipatan and even Madras. All India, save the apex of the Deccan, was his in name; but except in forts and cities, the possession was nominal in the south.

The empire of the Great Moguls began to break up after the death of Aurangzīb. His successors were for the most part weak and debauched; and the rising powers of the Sikhs, Jāts, and Marāthas were young and strong. The invasions of Nādir Shāh in 1738, and Aḥmad Durrānī in 1748, 1757, etc., were signs of the feebleness of the empire. Fifty years after Aurangzīb's death the Marāthas were supreme in the south, except where the newly-founded dynasty of the Niẓām kept them at arm's length, and were pushing their way through Gujarāt up to Dehlī; the Rājputs had ceased to acknowledge the Mogul supremacy; the Sikhs were gradually winning the mastery of the Panjāb from the Afghāns; the Jāts were practically independent near Agra; Oudh was virtually a separate kingdom, and so was Bengal; though the little patches of territory at Calcutta, Bombay and Madras scarcely portended the great future of the East India Company. The progress of the Company's arms need not be related here. The battle of Plassey (1757) and Buxar (1764) laid the ghost of the Mogul Empire, though the fiction of Mogul sovereignty was maintained till 1857. The last three emperors were pensioners of the British Crown; and Bahādur II, after upsetting his puppet-throne by joining in the Mutiny, died in exile at Rangoon in 1862.

A.H.		A.D.
932	Bābar, Zahīr-al-dīn*	1526
937	Humāyūn, Naṣir-al-dīn	1530
963	Akbar, Jalāl-al-dīn	1556
1014	Jahāngīr, Nūr-al-dīn	1605
1037	*Dāwar-Bakhsh*	1627–8
1037	Shāh-Jahān, Shihāb-al-dīn	1628
1068	*Murād-Bakhsh (in Gujarāt)*	1658
1068–70	*Shujā' (in Bengal)*	1658–60
1069	Aurangzīb 'Ālamgīr, Muḥyī-al-dīn	1659
1118	*A'zam Shāh*	1707
1119–20	*Kām-Bakhsh*	1708
1119	Shāh-'Alam Bahādur Shāh I, Ḳuṭb-al-dīn	1707
1124	Jahāndār, Mu'izz-al-dīn	1712
1124	Farrukh-siyar	1713
1131	Rafī'-al-darajāt, Shams-al-dīn	1719
1131	Rafī'-al-dawla Shāh-Jahān II	1719
1131	*Nīkū-siyar*	1719
1132	*Ibrāhīm*	1720
1131	Moḥammad, Nāṣir-al-dīn	1719
1161	Aḥmad	1748
1167	'Alamgīr II, 'Azīz-al-dīn	1754
1173–4	*Shāh-Jāhan* III	1759–60
1173	Shāh-'Ālam, Jalāl-al-dīn	1759
1202–3	*Bīdar-Bakht*	1788
1221	Moḥammad Akbar II	1806
1253	Bahādur Shāh II	1837
—1275	[*Great Britain*]	—1857

* Bābar and most of his successors had the Arabic name Moḥammad in addition to their Persian names. In the list, the names of usurpers and pretenders are printed in italics.

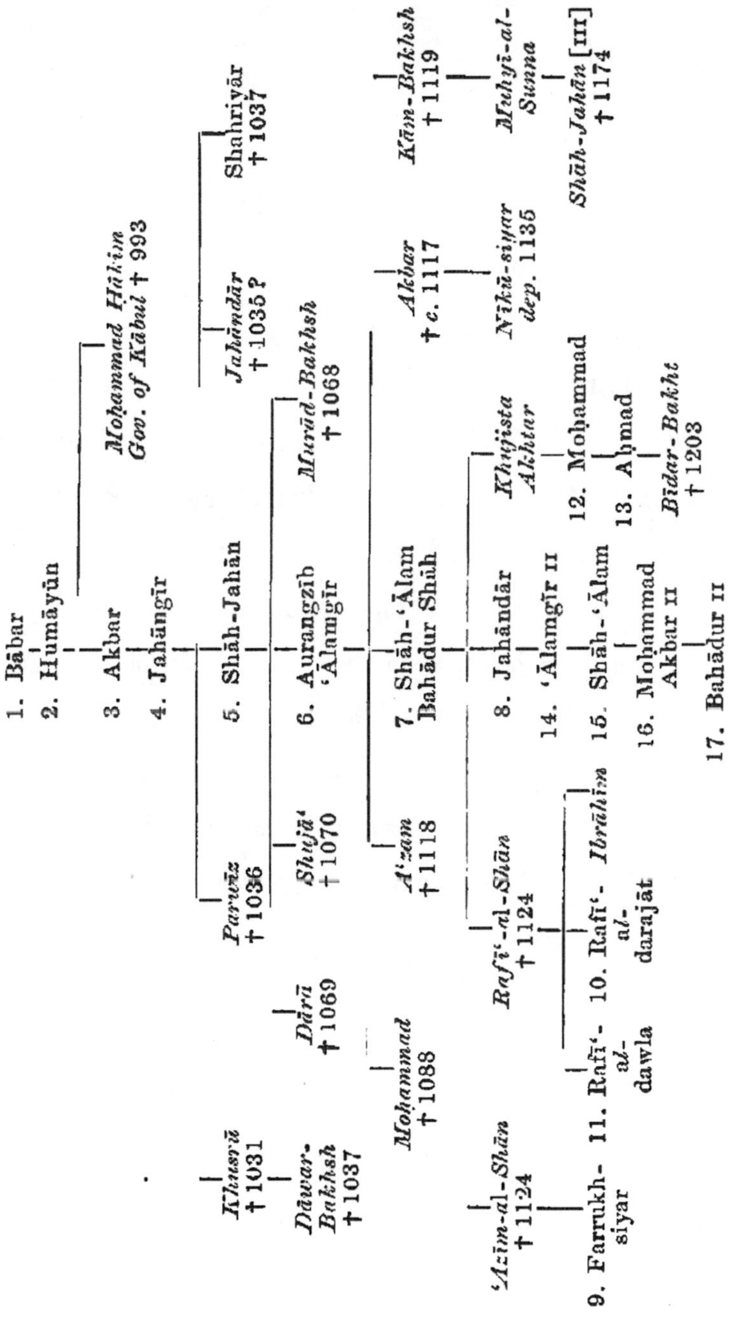

1. Babar
2. Humāyūn
Mohammad Ḥakim
Gov. of Kābul † 993
3. Akbar
4. Jahāngīr
Khusrū
† 1031
Parwīz
† 1036
5. Shāh-Jahān
Jahāndār
† 1035 ?
Shahriyār
† 1037
Dāwar-Bakhsh
† 1037
Dārā
† 1069
Shujā'
† 1070
6. Aurangzib 'Ālamgīr
Murād-Bakhsh
† 1068
Mohammad
† 1088
A'ẓam
† 1118
7. Shāh-'Ālam Bahādur Shāh
Akbar
† c. 1117
Kām-Bakhsh
† 1119
'Azīm-al-Shān
† 1124
Rafī'-al-Shān
† 1124
8. Jahāndār
Khujista Akhtar
Nīkū-siyar
dep. 1135
Muḥyī-al-Sunna
9. Farrukh-siyar
11. Rafī'-al-dawla
10. Rafī'-al-darajat
Ibrāhīm
14. 'Ālamgīr II
12. Mohammad
Shāh-Jahān [III]
† 1174
15. Shāh-'Ālam
13. Aḥmad
16. Mohammad Akbar II
Bīdār-Bakht
† 1203
17. Bahādur II

A.H. A.D.

1160—1311 118. AMĪRS OF AFGHĀNISTĀN 1747—1893

The modern history of Afghānistān as an independent State begins in 1747. After the deposition of the Ghōrids, the country ceased to possess a dynasty of its own,* and merely formed part of a larger kingdom. It became a province of the Īl-khāns of Persia, and then of the Tīmūrid empire; and after the establishment of the Moguls in India, it was sometimes part of their dominions and sometimes belonged to the Shāhs of Persia; or, more often, was divided between the two. Kābul and Kandahār were generally in the possession of the Moguls until after the death of Aurangzīb, whilst Herāt belonged to Persia. In 1737 Nādir Shāh, the Afshārid ruler of Persia, seized Kābul and Ḳandahār and made his memorable descent upon India. After his assassination in 1747 the Afghāns resolved to be independent of Persia, and chose Aḥmad Khān the chief of the Abdālī or Durrānī tribe to be their Shāh. The post of vezīr, or second man in the state, was conferred

* The line of the Kart Maliks were a local exception at Herāt (p. 252).

upon Jamāl Khān the hereditary chief of the rival tribe of the Bārakzais. Henceforward for nearly a century this arrangement subsisted: the Shāh was a Durrānī and the Vezīr a Bārakzai.

Aḥmad Shāh reduced all Afghānistān, conquered Herāt and Khurāsān, invaded India repeatedly, occupied Dehlī for a time, and annexed Kashmīr, Sind, and part of the Panjāb; but his Indian possessions gradually passed over to the growing power of the Sikhs, who had become masters of the Panjāb before the end of the 18th century. A massacre of the Bārakzais by Zamān Shāh, Aḥmad's grandson, instead of diminishing, increased the influence of the heriditary vezīrs, who exercised the chief power during the nominal reign of Maḥmūd Shāh and the early reign of Shāh Shujā'. Several attempts were made to oust them from their dominant position; but the blinding and murder of Fatḥ Khān Bārakzai in 1818 was the signal for the deposition of the Durrānī dynasty, and after some years of anarchy Dost Moḥammad, the brother of the murdered Vezīr, took possession of the throne (1826), as the first Bārakzai Amīr of Afghānistān.

During the decline of the later Durrānīs the claim of Persia to the possession of Herāt had been pressed by force of arms. Since its conquest by Aḥmad Shāh the city had been held by various Afghān princes, with little dependence upon the central government. In 1816 the Persians had attacked Herāt, but had been repulsed by Fatḥ Khān the Bārakzai. In 1837, urged on by Russia, the Shāh of Persia again advanced upon the 'key of Afghānistān,' and again, after a ten months' siege, protracted by the splendid defence of Eldred Pottinger, was forced to retire (1838). When Dost Moḥammad showed signs of encouraging Russian overtures, the British Government of India, excited by the narrow escape of Herāt, and alarmed at the unfriendly attitude of the Amīr, declared war, and the Afghān campaigns and disasters of 1839–1842 ensued. Shāh-Shujā', the representative of the deposed Durrānīs, was in an evil day restored to the Amīrate, and Sir William Macnaghten was posted at Kābul as British Resident. Dost Moḥammad had surrendered and remained passive, but his son Akbar Khān continued the resistance of the Bārakzais. In Nov. 1841 Macnaghten and Burnes were treacherously murdered, and of the sixteen thousand British troops and camp followers who left Kābul under a safe-conduct only one escaped to tell the tale of slaughter. The massacre was avenged by Pollock's army in 1842, and the Afghāns thenceforward, for nearly forty years, were allowed to manage their own internal affairs. Dost Moḥammad died in 1863, the subsidized ally of England; and the history of Afghānistān since his death has consisted chiefly in the struggles of his sons and grandsons for the throne. A second attempt to force a British Resident at Kābul upon the Amīr, as a check upon the envoys of Russia, led to the defeat and deposition of Shīr 'Alī, the murder of Cavagnari, and the campaigns of Stewart and Roberts in 1879–81. The Amīr 'Abd-al-Raḥmān, then established by the British, has since, on the whole, succeeded in holding the mastery over his refractory subjects.

A.H.	DURRĀNĪS*	A.D.
1160	Aḥmad Shāh	1747
1187	Tīmūr Shāh	1773
1207	Zamān Shāh	1793
1216	Shujā'-al-mulk (Shāh Shujā') . . .	1801
1216	Maḥmūd Shāh	1801
1218	Shujā' (2nd reign)	1803
1224	Maḥmūd (2nd reign; latterly at Herāt, to 1245)	1809
1233	'Alī Shāh (at Kābul)	1817
1233	Ayyūb Shāh (at Peshāwar and Kashmīr) .	1817
1245	Kāmrān (at Herāt, to 1258)	1829
1255	Shujā' (3rd reign)	1839
1258	Fatḥ Jang (fled the same year) . . .	1842

BĀRAKZAIS

A.H.		A.D.
1242	Dost Moḥammad	1826
1255-8	*Shujā' restored*	1839-42
1280	Shīr Alī	1863
	(Afḍal and 'Azīm at Balkh and Kābul 1865-7)	
1296	Ya'ḳūb Khān	1879
1296	'Abd-*al*-Raḥmān Khān *regnant* . . .	1879

* The list and pedigree of the Durrānīs is adapted from an article by M. Longworth Dames in the *Numismatic Chronicle*, III. viii. 325-63 (1888).

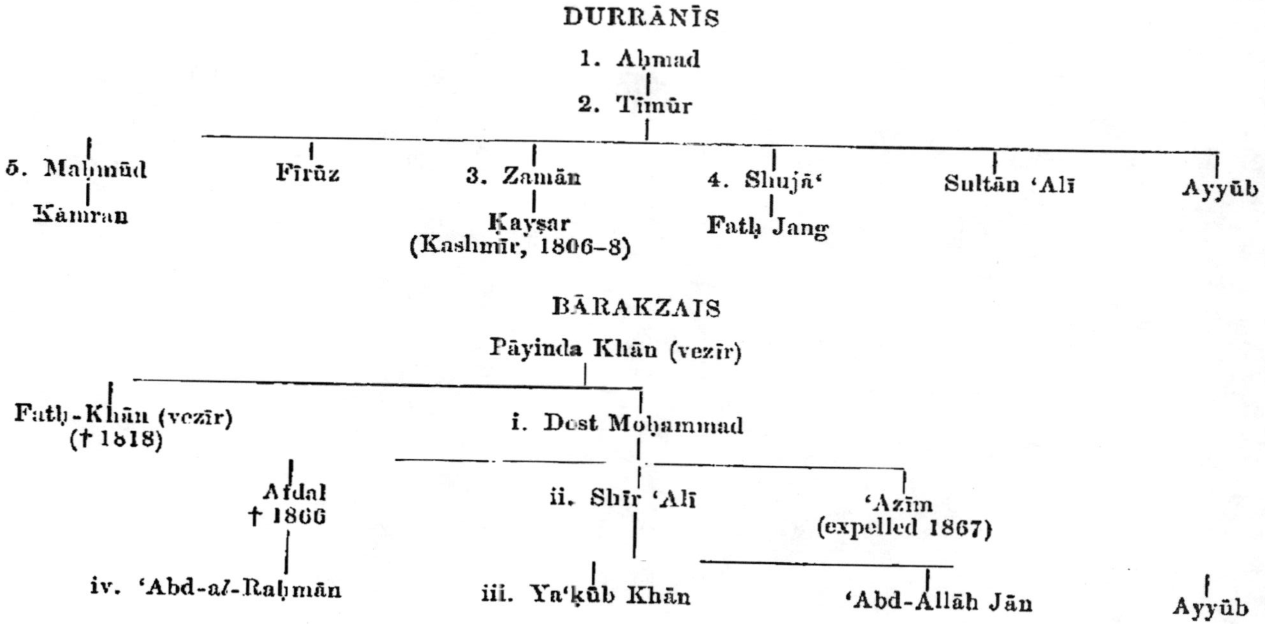
DURRĀNĪS
1. Aḥmad
2. Tīmūr
5. Maḥmūd
Kāmran
Fīrūz
3. Zamān
Ḳayṣar
(Kashmīr, 1806–8)
4. Shujā‘
Fatḥ Jang
Sulṭān ‘Alī
Ayyūb
BĀRAKZAIS
Pāyinda Khān (vezīr)
Fatḥ-Khān (vezīr)
(† 1818)
i. Dost Moḥammad
Afḍal
† 1866
ii. Shīr ‘Alī
‘Azīm
(expelled 1867)
iv. ‘Abd-al-Raḥmān
iii. Ya‘ḳūb Khān
‘Abd-Allāh Jān
Ayyūb

INDEX TO RULERS*

* The *first* number refers to the dynastic list in which the name occurs. In the case of identical names the alphabetical order of the dynasties is followed. Where two or more identical names occur in the same dynasty, the dynastic name is put in the plural. Prefixed words like Abū-, Banū, Ibn, must be sought under the second name.

THE END

BY STANLEY LANE-POOLE

The Life of Edward William Lane. 8vo, pp. 138. Williams and Norgate. 1877.

The People of Turkey. By a Consul's Daughter. Edited. Two vols. 8vo, pp. xxxi, 281; x, 352. Murray. 1878.

Lane's Selections from the Kuran. Edited with Introduction. 8vo. Frontispiece. pp. cxii, 173, 2. Trübner's Oriental Series. 1879.

Egypt. Illustrated. Fcp. 8vo, pp. xii, 200. Sampson Low. 1881.

The Speeches and Table-Talk of the Prophet Mohammad. 18mo, pp. lxiii, 196. Macmillan's Golden Treasury Series. 1882; reissue, 1893

Le Koran, sa Poesie et ses Lois. 24mo, pp. vi, 112. Leroux. 1882.

Studies in a Mosque. 1883. *Second Edition.* 8vo, pp. viii, 326. Remington. 1893.

Arabian Society in the Middle Ages. Edited. 8vo, pp. xvi, 283. Chatto. 1883.

Picturesque Palestine, Sinai, and Egypt. Vol. IV.—Egypt. 4to, pp. 121–234. Illustrated. Virtue. 1883.

Social Life in Egypt: a Description of the Country and its People. (Supplement to *Picturesque Palestine.*) 4to. Illustrated. pp. vi, 138. Virtue. 1883.

Selections from the Prose Writings of Jonathan Swift. Portrait Preface, and Notes. 8vo, pp. xxx, 284. Paul and Trench's Parchment Library. 1884.

Notes for a Bibliography of Swift. 8vo, pp. 36. Elliot Stock. 1884.

Letters and Journals of Jonathan Swift. With Commentary and Notes. 8vo, pp. xv, 292. Paul and Trench's Parchment Library. 1885.

The Life of General F. R. Chesney, R.A. By his Wife and Daughter. Edited, with Preface. Portrait. 8vo, pp. xxiii, 279. Allen. 1885; reissue, 1893.

The Art of the Saracens in Egypt. Illustrated. 8vo, pp. xviii, 264. Published for the Committee of Council on Education by Chapman and Hall. 1886.

The Moors in Spain. Illustrated. 8vo, pp. xx, 285. Unwin. 1887.

Turkey. Illustrated. 8vo, pp. xix, 373. Unwin. 1888.

The Life of the Rt. Hon. Stratford Canning, Viscount Stratford de Redcliffe, K.G. From his Memoirs and Papers. Three Portraits. Library Edition. 2 vols. 8vo, pp. xxix, 519; xviii, 475. Longmans. 1888.

Popular Edition. pp. xx, 377. Longmans. 1890.

Thirty Years of Colonial Government. From Papers of the Rt. Hon. Sir G. F. Bowen, G.C.M.G. Portrait. 2 vols. pp. viii, 460; viii, 467. Longmans. 1889.

The Barbary Corsairs. Illustrated. 8vo, pp. xviii, 316. Unwin. 1890.

Sir Richard Church, C.B., G.C.H., Commander-in-Chief of the Greeks in the War of Independence. With two Plans. 8vo, pp. iv, 73. Longmans. 1890.

Stories from the Arabian Nights. 16mo. 3 vols. pp. vii, 338, 331, 346. Six Illustrations. Putnam. 1891.

The History of the Moghul Emperors illustrated by their Coins. pp. clxxvii. Constable. 1892.

BY STANLEY LANE-POOLE

Cairo: Sketches of its History, Monuments, and Social Life. Numerous Illustrations. 8vo, pp. xiv, 320. Virtue. 1892.

Aurangzib. Rulers of India Series. 8vo, pp. 212. Clarendon Press. 1893.

The Mohammadan Dynasties: Chronological and Genealogical Tables. 8vo, pp. xxviii, 361. Constable. 1893.

The Life of Sir Harry Parkes, K.C.B., late H.M. Minister in Japan and China. 2 vols. 8vo. Macmillan. *In the Press.*

The Life of Saladin. Putnam. *In preparation.*

Lane's Arabic-English Lexicon. Vols. 6-8. Imp. 4to, pp. xxxix, 2221-3064. Edited. Williams and Norgate. 1877-1893.

NUMISMATIC WORKS

Catalogue of the Guthrie Collection of Oriental Coins. pp. viii, 38. Five Autotype Plates. Austin. 1874.

International Numismata Orientalia. Part II.—Coins of the Turkumans. 4to, pp. xii, 44. Six Plates. Trübner. 1875.

Essays in Oriental Numismatics. First, Second, and Third Series. Plates. 8vo. 3 vols. 1874, 1877, 1892.

Catalogue of Oriental Coins in the British Museum. Printed by order of the Trustees. 8vo. 10 vols. (Ouvrage couronné par l'Institut de France, 1881.)

Vol. I. THE KHALIFS. pp. xx, 263. Eight Autotype Plates. 1875.
II. MOHAMMADAN DYNASTIES. pp. xii, 279. Eight Autotype Plates. 1876.
III. THE TURKUMANS. pp. xxvi, 305. Twelve Autotype Plates. 1877.
IV. EGYPT. pp. xxx, 279. Eight Autotype Plates. 1879.
V. The MOORS and ARABIA. pp. lii, 175. Seven Autotype Plates. 1880
VI. The MONGOLS. pp. lxxv, 300. Nine Autotype Plates. 1881.
VII. BUKHARA. pp. xlviii, 131. Five Autotype Plates. 1882.
VIII. The TURKS. pp. li, 431. Twelve Autotype Plates. 1883.
IX., X. ADDITIONS: 1875—1889. 2 vols. pp. 420, 460. Twenty Autotype Plates, and General Index. 1889, 1890.

Catalogue of Indian Coins in the British Museum. Printed by order of the Trustees. 8vo. 3 vols.

Vol. I. SULTANS of DEHLI. pp. xiv, 199. Nine Autotype Plates. 1884.
II. MOHAMMADAN STATES. pp. lxxx, 239. Twelve Autotype Plates. 1885.
III. MOGHUL EMPERORS. pp cliii, 401. Thirty-three Autotype Plates. 1892.

Catalogue of Arabic Glass Weights in the British Museum. 8vo, pp. xxxv, 127. Nine Autotype Plates, Printed by order of the Trustees. 1891.

Coins and Medals: their Place in History and Art. By the Authors of the British Museum Official Catalogues. Edited. Illustrated. 8vo. pp. x, 286. Elliot Stock, 1885. *Second Edition.* 1892.

Catalogue of the Mohammadan Coins in the Bodleian Library, Oxford. pp. xvi, 55. Four Plates. Clarendon Press. 1888.